TRUE
GRIT

**THE
MAKING
OF A
LEGEND**

TRUEGRIT

THE MAKING OF A LEGEND

SYLVIE LINNANE

with Liam Hayes

IRISH SPORTS PUBLISHING

Published by Irish Sports Publishing (ISP)
Unit 11, Tandy's Lane
Lucan, Co Dublin
Ireland
www.irishsportspublishing.com

First published, 2012

A CIP record for this book is available from the British Library

ISBN 978-0-9573954-4-2

Printed in Ireland with Print Procedure Ltd
Cover design, typesetting and layout: Jessica Maile
Photographs: Inpho Sports Agency
Photographs of Galway 1980 triumph courtesy of The Connacht Tribune

DEDICATION

To the greatest love of my life, my wife Margaret,
and my children Shane, Darragh, Tadgh, Sylvie Og,
Aoibheann and my grandson, Brogan.

CONTENTS

ACKNOWLEDGMENTS

I was not sure if I would ever see the day when I would have 'my story' on a bookshelf, and because of that I never thought the day would arrive when I would have to formally, in black and white, thank all of the people who have helped me in my life, and, of course, in my hurling career.

It was a successful career, mainly because there were so many great people around me from the very start, and right to the end of my career – which came a little bit too suddenly for my liking. But, all good things have to come to some sort of ending.

It's a daunting job to have to list the names of all these people in my mind because it is such a long list.

It's safer to thank everybody from the bottom of my heart.

But, now, I do need to thank some people personally. Three men stand out, all unsung heroes of the GAA, who were magnificent supporters of mine and they represent so many other great people – in Gort, to begin with, and throughout Galway – who helped make it possible for me to achieve more than I often imagined was my due, on the hurling field.

These men are Stephen Killeen, Jerry Sheehan and Frank Lally RIP. They are the finest men, and they truly represent the finest community a man could live in, here in Gort. To everybody else in the parish, and in Gort GAA Club in particular, I offer a heartfelt thanks.

Of course, my colleagues on the Galway teams that I was fortunate enough to play on for well over a decade, have to be officially thanked, as well. I was surrounded by so many brilliant hurlers, from the first day I set foot in a Galway senior dressing room in the mid-'70s, and by men like our three-times All-Ireland winning manager, Cyril Farrell, and Bernie O'Connor and

Phelim Murphy, his selectors, who did such an outstanding job in making us the team we were – and a team good enough to win three All-Ireland titles.

I say in this book that we should have won more than three! And I blame some people for that in this book, but it's something which we all had a hand in, and none of us were blameless in leaving All-Ireland titles behind us. But, they were the best of years, each and every one of them, whether we won, or whether we were denied the Liam MacCarthy Cup.

On a personal note, I have to honour my parents, Mick and Celia, for everything they did for me in my life, and all my brothers and sisters, including my late brothers Aidan and Brendan, for being an amazingly loving family.

My brother, Martin, and I spent many a happy childhood summer with my older cousin, Mickey Connaughton of Carraclough, Kilchreest, Loughrea. Mickey played intermediate for Galway and was also a selector for the Galway senior hurling team. He took me along as a young lad to matches and training sessions, and it was there my dreams of playing for Galway first began.

Finally, I'd like to say the biggest thank you of all to my wife, Margaret, and my 'children' who are no longer children, Shane, Darragh, Tadgh, Sylvie Og and Aoibheann, for their love and generosity to me as a husband and a father.

I hope you all enjoy this book.

It's down to you all as much as me!

Sylvie Linnane,
October 2012

CO-AUTHOR'S NOTE

Two years ago, I received a hand-written letter from Paddy O'Grady from Cahermore in Gort, a gentleman I had never met. He informed me that he felt it was high time that Sylvie Linnane's autobiography was published, and in reminding me of Sylvie's outstanding achievements on the hurling field he noted… "He established a reputation as a firebrand and would have a lot of stories to tell. His teammates and opponents would have tales to tell, too, plenty of them."

I knew he was dead right.

Paddy had just finished reading 'Doyle: The Greatest Hurling story Ever Told', which the company I founded with my colleague, Kevin MacDermot in 2008, Irish Sports Publishing, had proudly launched just a couple of months earlier to huge critical acclaim.

I called Paddy a few days later, and promised him that I would, at the very least, sit down with Sylvie Linnane and talk about his memoirs. After that, Sylvie and I, and his wife Margaret, met again and again, and we agreed that there was indeed a book that should be written.

I had not intended to write the book myself. I had been a member of the Meath football team during Sylvie's years with the Galway hurling team. We both had our lives changed by similar managers, Sean Boylan in my case, Cyril Farrell in the case of Sylvie. We both won All-Ireland titles with Meath and Galway, in 1987 and '88, and we both failed to finish off the 1980s with two 'three-in-a-row's.

However, I had never met Sylvie and Margaret Linnane during that time, even though the Meath and Galway teams had holidayed in Gran Canaria and in the United States at exactly the same time, in exactly the same hotels.

On my first meeting with Sylvie and Margaret, I was intrigued. It was a real pleasure, and an honour, for me to be warmly received in the home of the most iconic hurler of that decade, not just in Galway, but in the entire hurling community in Ireland. I quickly wanted to know more about the man.

However, I also wanted to know more about a young boy who was one of a family of 15 which lived off a small holding of land. I wanted to know about his siblings and his parents, and I wanted to learn a great deal more about life in the south of Galway (and, indeed, the lives of young Galwaymen who found themselves in London) in the 1960s and '70s. Six young Linnane boys had left Kilmacduagh in Galway for work in London, Sylvie amongst them.

I wanted this book to tell readers 'who' and 'what' had made Sylvie Linnane – and tell the story of the 'making' of a boy, the making of a man and, ultimately, the making of a legend.

Also, I wanted this book to be more than a sports book. I wanted it to be a rich, cultural and social history of a time in Irish life that we seem to have abandoned, and left behind at lightning speed.

It was then that I decided that I wished to write this book myself.

I have a great number of people to thank, but I will mention only a few here, and the others I will thank personally. I want to thank Sylvie's great coach, Cyril Farrell, who was also in his time was my coach in Skryne, after I visited him in his home in Navan in the mid-80s when he was taking time out from his duties with Galway and asked, and pleaded, with him to come out to our parish and look after us for a year. Cyril was a gentleman then, and was warm and receptive when I knocked on his door in the last 12 months with questions to ask him about Sylvie Linnane.

I want to thank the Linnane family, many of whom have their stories told on the pages which follow and especially Micheal Linnane, who was the first of the Linnane boys to head off and restart his life in London. Micheal recounted his life story and the stories of his brothers and sisters with great care and affection, and brilliant honesty.

Naturally, I have Sylvie and Margaret Linnane and their family to thank most of all, not only for their hospitality on my many visits to their home in the summer of 2012, but for their understanding and support – as I explained to them that we had an opportunity to write a book which would be more than a sports book.

Finally, I would like to thank Paddy O'Grady for taking the time, two years ago, to put pen to paper, in an old-style manner in an IT world which has gone half-mad with the wizardry of communications, and recommending to me in the strongest possible manner that I should have a word with his close neighbour, Sylvie.

Liam Hayes,
October, 2012.

FOREWORD

I am a native of Dromkerry, Killarney, County Kerry. However, my employers saw fit to direct me to patrol the streets and roads of South Galway in the late 1960s.

I have a strong interest in Gaelic football traditions and I endeavoured to pursue these in my adopted parish. But, these aspirations did not always work in parallel with the hurling traditions in Gort Inse Guaire.

To overcome these 'tensions', I subscribed to the administrative side of camánaíocht. As secretary of the Gort Inse Guaire Club, I ventured through a learning process. Apart from the normal duties of rúnaí, particularly in the 1970-72 years, the honourable secretary was obliged to ensure that all underage players attended the venues of Championship games.

These exploits, generally take a route through the west side of Gort parish – various crossroads and other pick-up points had to be effectively serviced. Another vehicle would be secured to cover the east of the parish. It was important, too, to ensure that there were 15 players available for the game.

Cars were scarce and available drivers were sometimes as scarce as hen's teeth. You had one run at it and time was of the essence on these missions.

It was during one of these exploits that I drove up a hill to a Crannagh household. It was a relief to see five or six young players waiting for my hasty arrival. What inspired me most, as I approached them, was to see one of these youths playing ball against the gable end of a building which touched onto the verge of the road.

I immediately noted the artistry of stick work and ball control of this young player. I was happy in the knowledge that we had a player who had craft and determination to challenge the opposition.

I cannot recall the result that day, but the same young lad stood out a mile. It was a day of learning. Back at the ranch that evening, I had a discussion amongst the natives. I got a print-out of the geography.

This player was known as Sylvie Linnane.

I think I used the spelling 'Silvie' but that did not matter. When I first set eyes on him, he was not knocking the paint off anyone else's building but that of his own family. I believe it was later that same evening that I said to my conversationalists that that young lad would don the county jersey with honour, in future years.

He was no more than 14 or 15 years old at the time.

It was no surprise to me that Sylvie won every honour in the sport. He always upheld the qualities of honesty, fire, passion and determination. He had an excellent anticipatory brain. He was fair, fearless and courageous. He was always a genuine leader, sportsman and team player.

Sylvie was in the wars on a couple of occasions.

The Nicholas English saga was blown out of proportion. This fact was proved in his appeal hearing. I was a strong supporter of his defence presentation. It is a question of the interpretation of rules and the opinions of amateur officials. We witness much more serious breaches of discipline nowadays where there is little fuss created.

It is a man's game.

My name is Jerry (Jeremiah) Sheehan.

I live at Barrack Street, Gort, Co. Galway

I am a native of Dromkerry, Killarney, Co. Kerry.

Jerry Sheehan, October, 2012 (Retired Garda Sergeant).

PART ONE
Making of a Boy

CHAPTER

1

Micheal Linnane didn't know what had turned Mickey Connaughton's face yellow. Mickey was smiling. His face was pure yellow, but he looked to be in the best of health. He was standing beside Micheal, one hand in his pocket, the other hand keeping a firm hold of his suitcase. Micheal was looking at his travelling companion, and also looking all around him. The busy-ness of the huge train station had him enthralled. Mickey had told him Euston Station was big. But the place was bigger than a town. It helped wipe the tiredness from Micheal's eyes. Their long journey from Dublin, the boat, and then the train from Liverpool down to London, had left them weary. Before that, the day had commenced with a drive to the train station in Galway. They'd been on the move for almost 20 hours.

It wasn't just Mickey. Everyone was pure yellow in the face. But they were rushing about the place, with homes to go to, workplaces, public houses perhaps. What did Micheal know? He was in London Town. He was 17 years old. The son of Mick Linnane, from Kilmacduagh, in the south of County Galway, the second-eldest boy in his family, and the first Linnane to arrive, for good, in London.

It was the spring of 1958. Micheal Linnane would be followed to London by five of his brothers, by Johnny and Brendan, and then Colie, then Martin, and then, finally, Sylvie. All of them just young lads. Sylvie, too. He would be 16 years old when he spent his first night in Brendan's home in the middle of the biggest city in the world, as far as he was concerned.

• • •

Micheal Linnane, in London, would be stuck with the Irish pronunciation of his name. He had never been Micheal at home. He was Michael. Or he was Mick, as his father was… Mick Linnane.

In London, however, he had cousins. There was already a Michael Linnane working around the city and playing hurling. And there was also a Mick Linnane, who was also useful with the stick in his hands. He was told that it was to be Micheal, and that was good enough for him. Sure, what complaints could he have? Everything had gone nicely since he had first met his cousin, Mickey Connaughton, at a party in a neighbour's home that Christmas. He hadn't the slightest notion of heading to London when he first started talking to Mickey that evening.

"Do you want to come to London with me?" Mickey had surprisingly asked him. And Micheal didn't have to think long about it at all.

With his mother and father, he had never discussed the prospect of moving out. There was a good number in the house by then, nine brothers and sisters. His younger brother, Aidan, had passed away two summers earlier. He was 12 years old when he died, from a 'hole in the heart' as they called it, something which might often be dealt with quite expertly ten years later, but which had left Aidan, and mainly his mother, suffering and enduring his ailing condition in the last couple of years of his life. One baby had died shortly after being born. Another was about to be born, as Micheal readied himself for his move to England, and the very day he left Kilmacduagh he first got a lift into Galway Hospital to see his mother, and his little baby sister, Bernadette, just hours old, lying in his mother's arms. From the hospital, Micheal headed straight for the train station, for Dublin, and for London.

Mick and Celia Linnane would have another child while their second eldest son was living in London. Mick and Celia would have fifteen boys and girls in total, thirteen of them surviving, to live strong and healthy lives.

There were two bedrooms in the cottage, while another four children nightly climbed the little ladder to sleep beneath the roof, a curtain separating them from the adults' talking and playing draughts and cards, and sometimes dancing quietly enough below them. Micheal Linnane knew alright that it was time to move out. He was the third in the family. The oldest, Patrick, was working the farm with his father. And his elder sister, Mary, was looking for work and had talked about it at home. She had her exams done, and she was thinking of going to London? By the time Micheal had left, however, Mary had four job offers on her hands, and decided against the biggest move. She went to live in Tuam, where she started work as a telephonist.

Micheal had his suitcase at his feet as he waited in the station. There was not much in it, his everyday clothes, working clothes and a good suit. There was also a pair of second-hand boots, which the hurling club in Kilmacduagh had handed to him as a present, a decent pair. They'd been polished up and looked good. In his right trouser-leg pocket he had thirty-five Irish pounds, more money than he had ever possessed in his life. As soon as word had started to reach houses in the parish that one of Mick Linnane's boys was heading to London, people had started dropping in to Celia, and leaving small envelopes with his mother. Most contained one pound. Some had two pounds. He had the money in a small wallet he'd bought. It would be several months before he felt he was ready to go to a bank and open up his first account, so, in the meantime, he moved his money from one pocket to the next.

• • •

The old sodium street lamps were everywhere Micheal looked, and walked, that first evening. The thousands and thousands of lamps turned the night sky orange, but the hands and faces of people passing him by on the street were all coloured yellow. It wasn't just Mickey, who walked briskly by his side, who looked like he had been doused in a barrel of the yellow stuff. They made their way through a pea-soup fog that cloaked the lingering smell of coal, but the place was amazing, startling to Micheal. The brightness, for starters! In Galway, night-time was a shuddering darkness, and had been all his life, but, in London, night-time was a sudden illumination of people and noise, and of all those most fanciful of old buildings. One minute a bus would be in front of him. The next minute it was gone. In the days to come, he would understand that he'd have to move faster than he ever did at home. Everybody was bustling about the place. Everybody was in a hurry, and nobody really spoke. He didn't mind. He was in London to work.

And there was good work in London. The great city was moving into the countryside while, in the old town of London, around the likes of Blackfriars, there were still ruins left over from the war and buildings half falling down, where the homeless found some comfort. The Irish were working hard in the city, and Micheal was warned that he would have to be up to a hard day's work straight away. In the first few days and weeks to come, he'd see big, hardy, muscled fellas, Irishmen and Englishmen, men twice his age in their 30s and 40s, with huge chests on them, and with the mightiest of hairy locks clamped either side of their faces. They looked ferociously strong. But Micheal Linnane quickly found that a 17-year-old boy, reared on a small enough farm in the south of Galway, had almost as much strength stuffed into his skinnier body. Twelve, and fourteen and sixteen-hour days, working to the orders of Mick Linnane had made him fit for any man's choice of work.

Micheal had been met by two of his first cousins, Michael Linnane and Bernard Roche, that first evening. They already had a room picked out for the lads, and paid for. One week's rent. It was a fair-sized room, with two single beds, and a nice little kitchenette. The house was divided into four rooms for rent. The beds weren't soft, but they weren't bad either. Micheal and Mickey Connaughton had just sat down on the two beds, when there was a loud banging on the door downstairs.

"Is Micheal Linnane here yet?" he heard a man ask, though it was more of a shout to Micheal's ears.

"Jesus Christ, there's something wrong," Micheal said, looking over at Mickey. "Is there someone…DEAD?"

His name was called from downstairs.

The man asked if he could come up to the room. He wanted to talk to Micheal, and to Mickey. Micheal led the stranger back up the stairs and into the room, where, by now, Mickey was lying back on his bed.

"I'm Martin Diggins!" said the stranger. 'From Kerry, to start with… but I'm with St Monica's hurling club here!"

Micheal and Mickey listened.

"If you sign here ... we've got jobs for you ... Monday morning like!"

Micheal and Mickey signed the two pages of paper. Diggins said he'd back to see them again the next day. He'd tell them where they were working, he'd get them over to training. Micheal and Mickey thanked him, and Diggins left. It was only a 10-minute visit, and an even shorter conversation. A month would pass before Micheal asked how they'd known that he had arrived in London? Martin Diggins kept his reply to that question very short indeed.

"Contacts!" he smiled.

In truth, Martin Diggins was married to a girl from Kinvara. She was a distant relation of the Linnane's, in fact, and she'd advised Martin all about Micheal and Mickey Connaughton and their travel plans.

• • •

Johnny Linnane joined Micheal eighteen months later. As new boys and girls arrived in the Linnane household in Kilmacduagh, the older Linnanes had to be on their way. It was part of Irish life for families in small homes on small parcels of land in the west of Ireland. Upon arriving in London, life, however, was that little bit easier for Johnny as he found his feet and discovered a whole new world, and his place in it.

The brothers would, of course, live together. Before Johnny's arrival, Micheal had discovered a natural flow to his working life and his domestic life, as well as his hurling career in a new country. Mickey Connaughton had quickly met a man who was working in the steel-fixing business, and he had moved north of the city. Micheal and Bernard Roche had decided to share the expense of a roof over their heads instead, and that roof was in Finsbury Park, in a part of the city which was more the natural home of Arsenal FC, than Tottenham Hotspur FC.

The pair of cousins had their needs sussed out. If they cooked chops or something which could be flashed onto a pan one evening, then they would also decide to put in a more worthwhile piece of meat into the oven on the same evening. That way, when they arrived home from work later in the week and had little time to grab a bus or a train, which had the nasty habit of refusing to wait around for any young hurler from Ireland, they had their meal already prepared. A few potatoes, and some veg, and, as soon as they had downed their food, they'd be off to catch some or other means of wonderful transport that criss-crossed the city so brilliantly.

They might have to get as far as New Eltham, a vast swathe of common ground in the south-east of London. That was the home of the GAA in the city for a time, and it was an awful bloody journey for lads who had been out of their beds at 4.30 that morning, who had an eight-hour working day, and three or four hours of journeying to and from work, already under their belts. On Sundays, the club would have a car to fetch them, or even put on a bus when there was enough money in the kitty. But, midweek, in the evenings, they raced to The Underground. Life, indeed, had presented them with choices, and forms, of transport they had never imagined existed a year or two earlier when, mostly, the eight-mile trip from Kilmacduagh into Gort had to be taken on foot and, occasionally, by trap. The Piccadilly Line was the best. Every five minutes, there was a train on hand, but, if they had to depend on the Northern Line, the wait on the platform was extended to an unholy fifteen minutes.

The good men and women of suburban London would indeed look at young men carrying sticks in their hands, as they walked onto the train. Micheal got looks. Every single week there'd be a hard stare, from some busybody. But nobody ever spoke to him, nobody questioned him, ever! Not once over the next two decades did he encounter a problem with the people of London Transport, or their paying customers, for existing as a hurler deep in the bowels of the city. It was different in the broad daylight.

The lads would try to get an hour of hurling in on Finsbury Park, when they didn't have to hike it across the city for a formal training session with St Monica's. The magnificent facility was on their doorstep in central north London and, since it had been laid out in Victorian times. it had a very formal appearance, and hard and fast rules. Young men pelting small balls around the place, and swinging sticks of ash as they ran around in circles, was neither amusing nor tolerable. Hurling was not quite cricket. The English game didn't have grown men racing after one another with their sticks. And it didn't have any violence on display. There were nets for the English game in Finsbury

Park. There was cricket, there were formal gardens, beautiful avenues and even an arboretum with a fantastic mix of unusual trees. There was a lake, boating, a children's play area, a café, and place for art exhibitions, but there was no space for a hurling pitch, not one.

Micheal and Johnny, and whoever joined them, would wait until the park's wardens were well out of sight before getting into the thick of a good puck around. Uninvited and unrehearsed games of hurling were, seemingly to onlookers, the most violent occasions ever witnessed in Finsbury Park until, that is, 1967, ten years after Micheal Linnane had first arrived in London, when Jimi Hendrix decided for the first time ever to burn his guitar on stage in the same park.

• • •

The first time a Linnane played a game of hurling in London, Micheal found himself in the unfamiliar territory of the half-back line. His natural preference, at home in Kilmacduagh, was to be further up the field. But what was even stranger to behold, as Micheal stood his ground in the No.5 shirt of St Monica's and awaited his immediate opponent was the sight of three well-known Galway hurlers walking in his general direction. The three of them were 'countymen' who had landed in London a fortnight earlier. Micheal knew it would be a difficult day, but he had had a run out for the Galway minor team himself on one occasion before having to leave home. He stood as tall as he could, and he knew he had young Hanrahan on the far side of the line, and he'd seen that the Waterford lad could hurl as well. In between the pair of them was Mickey Connaughton. Mickey was a naturally hard man. He'd hurled for the Galway seniors for a short time, but he'd lost the sight in one eye many years earlier when a stick was swung wildly, and far too high.

St Monica's had Brothers Pearse to deal with that evening, one of the oldest GAA clubs in the city, and a club which seemed to never forget the troubled history at the time of its birth. 'Pearses' was put together in the 1920s, at a period when Ireland was finding its way out of a War of Independence and a Civil War, and England had extracted itself from The Great War. Yes, 'Pearses' had a reputation for being war-like. And the club's unique mixture of brilliance and brute force was never summoned forth with more passion than it was in the late 50s and early 60s. Some months later, out in New Eltham, Micheal would witness the most ferocious game of hurling he was to ever experience in his whole life. He was a spectator, luckily, but even standing and watching in his street clothes did not necessarily mean that a man was entirely separated from the fighting that broke out between Brothers Pearse and Sean McDermott's that Sunday afternoon, and spilled all over the sidelines. By the end of the sickening game, Micheal swore to himself, as he waited on the platform for his train home, that he would never play hurling in London again. Men had been lying, as if they were dead, in several places. There were two ambulances at work. There were faces and arms, with blood dripping from them. He was certain that he'd hear a day or two later that someone had been killed.

St Monica's lost by four at the final whistle. The first member of the Linnane family had survived his first game of hurling on British soil, and had acquitted himself well enough.

CHAPTER
2

Harold Macmillan was elected Prime Minister of Britain within twelve months of the first of Mick and Celia Linnane's children arriving in London. Macmillan succeeded Anthony Eden, who had resigned in January of 1957 and left the Conservative party in a bit of a pickle as they had no mechanism for choosing a new PM literally overnight. It was left to Queen Elizabeth II, upon direction from Winston Churchill and others, to appoint Macmillan who, before he left office six years later, would be remembered for five shortish words, more than anything else. With some growth in the British economy at last, and incredibly low unemployment numbers, Macmillan informed his people that they had "… never had it so good!"

It was not quite true, but Macmillan's government was a government with its sleeves rolled up high. They got things done. At the beginning of the 1950s, Macmillan, under Churchill as PM, had held down the post of Minister for Housing, and his surly old master gave him the target of building 300,000 houses per year. Churchill told Macmillan that the job would make or break his political career. Macmillan achieved his target a year ahead of schedule. They were building houses all over England, and principally in the south of the country, as if there was no tomorrow. London boomed. The car factories were busy as bees. The aircraft factories were beginning to do a roaring business and in London docks there were 30,000 people fully employed. The

Irish were massing in England to take up work in the building trade. Other peoples were arriving as well and, by the mid-50s, 20,000 West Indian men, women and children, were landing in the country every year.

That was the England in which Micheal, Johnny, Brendan, Colie and Martin Linnane would find work for all the hours God gave them. Sylvie Linnane was the last of the Linnane boys to arrive. By the time Sylvie got his legs under him in London in 1973, Edward Heath was PM. Harold Macmillan had resigned after being misdiagnosed with inoperable cancer of the prostrate, Alex Douglas-Home had held the job for just under 12 months, and Harold Wilson had seen out the first of his two periods in power for his Labour government, before Heath arrived at 10 Downing Street in 1970.

• • •

It wasn't politics that entertained the Linnane boys, however. In London, and in north London in particular, it was football. It was Arsenal and Spurs. And, living just around the corner, more or less, from Highbury, the marble-halled home of Arsenal FC, the first port of call was to see 'The Gunners' doing what they did best. However, Arsenal played the game the Arsenal way in the late 1950s and early 60s, and that was simply dead-beat and quite boring. If Arsenal scored early in the game, then, straight away, they'd shut up shop. Unlike what their proud, old nickname promised, Arsenal did not blaze away at anybody with their big guns. Arsenal defended and defended, and Micheal and Johnny Linnane could not stomach that sort of football at all. On their first visit to White Hart Lane, which was a slightly further stretch of the legs for the boys, they immediately fell in love with Tottenham Hotspur.

Spurs would attack and attack and attack, with a boldness and a fearlessness, which might have been more at home on a hurling field or a Gaelic football field. At times, the Linnane boys would be praying for Spurs to defend, but the team built at White Hart Lane by the wily little Yorkshireman, Bill Nicholson, seldom answered those prayers. As it happened, Nicholson, too, came from a big family. The Spurs' manager was the eighth of nine children and, for him, it seemed that life, and a game of football, was about making the most of every single day that a man was given. He had left school as a little boy. He worked in a laundry at first and, much like all of the Linnanes, he was on the cusp of his 16th birthday when he first arrived in London by train from the north of the country. He began by earning £2 per week as a ground-staff boy at White Hart Lane but, by the time Spurs won the First Division Championship in the 1950-51 season, he was working away, up and down the field, at right-half on the first eleven. Exactly 10 years later, with Bill Nicholson as first team boss, Spurs became the first English team in the 20th century to win the First Division Championship and the FA Cup. Spurs won 'The Double' and two Linnane boys were with Spurs every step of the way that historic season.

Spurs ran at every team that season. They won their first 11 games and, by the end of it all, they'd scored 115 goals in 42 games. The following year they won the FA Cup again. They also came within a hair's breadth of a European Cup final. Benfica beat them, but only just, and the season after that Nicholson wrapped up another piece of history for the club when Spurs became the first British club to win a major European trophy, drubbing Atletico Madrid 5-1 in the final of the European Cup Winners' Cup.

While Arsenal laboured under the management of Jack Crayston, and later George Swindin and Billy Wright, Spurs left everything in Bill Nicholson's hands. His team in those years was sublime, and honest, from the stoic figure of Scotland's Bill Brown in goals, to the fast legs of winger Cliff Jones up front. Jones threw himself into everything and, usually, came off the worse for wear, but Spurs also handed out lots of pain to opposing defences with the battering-ram instincts of goal-scoring machine Bobby Smith. In between, there was Danny Blanchflower and Dave Mackay, the sort of footballers who liked to put manners on their opponents sooner rather than later in games.

GAA men of both creeds felt at home in White Hart Lane.

• • •

The lads had moved to Tollington Park by then. They were promised that there was a lovely flat going at the end of the road. It looked good when they got there to throw their eye over it. The landlady was a Limerick woman, a kind-hearted soul who, the following Christmas, cooked up the full works of turkey and ham for the Linnane lads a full fortnight before December 25. She'd heard they were going home to Galway for Christmas, and she didn't want her boys to miss out on their Christmas in London.

There was a sitting-room, and fairly large it was too, in the flat, which made it more of a home. Not that they got to relax much in their new surroundings. Work was hard but it was the hours that were a real devil. Home was a place to eat, and usually eat fast. And home was a place to sleep. The lads didn't drink alcohol. Sure, they hardly had the time.

It would be pitch dark when they rolled out of their beds every morning. It reminded Micheal of getting up in the middle of the night, back at home, when himself and his brothers would be lined up by their father to bring the sheep and cattle to the fair in Ardrahan or Kinvara three and four miles away or, better still for the boys, the long night's walk with the animals into Gort. They'd be out of their beds at one o'clock in the early morning and their mother would have a pot of steaming porridge prepared. They needed full stomachs as they would not get to The Square in Gort for four or five hours. It'd be 5am or even 6am before they got a sandwich in the town. Every morning in London, those first few years, was like the morning of a fair day back home in Kilmacduagh.

Every morning, the boys would be out of their beds at 4am. If they were not out the front door of the house by 5.10 am, they knew they'd be in trouble. They needed to be on the platform at Finsbury Park Station by 5.20am otherwise they'd be mad late for work. It didn't matter if they were out at a dance the night before or a small party in someone's home, they still had to be on that platform by 5.20am. And, once they got home from work, they had to get out the door to training two evenings each week. Weekends also refused to let the Linnane boys let their hair down and stop looking at the alarm clock Micheal had bought, and that served them best for years. Hurling in London was a serious piece of business, and it was no use anyone arriving at a game with a head thumping every five or six seconds. With so many Irish flooding through the GAA clubs in the city, the quality of the game, the stick-work, and the strength and athleticism of teams was as high as any club in Ireland. Even higher, some years.

London was a place where a hurler, no matter what his name, no matter where he was from, had to prove himself all over again from the very beginning. While, at home, a sense of place and the boundaries of a parish where a man was born and reared, defined him, London was a whole new story in his life. A hurler no longer had the same clubmen, the same countymen, wrapped around him. Instead, he had to represent himself and his parish and his county of birth amongst a whole pile of strangers. At the very beginning Micheal Linnane had found himself with some Galwaymen, but there were also five Corkmen, five Tipperarymen, three men from Westmeath, and a big fella from Limerick at training those first few weeks. A boy in a man's world had to hold his ground and he had to do so from the very start or he'd have no chance. Micheal, for one, didn't touch a drop of alcohol at all for his first seven years in London. He hadn't the inclination, but neither did he have the time, day or night, to even think of finding himself a public house from so many public houses on every street corner with their tempting, descriptive names, and moseying in there once or twice a week. First time he touched the strong stuff was the night that he and Mona became engaged.

• • •

The Linnanes became St Gabriel's men. The blue and yellow sash was worn by all six of them, from Micheal to Sylvie. It was, of course, a Galwayman's GAA club, and was founded in a room above the Windsor Castle Public house on Harrow Road, on October 11, 1960. There were 15 people present, 10 of them hurlers.

A few weeks earlier, the first talk of a club was heard at 64 St Margaret's Road, in the home of Martin and Bridie Treacy, a haunt for musicians and GAA men and women for years. The toughest job was to get players into St Gabriel's from other clubs, and from Brothers Pearse in particular. The easy job was to get a set of jerseys, it was thought. These were to be blue and gold, as the only Tipperaryman present at the first general meeting suggested his home county's colours, with a gold sash rather than a gold band. Each man at the meeting agreed and hands were buried into pockets as £1 per man was collected to buy a first set of jerseys. They were told there was a good shop on Fleet Street for jerseys, by the name of Jack Hobbs.

However, nobody did jerseys with sashes in London. So, Joe Leahy, from Loughrea, whose wife was a dressmaker, volunteered to finish off the job. The jerseys cost 17 shillings and six pence. Socks were another two shillings and six pence. The Leahys cut the gold material into strips and sewed it on for free. There was also more than enough money to buy a large suitcase, coloured a striking blue, which had enough room for jerseys for two or three teams, and which served the club splendidly for a good 10 years.

That trouble out of the way, delegates of the new club had to turn up at the first London County Board meeting of the year, in 1961, and submit papers with requests for transfers. The chairman of Brothers Pearse was told that there were 10 transfers requested from his club. He made no comment, but asked for the 10 names to be read out. London secretary, Jerry Daly, began with the name of Patrick Grealish, and then followed on... Peter Crehan, Richard Power, Peter Fitzgerald, Charlie Graham, William Gorman, Michael Greally, Patrick Shiels, Tom Malone ... and Patrick Joseph Noone. The chairman of Brothers Pearse Hurling Club nodded his head.

Two Linnanes played for St Gabriel's that year. Micheal was usually found in the centre of the field. Johnny arrived in London as a half-back but, like his younger and ultimately more famous brother, Sylvie, he dropped back into a corner slot for the final years of his career. Johnny had a dash to him, and he was as aggressive as they come when he needed to be. But Johnny also had control of a ball that was rare amongst defenders. On the St Gabriel's team, he was supreme with ball and stick. And his vision in moving the ball about the field often left his team-mates as baffled as they were delighted. He won seven London titles with the club before his career was done, but, by the end of that same career, Johnny's body was also just about done. He met with a cruel run of injuries. Amongst them was a broken leg and further damage to cartilage and ligaments. Micheal, Colie and Brendan were fine hurlers, but Johnny Linnane was something different. So, too, Martin Linnane. In the year in which the now-legendary Sylvie Linnane was named Galway Hurler of the Year, his brother, Martin, was the unanimous choice as Britain's Hurler of the Year.

· · ·

It was the summer of 1973, and Sylvie Linnane had a plane ticket in his hand, with the name Mr S. Linnane, and Heathrow, printed in their appropriate boxes. There was still a good amount of work to be found in London and his brothers were doing well there, though Micheal had already come home to Galway for good, a year earlier, with his wife and two children.

He was needed at home. Mick Linnane had not been fit for work for a few years, as a heart condition had brought the man who had been as strong as a bull all his adult life, almost to a standstill. Micheal left behind him a lovely four-bedroom home in Wembley and a business that was thriving very nicely. The Linnanes were contracting in building works all over the city and around it. There were a dozen houses started in Newmarket. There was a block of flats in Lewisham. There were roads and sewerage works in Southend. There was work in Staines going on and at Pinewood Studios, the Linnanes were doing some ground-work on building the set of Baker Street for a new TV series of Sherlock Holmes.

Micheal Linnane found it harder to leave London than he had leaving Galway almost two decades earlier. He'd lived longer in London than he had lived in Galway. It had become his home.

Micheal brought his wife back for a visit to Kilmacduagh before making their final decision, the biggest decision of their lives.

"You better have a good look at what's there." he told Mona.

He'd already warned her that they would be giving up everything they had worked so hard for in England. The Linnane home place was still the same size. There was little space, no luxury and no prospect of any for a couple of years at least until they had got back on their feet and sorted everything out at home.

"You have your house here," he reminded Mona, "… your beautiful home, bathrooms, toilets … everything our family needs."

But Micheal and Mona, after a three-day visit home, were one hundred per cent certain that there was only one decision to make.

Things had changed in England. Edward Heath was looking to curb the powers of the unions and he was facing a fight. Unemployment was rising fast. The post-war low in England had been 215,000, or just under one per cent of the population. One miner's strike had ended and another would commence the following year. The Troubles in Northern Ireland were at their height, and costing the British taxpayer. There was a worldwide oil crisis. The Irish economy was on its knees. The world economy, meanwhile, had landed on one knee, and England was beginning to suffer like everywhere else.

CHAPTER 3

L218, 307

Sylvie wanted to go to London. The decision was his. And he knew that he had brothers and sisters there to help him. Johnny, Colie, Brendan and Martin were still living in the south of England. And the boys had also been joined by Sheila and Anne.

It was Brendan who'd asked Sylvie if he had thought of joining them in London. Brendan had been home for three weeks. The Linnane boys always came home from London twice each year – for a good summer break and the races, and for a short stay over Christmas.

"What would you think of coming back with me?" Brendan had asked, out of the blue, one morning. Sylvie was surprised, but neither did he think it a bad idea. It would be an adventure, for a start.

"I'll have a go at it!" he replied, quickly enough.

The first week in London, Sylvie stayed in Brendan's perfect home in Enfield, outside the city, but he wanted to be his own man as well. By the start of his second week in London, 16-year-old Sylvie had found a bedsit on Holloway Road. It was simple, comprising a bed and a tiny kitchenette, and it was only a stone's throw from the house in which Micheal Linnane, at 17, had spent his first week in London almost 20 years earlier. Like Micheal, Sylvie had filled a bag with everything he had at home. It wasn't a massive bag in the end. He had all his clothes, or all the clothes that were any good, and some possessions. On one or two nights, in those first two or three weeks, he felt pangs of loneliness, and it was a strange emotion, like something tearing at his heart. He hadn't been prepared for that. It had never dawned on him that he'd miss so many of the little things that had idly cluttered up his life, never mind missing the people at home. But, he was going to make a good life for himself. That was his mission in London. That was what it was all about.

His first weekend, Sylvie was needed back home in Galway for a game. It was the same the next weekend and, with the club asking him home and the Galway minors gearing up for the Championship, Sylvie found himself heading to Heathrow every Friday evening when his day's work was done and being picked up by somebody at Shannon later that night.

He liked London, and he felt he could make a home and a life there for himself, as his brothers and sisters had. But he also knew the hold of his parish and his county was strong. The rest of the family thought him a 'home-bird'; he knew that too! And, at home, by then, he also had found his way into the affections of a local girl, Margaret Nolan from the parish next door, from Gort, whom he'd met in the Classic Ballroom in the town a few months earlier. He liked her a lot. However, Margaret was still in secondary school and had let him know, in no uncertain terms, that she was not interested in going anywhere yet.

The weeks went fast in London. It was only five days, after all, and for two of those days Sylvie Linnane was reporting to the 'Scrubs' on Tuesday and Thursday evenings for training with St Gabriel's. It wasn't all that different than home, after all. He'd no friends around him, but there were lots of new faces on the building sites through the day, where he spent his hours labouring and clearing ground, and more interesting faces and hurlers out on the field in the evenings, hitting the ball about, and he was getting less lonely.

The 'Scrubs' was right behind the famous prison, a huge open space, in north-east London, a couple of hundred acres or thereabouts. And, at the western end of the common ground was HM Prison Wormwood Scrubs, which had been built a century before and looked every inch the sort of place that had missed out on every single advantage, and advancement, that had ever happened over the last one hundred years. It had a scary look to it, as far as young Sylvie Linnane was concerned, and was a place best ignored.

At the end of his sixth week in London, Sylvie took time to ask himself what on earth he was doing tearing over to England and tearing home again? He should be playing hurling in one country or the other, and that left him with no choice. He should be living his life in one country or the other. Again, there was no choice there either. He tore up his return ticket to London. It was best to tear it, that way the firmness, and finality of his decision was less likely to ever be second-guessed in the weeks and months ahead of him. Micheal thought it was a good decision. And that counted in Sylvie's head too. The next week, Micheal found Sylvie a job in Ennis, where he was due to start work with the Lynch construction company.

• • •

Micheal had never wanted Sylvie to go to London in the first place. He was too young, and times had changed in Ireland and England. And, besides, he was too good a hurler. Every year he had come home from England, for a holiday, Micheal was surprised by Sylvie! The things he could do with the ball at his feet! And when the ball was at the end of his stick, the little lad was magical. And, every year, when he went back to London, Micheal would find himself telling the lads in the club over there how good the little lad was, how good he was going to be. Micheal knew that Sylvie was going to be the best.

London was the wrong place for Sylvie, Micheal knew that for certain in his heart. It would be a shame for him to leave Galway. Pure shameful. Nothing in Ireland could stop him, not on the hurling field, but in London, you'd never know!

Micheal had seen very good hurlers in London being destroyed with bad belts, from one fella or another; there was always someone who might do damage.

Anything could happen.

Micheal remembered that almost everything had happened during his time in London. Before one London final, he was belting the ball around with his own teammates. They were waiting for the referee to call the game to order, and for the two teams to get into their places. There were boys in their street clothes also on the field, hitting balls too. And that was normal enough in London, until the referee ordered the pitch cleared. Micheal Linnane was talking to the Gabriel's chairman, listening to him tell him to go for his scores early on, when, next thing, suddenly, Micheal crashed to the ground in a heap. He lay there. Dazed, confused for a few seconds. The selectors were around him.

"You were hit...!" he heard someone shout.

"One of those lads... over there!

"Hit Linnane with the stick... he did!"

Micheal rolled onto his side. His head was thumping. The back of his skull was painful, and there was blood to be cleaned up from the side of his face and his neck. He was helped to the sideline as the game was about to start. Later, in hospital, his wound would need 11 stitches. But, that was later. Micheal lay on the sideline watching the final. His head was bandaged up, rightly bound up in white tape and rolls of faded purple bandaging. Maura Malone did a fine job stopping the blood alright, but St Gabriel's were three points down with five minutes left in the game. Micheal came onto the field for those last five minutes. Gabriel's lost by one.

Micheal knew that he had not being struck by accident. He'd been taken out early, before the game had ever started. The hurling fields which had grown up all over London in his 16 years there were no place for an outstanding hurler with rich promise, not the likes of Sylvie Linnane.

• • •

It was a mild and warmish spring day in 1980. Sylvie was digging the foundations for his new home. It was hard work, but satisfying. And, as soon as he had finished his long day, Sylvie decided that he had earned a pint. He drove into Gort, and sat down at the bar in the Silver Spruce. That's where he was when he was told that Brendan was dead.

Johnny had called home from London.

Brendan Linnane was the quietest of the Linnanes, and maybe the smartest as well. He had completed his secondary education at Our Lady's College in Gort, before he had found himself a fine job in London, and all over the south of England, working with Murphy's as an agent and overseer of construction works. He was on the hurling field when he died.

A St Gabriel's training session had just started when he fell to the ground. Nobody had been near him; nobody had touched him. It had been the birthday of his four year-old twins that same day, and Brendan had left the party, but promised to return after training for the cutting the cake. He died from heart failure, and it happened within minutes. Johnny was at the field, watching, and Johnny got his younger brother into his van and brought him to the hospital, around the corner from the 'Scrubs', in a matter of minutes. There was nothing the doctors could do.

Brendan Linnane was different to the others. So exact about everything, and so needing to do things right. He would obsess about doing things right. He was a good young hurler at home in Kilmacduagh. In London, he was a strong centre-fielder with the Gabriel's. When he won a ball in that big fist of his, he might be slow releasing it. But that's because he never wanted to waste one ball. He always wanted to find his man, and Brendan Linnane usually did. He was 32 years old.

• • •

Sylvie always felt close to Brendan, and probably closer to him than any of his brothers, tough they were all too good to him, most of the time. When each of them left for London, Sylvie and the rest of the gang in Kilmacduagh were never forgotten for long. There were the two sets of holidays, summer and Christmas, but there were always parcels, and letters with a few bob in them. Whatever winged its way from London to Kilmacduagh was usually worth getting your hands on.

He'd never really known Micheal or Johnny before they went. They were so much older than their baby brother. He was reared, and had made half a name for himself as a hurler in South Galway before the first of the Linnanes came back home to Galway for good. He didn't have any strong memory of Micheal before he'd left for London. Neither did he feel he'd known Johnny, so he never missed either of them terribly. But the hullabaloo every summer, and then Christmas, brought two of his biggest brothers back into his life, with extra drama and excitement attached. With Colie, Brendan and Martin, it had been different. He knew them as brothers, and he missed them always.

When they all came home, Sylvie, especially, was ready for the big matches in the field beside the house. Everyone played, boys and girls. In the matches, no quarter was given, or expected and, even if Sylvie was one of the smallest on the makeshift pitch, nobody took any extra care with him when there was a ball to be pulled on. His sister, Anne, was to one to watch. Sylvie found that out early on, and had enough bruises on his legs after games that were usually down to her excitement and competitiveness.

He'd wait for weeks for those matches. He'd be waiting to show all of his brothers a thing or two, things he knew how to do with a stick and a ball. Their praise was special. Any words, from any of them, would not roll off his back for days, and if Brendan told him how good he was getting, then Sylvie's boyish chest would be filled to the very brim.

It wasn't just the boys who made a hero out of him when they came home. The girls too. Mary was in Dublin working in the Civil Service and she never forgot anybody at home. Sheila and Anne in England, Carmel in Dublin, and Bernadette up the road in Claregalway, taught Sylvie great lessons in generosity and care and love, which he would carry with him for the rest of his life. As a young man making his own way in the world, Sylvie would think of his sisters as being too good. That was the simple truth, he told himself more than once.

• • •

As a boy growing and striving for early manhood, Sylvie was part and parcel of a family that had become smaller and smaller as every second year passed by. His mother and father were left in the three-roomed cottage along with Patrick, the eldest of his brothers – who was also his Godfather, and who would later act as Godfather to Sylvie's son, Tadgh – Martin, Anne and Gerry. It was a much quieter and more comfortable house. For starters, there was space.

More space, in fact, than could be found in Killomoran National School, a perfectly normal two-room, two-teacher building, with fourth, fifth and sixth classes in the Master's room and everyone else in the other half. About 30 children in each room. Toddy Byrne was the Master. He'd taken over from a cranky predecessor, in the estimation of more than one of the Linnane boys. Micheal received 20 of the best across the palms of his hands for whacking a ball over the school wall with a bit of a hurling stick one day. The others had less dramatic tales of woe and mostly received only a tongue-lashing. Very often, such lashings would be wholly deserved. But, Master Byrne was different. For starters, he was a hurling man, and if one of his boys lost a ball over a wall, Toddy Byrne was liable to applaud his strength or condemn him for lack of vision, one or the other, but a feat like that would never have been even close to a corporal punishment offence. Sylvie was a 'lively' little fella in the classroom and any punishment he, or anybody close to him, received from Toddy Byrne was asked for and duly received without a word of complaint.

Sylvie's favourite days at Killomoran National School were in the summer time. He could race to and from school in his bare feet. And race he did, as there was always work to be done at home: the herding and watering of the cattle, the lambing, something or other, which Mick Linnane had in mind for Sylvie and his brothers and sisters and which had to be done at a precise time.

Secondary school education for most of the Linnane boys and girls was in their local 'tech', St Colman's Vocational School, and that included Sylvie although his time heading into school in Gort was short-lived. He was two months into his second year in the tech when it was time to leave. He was 15 years old but he was able to do the work of any man on the farm and Mick Linnane needed young Sylvie to do more than his share. There was too much being left to his mother. His father had suffered a heart attack the year before when he was still a young man, in his late 50s, and, although he fought hard to get all of his strength back, he was never the same man again. High blood pressure and too many heart attacks ran in the Linnane family. The milking and the work in the fields were beyond him. Sylvie watched his father go downhill quickly after that first stab at his heart. Mick Linnane would be in and out of hospital, almost every second year. Sylvie blamed his father's fags for doing most of the damage, and watching his father so harshly debilitated and often struggling manfully for a breath, left Sylvie with a lifetime's revulsion at smoking. Mick Linnane had liked his Carrolls. Though he also liked his Aftons, and he was partial to Player's as well.

Mick also liked his horses. He always allowed himself four or five on the farm, and he was known to keep an eye out for a good horse. He'd have two horses for the ploughing and the others he'd be breaking-in and training. With a horse under him, Mick would take walls five and six feet high. The horses Mick Linnane sold on won many shows in Galway and in neighbouring counties. Between his horses and hopping on his bike and heading to Gort, he was as fit and strong a man as could be found in Kimacduagh. But, after his first heart attack, Mick would not be able to walk half a mile without stopping and holding up at the side of the road, his arms resting on a gate for a few minutes.

His wife had children underfoot all of their married life, but that did not stop Celia Linnane from joining Mick and her elder sons, helping with the hay, and bringing in the crops. In the house, Celia had the girls to help her with the cooking. Meals were like clockwork and were normally huge. Cakes of brown bread and tarts would be baked extra large. Come dinner time, two tables were set in the middle of the kitchen floor, side by side, and they would always be filled. It didn't seem to matter if Celia Linnane had spent half of her day in a potato field, doing an extra share of the work out there in addition to feeding the turkeys, geese, ducks and the chickens, the washing would still be done, everything would be baked for the evening tea, or for the next morning. There would be no help from outside. And Celia would still be smiling almost all of the time, every time her children looked in her direction. They knew, too, that their mother would not go to her bed without, first, having a game of cards. Or a game of draughts. She loved people having a little dance in her house, too. With the littlest ones asleep in the loft over her head, and everyone tired from their long day but no longer hungry, Celia Linnane needed to end her day on a light note, and with a 'thank you' for everything it had held.

• • •

The Linnane home place amounted to 40 acres, when Mick Linnane from Ballynastaig and Celia Diviney from Crannagh began their married life. The young couple had never imagined so many boys and girls around them, although large families were not unusual in rural Ireland in the 1950s and '60s. They'd been blessed with children for the first 25 years of their married life. As their family grew, in numbers and in size, Mick also needed to rent another parcel of land, roughly the same size, a couple of miles away in Labane.

Getting your hands on good land to rent off an elderly neighbour was sometimes a tricky business, and keeping hold of it needed just as much attention. Mick Linnane needed every acre in his possession to feed and care for his family. Between the two farms, there were sheep, cattle, lambs, pigs, and always enough pigs so that two or three could be killed for the family to eat through the year. The Linnane boys and girls were reared on bacon and cabbage, five days a week. It would remain Sylvie Linnane's favourite dinner for the rest of his life. There was fish on a Friday and chicken on a Sunday. Every week, all year long. Growing beet, potatoes, barley, wheat and oats, Mick Linnane had fields on the farm to be worked six days a week, and no end of jobs to be done seven days a week. Sylvie, like all of his older brothers and sisters, didn't have to be asked twice to attend to his individual chores. By the time he was seven years old, Sylvie had his share of the work laid out for him, and his father and mother expected everyone's share of their work to be done, and didn't expect to have to ask for it to be done. Not twice. Not even once.

Out in the fields was the toughest of the back-breaking work, and thinning beet broke the backs of the Linnane boys faster than anything else. There was always more than ten acres of beet on their own land, but when that work was in hand, the Linnane boys went out on 'hire' to their neighbours to thin more beet. It was the central component of the farm, and, for Mick Linnane to have enough money to see Celia and everybody happily through Christmas, there always had to be more than enough beet to work. The Government loved beet too. Sugar factories had been built, starting in the early 1930s in Carlow, Mallow, Thurles and also in the west of Ireland, to the heartfelt thanks of the farming community in Athenry, Ardrahan, Gort, Mountbellew, Ballygar and Glenamaddy, amongst other parishes. The sugar factory built in Tuam demanded 13,000 acres of the best of beet brought to its doors by the end of each year. The factory fed itself on 17,000 tons of washed beet every day, carried to Tuam by 240 railway trucks. Great Southern Railways had built 800 new trucks and bought 50 new lorries to bring the beet in as smoothly and efficiently as possible. At the height of the season, six hundred men were waiting to start work every day.

The beet had to get to Tuam on time. By the middle of September, at the latest, Mick Linnane needed everyone in the house out on the beet fields every day of the week, Sundays as well, and he'd lead the work himself until well after dark. It was the sort of work a man didn't want to leave behind at the end of the day, as he knew there would be so much more to be done the following morning. The harvesting, or 'campaign' as locals liked to eloquently call it, went from September to the middle of January, but the important thing was to get paid in early December. That was vital, but it was not always possible.

That's when Mick Linnane, farmer, would turn himself into a bold, efficient businessman. He was an amazingly smart businessman, with an equally amazing head for figures. Mick always knew where the money to feed his family and buy whatever needed to be bought was coming from, and he had everything added up in his brain. If Mick sold 10 or 15 sheep at a fair, he'd nearly always have the same number to bring home with him, and have a good sum of money left from his trade still in his pocket, for Celia or for the next family expense. Not that Patrick and Micheal and the older boys, or Sylvie either when his time came, admired their father's sharp business acumen when they were informed at the end of the day at the mart that they had a good few animals to walk back home.

After watching his boys and girls working in the beet field for two months, thinning the beet by hand, crawling on their hands and knees up and down the drills with sacks tied to their legs for the thistles and scutch grass, and then crowning the beet for days on end with their knives, it would be a poor show if a family didn't get paid in time for Christmas. But, to be sure of getting paid by Christmas, a man would need to get his beet away to the factory by the earliest day possible in December. Not to get paid on time for all of that work, for that twenty tons of beet, would be an awful poor show.

And Mick Linnane didn't put on poor shows.

PART TWO
Making of a Man

CHAPTER
4

Sylvie Linnane had to be out of his bed by midnight. His mother was going to call him. He had the sally rod ready and waiting behind the kitchen door. He'd been preparing that stick for days, since he'd found just the right one the week before. He'd been so excited going to bed that he could barely keep his eyes closed but, slowly, surely, he'd fallen into a deep sleep, before Martin had shaken him.

"We're off!" announced Martin.

First, the pair of them had to have something to eat. Their mother had prepared a large pot of porridge, and the two of them walloped it down. Before they went anywhere, however, their father had to talk to them. Mick Linnane was waiting outside in the yard. There were no cows, only a gang of sheep to be brought into Gort. Later in the morning, before the first light of the day, Mick would get on his bike and he'd follow the two lads into the town. Fair day in Gort was a crazy, busy day, from the first hour of the morning, with the whole centre square of the town and the streets feeding the square wall-to-wall with farmers and the animals they had sold and bought. The noise itself would be hard for the two boys to battle on their own. Mick would be there with them, making sure they got a cup of tea and a sandwich or something quick to eat as soon as the sheep were safely tucked away in their pen.

Martin and Sylvie were out the gate by 1am. The journey, all eight miles of it, usually took the guts of five hours if everything went smoothly. If not, they could be stuck on the road an hour longer. And the two lads didn't want that, because they knew that, if the day went according to their father's wishes, they would be bringing some animals home as well. For the first hour, always, the sheep would be frisky, which was fine. They'd snap along at a decent enough pace on their short legs but, come the second hour, everything would slow down. Sometimes, by the third hour, the walk would almost come to a standstill, which was not good. Martin and Sylvie would be getting hungry again by that time, but the sheep would be tired. If one or two of them decided to have a little sit down, they had to be shifted smartly. The fatter sheep, and the ewes, never fancied the long journey to Gort. But, for Martin and Sylvie, it was all about movement, just keep moving, that was the only secret to a good morning's walk to the fair whether it was the long walk into Gort or half that journey again to Ardrahan or Kinvara.

For weeks, ten-year-old Sylvie had been looking forward to the walk and to the fair but, after three or four hours on the road, the excitement always wore off, and he'd grow as impatient and demanding of the animals as his father or his older brothers were so often on similar journeys.

The reward was great, however.

He'd have a few bob in his pocket the next day. And, when Pudney Piggott's red van came up the road the following Thursday, Sylvie would soon have in his fist a bagful of something very interesting and tasty. Paddy Piggott was fondly known as Pudney. He and his red van were famous on every road in Kilmacduagh, and in all of the parishes around. Celia would have business with Pudney as well, as his van carried everything a cook would wish for a table. Celia bought from Pudney and traded with him. Fresh eggs were always demanded by Pudney's customers and Celia had a tray of fresh eggs to trade every time he pulled up at the Linnane gate. In their anticipation, Sylvie and his brothers and sisters always swore to their mother that they could hear Pudney Piggott's van two or three miles down the road. Maybe so, it did make a noise and was full to the brim with everything that twinkled in their imagination.

• • •

The last fair ended in Gort in the spring of 1967. It was also the last of the great street fairs in the west of Ireland. More than that, it was the ending of a way of life for small farmers, who also fancied themselves as the sharpest of businessmen when they put their minds to it. Monthly, there had been fairs in the town, but quarterly the entire town was consumed by livestock and their owners, on March 17, May 10, August 11 and November 7. Those were the four dates every farmer in the south of Galway was happy to spend far away from his own fields.

Agriculture, and in particular livestock, had changed the face of Gort for the previous 150 years. In the 18th century, Gort was strictly a poor man's town. Early in the 19th century, its status rose and, as soon as the parish priest, Fr Michael Duffy, played the largest part in ridding the town of some particularly notorious faction fighting which favoured fair greens and market places and often race courses, Gort never looked back. Farmers could stand their ground at the fair and, whether they knew the approximate weight of an animal or not, they had only themselves to blame if they did not get what they were due by the close of the day. However, the shrewdest and most cunning of dealers, warily known as 'tanglers', ruined a good many fair days for unsuspecting farmers. But, Gort was a thrilling place to be by midday on fair day, with the excitement at its peak and with money in people's pockets for the clothes and wares that were piled high on the street stalls. The day's business would be mostly completed by then, as sold cattle had already been driven to the railway station by 7am when the first 'special' left for Sligo, carrying its livestock destined for the North. A second 'special', carrying cattle for shipment to England, left shortly after that, for the North Wall in Dublin.

By late afternoon, hotels and public houses would be enjoying a roaring trade. Gort, on fair day, was a man's town. Few women turned up on fair day, though widows would have to attend and make the best of it. However, for the men-folk, the remainder of the afternoon, and the entire evening, were hours for a celebration, which had been well earned – though, of course, many a splendid animal, which had looked worth every penny when inspected with the help of a flashlight in the earliest hours of the morning, would suddenly appear not quite so outstanding in broad daylight.

For younger men and small boys like Sylvie Linnane, there was typically another long, four- or five-hour walk home with a fresh gathering of animals in front of him for company.

• • •

A game of hurling had become the number one event in Sylvie Linnane's young life. Any game, anywhere. Even on his own, when he belted the home-made ball against the gable end of the house, or at the side of one of the sheds. It didn't matter that he hadn't got his own hurling stick. Hand-me-downs were fine, home-made just as good. Walking his father's animals to the fair in Gort was the number two event. Number three was killing a pig.

Mick Linnane would slaughter his own pig, as would his brothers, Paddy and Tom. There were several men who cycled to many a parish to do the honours for a family and charged just one pound. It was a job that had to be done right. And it had to be done expertly and efficiently, especially with an animal that size. He had to be fasted the day before. Mick would then stun the animal with a belt of a sledge hammer, right on the tip of his forehead. His leg would be tied. That was one job for Sylvie and the smaller boys. They'd also have the job of shaving the animal a little later. The bloodier bits and pieces to be done were left to Mick and his brothers. The animal would have fallen over after being stunned and would be placed on a high cart. Celia Linnane would be there, too, with one of her basins from the kitchen. She did not want to see one drop of the animal's blood wasted. Sylvie and the younger members of the Linnane family loved their mother's black pudding. Soon enough the children would have the bladder. They would be waiting for a kill for weeks, waiting to get their hands on that bladder. And, soon enough, it would be blown up and the ball would be in play.

Sylvie would have watched his father expertly drive the sharpened knife straight down the throat of the animal, in seconds, plunging it into the pig's heart. Death was instantaneous. The animal had known what was on the cards alright, and the noise, the continuous shrill it made as it was tied up and dragged to a tree, could pierce a little boy's ears, but Sylvie never covered them. It was a job, he suspected, that he, too, would have to do one day, just like so many of the other big and amazing jobs he watched his father get through every day of every week. He always watched up close. The gush of blood from the animal's throat would steady into a strong flow as the basin filled. Shaving the pig was the hard part, taking all the hair off the body of an animal of 20 stone. It was boring, but it had to be done. The gutting was more interesting, as was the butchering, and he continued to watch as Mick Linnane finished off the entire job himself, from nose to tail. Nothing was wasted and there would be food for the next three or four months. All thanks to one good, big pig.

Some of the portions would be salted in a barrel. Others would be hung up from the rafters over the fireplace, wrapped in brown paper and newspaper, and left there for weeks, curing. The head and the tongue of the animal were the first to go into a meal. The nicest part of the pig, the succulent pork steaks, would be divided up and delivered to the neighbours. The Linnanes, like every other family, always shared their kill. It was the thing to do, a fine custom. It brought good luck and respect to a family for its generosity, and Sylvie and the younger Linnanes were dispatched the next day with the offerings, which were always received with thanks, and a little something for the child at the doorway.

• • •

Sylvie did not know enough about his father as a hurling man. They seldom talked about the game, or any games Sylvie played for Gort, as he moved swiftly from the club's juvenile teams to minor teams and onto the senior team at 17 years of age. When Sylvie played centre-field for Galway in the 1973 All-Ireland minor final, Mick Linnane, once more, didn't open his mouth to his second youngest son about the big game, even though he was so proud to see his boy walk out the door that Saturday morning as he headed up to Dublin with his team-mates. Mick watched that game on the television set in the kitchen. He never went to games. The journey up to Dublin, and the excitement of the game, and the cruel twist at the end of that one game in particular, might have killed him. It certainly wouldn't have done his damaged heart any good. Neither did Sylvie ever to get to sit down and ask his father about his own hurling career.

Mick Linnane was a fine hurler in his day. He had a short run with the county, but his greatest day on a hurling field was in 1934 when he, and his brother Paddy, helped Gort to the Galway senior hurling title, their first since 1916 and their third county title in total. Gort had taken out mighty Castlegar on their way to the county final, and had a tough battle with Tynagh in a final played in Renmore that was full of goals, seven of them in total. Gort won 4-4 to 3-1. Two years later, Gort got back into the final again, but on another day when goals were plundered hard and fast, Castlegar swiftly took their revenge in an eight-goal game, winning 6-6 to 2-5.

Mick played wing-forward and moved in to corner-forward also that day in 1934, and got on the scoresheet before the end of the game in one of the most historic and emotional victories in the history of the club. He scored a goal and a point. However, when Mick had received the call from the county selectors a couple of years earlier, he had been working in his sister's public house, ten miles closer to Loughrea, in Kilchreest. The local club had asked him to play with them and Mick felt that he couldn't say no. For starters, it would have been bad for business, but it was common knowledge that most lads played for two or three different teams, in their own county and far outside of it, whenever they got half a chance. While still a Gort man, Mick lined out with his new friends and customers in Kilchreest and, surely enough, the county board got wind of it. He'd played under a false name but he was still found out. His chance of starting a decent career with the Galway hurling team ended when the suspension of a couple of months was handed down.

Mick Linnane had become a changed man, a more subdued man, after he had met his first belt with his heart. That first one had knocked the man back. The older Linnane boys, Patrick, Micheal and Johnny, had known their father as a far more passionate hurling man. He had let them know, from time to time, of the little details in his hurling life. How hard they had trained that summer in 1934, and how the club had arranged for a man to look after the everyday chores on the Linnane farm while Mick joined his team-mates for a long fortnight of full-time training in preparation for the county final. For years, he had travelled with his older sons to Croke Park to see some of the greatest hurling teams in the country.

Patrick was the first member of the Linnane family to drive a car and Micheal also drove, but their father had never cared to get behind the wheel himself. As his heart continued to trouble him, he left his home less and less. He was afraid to go anywhere in case he felt ill or collapsed. He felt it better for himself, and better for his family, if he stayed at home. People would talk to him about his boys and how strong they were on the field. And more and more people would come up to him, after Mass, or any social gathering in the parish, and look to talk about Sylvie in particular. They would tell him how good Sylvie had been the previous Sunday or how great he would be for Galway, some day. Mick would not necessarily agree with them, he was not one to flatter himself or encourage others to flatter his sons. But Mick knew that young Sylvie had something as a hurler that neither he himself, nor his brothers nor anybody else in his own family, had ever been able to discover in themselves.

• • •

In 1977, when he was 70 years of age, Mick Linnane died from one, final, massive heart attack. Celia outlived her husband by 31 years and remained a proud, loving matriach for all of her children and grandchildren, and her great-grandchildern. She was 94 years old when she died in 2008.

Mick Linnane passed on a Friday evening. It was June 23, and a fine summer's evening as Gort hurling club held one of their weekly training sessions. Fridays promised the club a full attendance at training as the younger lads who had moved out of the parish to find work, or who might have been living as far away as Dublin, would all be home for the start of the weekend. Early that Friday evening, Sylvie drove home from Lucan, on the west side of Dublin, where he was living. When he got to the family home in Kilmacduagh, he had just time for a quick bite to eat before getting to the hurling pitch. Micheal Linnane was the team coach, the man with the whistle. Sylvie didn't have time to get into Galway city to visit his father in hospital before the training session. Instead, he decided to drop in first thing the following morning.

Mick Linnane had already been in hospital for two weeks. Micheal had been in that morning to say hello to his father, and give him a nice clean shave. Micheal was finishing up his training session, with the hurling over, and Sylvie, Martin and Gerry Linnane and the rest of the team were doing their last couple of laps of the field, when a car came into the grounds faster than it should. Word was quickly sent out to the lads to get in straight away. They changed back into their clothes and the car raced them to the hospital. When they reached the corridor, just yards from their father's room, they were told that Mick Linnane was dead. They were too late.

Sylvie had loved his father with all his heart. Even though they did not get the time to talk very much, and even though neither father nor son had the inclination to sit down together and talk about their lives, and talk about work and hurling, and talk about everything else and anything at all, Sylvie had always felt safe in his father's company. Mick Linnane's strong, forceful, assured presence had guided Sylvie all through his young life and into manhood. Often, walking with his father was enough for Sylvie. They'd go to Mass in Labane, because Mick Linnane had his rented land nearby. Celia and the rest of the family would to Kilmacduagh Church, but Mick and Sylvie, or whichever of his sons he asked to help out with the herding, would head off on Sunday morning in the opposite direction.

On so many evenings, Sylvie would watch his father play cards with his mother and their friends. They would get up to such fun and mischief over a game of '25' in the family kitchen. He'd see his father ride off on his bike to Bradley's pub for a pint or two, but come home early, safe and sound, to his family. Come winter time, when Sylvie was only a young lad, Mick Linnane would rent a television set every year for the few dark months that were in it, for Celia and his boys and girls. He didn't take much interest in it himself. Mick Linnane preferred his radio, or a newspaper. And, most of all, he loved a quiet, honest-to-God chat with any of his closest neighbours. His father had never seen Sylvie play and his father had never asked Sylvie about one of his hurling games, not that Sylvie could ever remember; but Mick Linnane's second-youngest son would not have changed anything.

• • •

Sylvie would have done anything to be at his mother's side when she passed away. Celia Linnane spent the final years of her life with her daughter, Bernie, in Claregalway, but her final Christmas had been spent in Sylvie's home. He could see over those few days that she had failed and, by February, she was in the Regional Hospital in Galway. Sylvie and Margaret visited her daily. The last time he ever spoke to his mother she had been in good form and seemed to be getting stronger, but the next day he got a call to go to Galway immediately.

When he walked into his mother's ward, her bed was empty. He turned to Margaret and she went to find a nurse, but before she could do so another elderly patient walked over to Sylvie and, shaking his hand, sympathised with him over his loss. That was how he discovered that his mother had died. Celia Linnane had had a good life. It was a hard life, too, and Sylvie and his brothers and sisters knew that to be true. They did not believe that any woman had ever worked as hard for her husband or for her family.

She had been a young woman when she got married, just having turned 22 years old. Her life, after that, was always busy, usually hectic, and she was burdened with more work than she would ever have wished for, and blessed with far more children than she ever thought possible, but nobody in her home had ever seen her in a dark mood. Celia Linnane's life had been packed with cheerfulness and good humour and a love for her children which, remarkably, could not have been shared more equally if the woman had taken a sharp knife out of one of the kitchen drawers and cut that great love she bestowed into the most exact and perfectly even pieces.

CHAPTER
5

"Is that Sylvie Linnane out there?"

The matron had stormed through the door and landed at the side of Margaret Linnane's bed. The midwife and the sister didn't have time to offer any replies and Margaret was in no mood to talk to anyone. The throes of labour had her undivided attention. But, out of the corner of her eye, she could see that this woman who had just marched into the room was not to be ignored.

"And … is this his child being born here?" she continued, before anyone could confirm or deny that Sylvie Linnane's wife was indeed about to give birth to the couple's fifth child and only daughter, Aoibheann.

There was still no answer being provided to the matron, and she wasn't waiting around for one either, as she spun on her heels and marched back out the door she had just entered twenty seconds earlier.

It was Sylvie Linnane who was in the waiting room, alright, thirty yards down the corridor, minding his own business, sitting there, arms crossed, waiting patiently enough for someone to come to him with some more news.

"Come in here, you!" ordered the matron.

Sylvie jumped to his feet. He didn't know what was wrong. Was Margaret in some trouble? Or, was it the baby? He was at the matron's heels immediately, hot-footing it towards the labour ward. He was worried, panicked, but when he arrived into the room and found Margaret under pressure, but looking strong, and holding everything together, his head began to spin on his shoulders. He wasn't sure why he had been summoned so sharply and urgently.

"Get in there and stand next to your wife." he was told.

The matron pointed to the top end of the delivery bed.

"Your baby is about to be born!"

Margaret Linnane looked up at her husband. He was in a bit of a sweat. He had never been at the birth of any of the four boys. Their first, Shane, was born in 1978. Darragh and Tadgh came in quick succession, in 1984 and '85. Three years later, Sylvie Og was born. Margaret did not ask her husband to be at any of the four births. She didn't want him there. She was happier to finish what had to be done on her own.

And Sylvie Linnane was more than happy on each occasion to accept his wife's decision. But, in Galway Regional Hospital, as his beautiful and only baby daughter was about to enter the world, Sylvie did not know what to say and dared not disobey. He wasn't shy about arguing with referees, but he nodded submissively to the matron. He obediently took his wife's hand whenever she let him hold it and braved the experience to its happy ending.

It was 1992, and Sylvie Linnane was two years retired from the Galway hurling team that had gripped the nation's fullest attention, for all sorts of reasons, for an entire decade. His was a household name all over the country. In Galway, for those 10 years that brought such exquisite joy, and much heart-break, he was known as Sylvie. His surname had been an unnecessary addition ever since Galway's highly-charged breakthrough to win the first of three All-Ireland titles in a ten-year period, in 1980. If a man or woman mentioned the name Linnane in conversation sure hurling folk might wonder who they were talking about.

There was only one Sylvie in Ireland. Born on St Sylvester's Day, December 29, 1956, but always known as just Sylvie.

He won it all and did it all. But the proudest and most personally satisfying day for Sylvie was the day, in 1995, that he slipped the green and gold jersey over his head in the Gort dressing-room and took one look over to his right and saw his eldest son, Shane, already fully togged out: There he was, with his hurling stick in his hand, ready to run out onto the field with his father for the first time.

Sylvie thought of Mick Linnane, his own father, who had never talked to Sylvie about hurling and had never seen Sylvie play – for Gort or for Galway. That was a different time, and a time when fathers and sons had different relationships. Change was a good thing.

· · ·

The Catholic Church thought it a good and proper idea to have one parish of Gort, by bringing together Kilmacduagh, Kiltartan and a chunk of Gort town and its surrounding countryside, but most self-respecting GAA men demurred. Actually, for a long time, only over their dead bodies, would they hand up their beloved jerseys. It was the turn of the century in South Galway.

Three GAA clubs remained in the parish and would stand strong for another half a century, getting through some unfinished business with rival parishes and, most importantly, with one another. Gort presented themselves in blue and white; Kilmacduagh favoured red, with white cuffs; while Kiltartan wore blue, with gold cuffs and gold collars. There was a lot of history in those jerseys, victories and defeats, and blood washed out of them often enough.

Men from the three parishes had come together, briefly, long before then, answering the call of no lesser man than Michael Cusack who, in that great year of 1884, placed the final great brick in the wall which became the Gaelic Athletic Association. Twelve months later, Cusack made it his business to ask Dan Burke, of George's Street in Gort, to get a team together from South Galway to take on North Tipperary. Cusack wanted the game played in the Fifteen Acres in the Phoenix Park, and that's where three gentlemen from Gort, and a pile of lads from Kilmacduagh, Beagh, Kilbeacanty, Peterswell and Kiltartan found themselves on the early afternoon of February 16, 1886. The match was billed '… for the Championship of Ireland' and, even though the secretary of the fledgling association had his hand in the organisation of the game, it never did get recorded as the real thing: an All-Ireland.

Burke and the Gort captain, Edward Treston, picked the team, which was less difficult once they had dealt with Ardrahan. Ardrahan wanted six of their men on the team of 21 hurlers, but Gort would not go with that, and so it was decided to summarily leave Ardrahan out of it entirely. Cusack wanted the teams to be dressed properly, and distinctively, and the Galway boys got their hands on a roll of corduroy cloth that was for sale. A local tailor made knickerbockers for everyone and the team set off from Gort by train. Cusack himself met them at Broadstone Station, and hosted a meal for the two teams in the Clarence Hotel on the quays. After the meal was washed down, the rules were discussed. No tripping and no wrestling, nobody wanted that. But, mostly everything else was acceptable.

The South Galway lads went down by 1-0 to 0-0 in the game, which was obviously far from thrilling and, indeed, much greater intrigue and uncertainty attended to the fixture the day before when it was discovered that both teams brought with them sliotars of different sizes and weights. Tipperary used their heavier sliotar in the first half. Galway had their smaller, lighter ball in the second half, but it was with this ball that Tipp scored the winning goal.

Gort won their fair share in the first half of the 20th century, the club's most memorable three years being 1914 to 1916, when a Galway county final was won, lost and then won again. Almost two decades zipped by, before Mick Linnane and his Gort team got their hands on the county title for the third time, in '34. Kilmacduagh were 'South' Galway champions once, as were Kiltartan, but Gort won eight of the same Championships over their neighbours. Gort also fought hard for a county title in 1948 but lost out to Castlegar. For many years, county titles were mostly the stuff of dreams, and wholly elusive, for the hurlers from all three clubs, until, in the 1960s, the introduction of the 'one parish, one club' rule allowed all three clubs to hang up their old jerseys, in which they had fought so long and hard. Green and gold was the colour, as the best hurlers from the three clubs duly started off on a whole new journey in search of lots of county titles, minor and senior.

It was a journey, however, that began slowly and never really picked up the pace that was required. Neither did the new club develop a strong sense of entitlement which so characterised Castlegar, or even Ardrahan and Kiltormer and their likes, when quarter-finals and semi-finals promised so much to, and demanded even more from, those who entered them.

The 1960s closed down with no senior title. The 1970s came and went the same disappointing way.

• • •

Sylvie Linnane was eight years old when he made the decision, all by himself, that he needed his first hurling stick. His own, a new one, properly measured and all. One which he could hold in his hand and know that no other boy or man before him had ever failed with that stick or blamed the stick, which no other boy or man had thrown to one side because the stick was cracked down the middle, or had completely smashed into two separate pieces.

There was a reason he needed a new hurl.

He got on his bike, one Monday evening, and knew exactly where he was heading. Pat Monaghan was the man who made hurls. He was old and his reputation had reached the ears of young Sylvie a couple of years earlier. Now Sylvie had a nice few bob in his pocket. A parcel had come home from England, from Johnny, and Sylvie was sure he had enough. Two shillings and six pence.

"Will you make me a hurl?" Sylvie asked, without bothering with anything like a 'hello' upon arriving at Pat Monaghan's house.

He'd found the old man in his work shed at the side of the house and had knocked at the door, which was already half-open. The master craftsman recognised the young boy quickly enough. The red hair was the giveaway, he'd seen him every so often with his father, Mick Linnane, when they were working their land close to his house. The little boy would always have a hurling stick in his hand, even if he was much too small for the size of it. Sylvie was also going herding after ordering his new hurling stick, and he was killing two birds with one stone, but he knew he was talking to the right man. Pat Monaghan had a funny, happy smile on his face as he received his new order from the little fella.

"Come back to me in a couple of days." said Pat Monaghan.

The following Wednesday, Sylvie was back. The two shillings and six pence was still intact, but Pat Monaghan refused to take any money from young Linnane as he handed him his new stick.

"I have a feeling you'll make good use of it!" he said, as he closed the open palm in which Sylvie had his money displayed, and handed over the most beautiful, brilliantly sculpted piece of wood Sylvie thought he had ever seen in his whole life.

The following Sunday morning, there was an 11-a-side game of ground hurling in Ardrahan. Sylvie was back on his bike, his new hurl tied to his back, heading for Ardrahan. He didn't know anyone in the field when he arrived, but he quickly walked up to the nearest man, called Frank Lally, with a sense of purpose, keeping his face serious but also hopeful.

"You want to play with us?" he was asked, before he could open his mouth. Sylvie nodded his head, and said he did. It was his first game of hurling. He started on one of the teams, and had scored two goals by the end.

He'd seen his brothers making hurls before. They'd get a good piece of ash. They'd have found some good promising trees a few months earlier while they were out hunting, and they would have kept an eye on them. When the time was right, they would bring home the branch, and try to get a good turn on it first of all. Sylvie would see them clean it down with a hatchet, and continue shaping it for a few days. Those were the hurling sticks which, weeks and months later, he would find around the house and get his hands on. Those, or bits of broken sticks, which he'd tape tightly back into one stick, and hope for the best.

During Sylvie's lifetime there were some hurls he loved. Like a Randall hurl. He never took a Randall hurl up into his hand where he didn't feel that he possessed a greater power. Four generations of a Wexford family, and always magical. It had a flexibility, and a strength. And he could always drive a ball longer. It was smashing for a sideline cut. He guessed it was the older ash trees they used but, definitely, Sylvie would have walked with the greatest of confidence into any war, on any hurling field in the world, with a Randall stick in his hand. He'd received two or three Conway sticks as well, every so often, from friends in Ennis. It, too, was nothing less than mighty when he gripped it.

He never had to mess or fuss around with a Randall or Conway stick. Others, Sylvie would always like to work on, long before he'd select his three sticks for a Championship game, and mark each, 'S Linnane 1', 'S Linnane 2', and 'S Linnane 3'. Everyone did their own thing with a hurl they wanted to make special. A bit of lead in the bas helped with line balls – some hurls were a little light, and needed it, they needed better balance. And there were some hurls that Sylvie would take into his hands and, like a stubborn, indisciplined, cursed animal, would find himself giving up on and throwing to one side after 20 minutes. It didn't matter what grip he'd put onto that sort of hurl. It didn't matter if he spent good time shaving the end of it so that he could lift the ball faster. Some sticks just did not have it in them.

But, the good ones! He'd wrap them in damp towels, if he was getting on a plane to play a game in some far-off city in America. A man would hate to have a stick shrink. And a man would dream up ways and means of making a stick stronger, bolder, and even more magical than the next man's. As a young lad, Sylvie was told that if he put a stick up a chimney that the soot would seal it even harder. In his time, Syvlie put many sticks up the chimney but, as an older man, he'd see his younger sons getting their new hurling stick and hanging it from a washing line, and leaving it there for three or four days, on the line, one single hurl hanging there all on its own. And Sylvie would shake his head, and wonder: What does the young lad think he's doing with that stick?

Sylvie's very first hurling stick, which Pat Monaghan kindly made for him, lasted by his side for three and a half years. It was the greatest, most perfect hurl he ever possessed. That was until the late 1980s, when Galway were chasing down All-Ireland hurling titles thick and fast, and Sylvie owned another stick he was prepared to live or die by on the hurling field. He had held hundreds of sticks in his hand, down through his boyhood and manhood, but only two sticks would ever be remembered. The first came to a sorry end, as all sticks do, eventually, smashed clean in half as he sought to drive the ball up the field in a game against Castlegar's Under-14s. As sharply as a 'no' from a pretty girl, that loss broke his heart for a good month.

He never found out what happened to his second hurl. The 1988 All-Ireland final had just ended, and the people of Galway were rejoicing in Croke Park with their players after a magnificent, sumptuous victory over Tipperary. The Liam MacCarthy Cup had been presented, the speeches were done and dusted. Sylvie was leaving the field, through the Hogan Stand tunnel when a little lad grabbed him, and begged for an autograph. Croke Park, with a heaving mass of people, half of them looking to clamber over someone or other, was no place for stopping and writing your name on a piece of paper.

For starters, there was no elbow room. There was hardly enough room to breathe, for Chrissakes, but the young boy was begging him. And, besides, Sylvie was not going anywhere fast.

He grabbed the match programme and took the pen from the boy. As he did so, he let his hurling stick out of his grasp and left it standing against his hip. He signed his name, just as another shove came from behind him. He looked back, but the stick was gone. It was nowhere in sight.

It had 'S Linnane 1' written on it. But it was gone, long gone in seconds, and Sylvie Linnane never heard tell of it again.

CHAPTER

6

Sylvie Linnane was now a real hurler. He was up and running, and there was no more need for him to imagine himself being out on the field, winning ball, and thumping over points. All the imaginary games he played around the farm, all of the passes he had made against the gable wall, the goals he had scored when he aimed the ball right into the top corner of the shed door… all of those games, the whole lot of them, were now redundant. He had a jersey on his back. Other lads were shouting at him for the ball. Better still, other lads were trying to get the ball off him. The thrill of the game had begun.

Sylvie walked off the hurling field in Craughwell, in July of 1970, with a cup. A silver cup, the first cup he had ever got his hands on. It was also Killomoran National School's first cup. They had beaten Leitrim National School by two clear goals, 4-1 to 2-1, in the 'Two Teacher School' county final. It was a simple enough way, and the fairest way, perhaps, in letting schools take to the field against one another. Seven-a-side, and even a two-teacher school could get seven good hurlers, surely? That was the theory of it. Killomoran were off to a good start in picking seven boys, because, for starters, there were two Linnane's, Sylvie and Gerry.

That summer, Syl Linnane scored nine goals and six points in Killomoran's four games, against the schools from Leitrim, Killina, Kiltiernan, and Ballyturin. Sure enough, he was the talk of every match, and he got his name all over the match report of the final in *The Connacht Tribune*. The newspaper was handed to everyone who came into Mick and Celia Linnane's home that week. It was the first time Sylvie would read his name in a newspaper, and that name was 'Syl'.

• • •

The first thing Cyril Farrell noticed about Sylvie were his wrists, the boy had amazing wrists. The second thing he double-checked, immediately, about the boy with the great wrists was that he had the reddest head of hair that the Galway minor hurling coach had seen in a long time. Third thing was the small lad's aggression. He was fiery, no doubt. Sixteen years old, and getting stuck into everything, and coming back for more, every single time it was asked of him. He was fast, too, and he could probably play anywhere. The only work a coach might have to do with a young lad like that, thought Farrell, was cool him down a bit. Though, not too much; that would be a mistake.

Cyril Farrell was learning his trade as a coach. He was still a young man himself, only seven years older than Sylvie Linnane. Farrell was doing his bit with the students in UCG, he was 23 years old, and he had JP Cusack as team manager of the Galway minors keeping an eye on him, as well as Brendan Murphy, Sean Fahy, John Furey, Gerry Corbett, and Noel Treacy as the team's selectors. Six men had a say in who was going to play for Galway in the 1973 All-Ireland Minor final. Cyril Farrell wasn't one of them.

They hadn't picked Sylvie for the semi-final, the month before, when Galway had surprised Tipperary and everyone watching, including some of the grown men in the Galway dug-out, by winning a storming game by 3-14 to 3-10. Sylvie had been told to whip off his track-suit during the second half. He was told to hold the middle of the field, and stop the ball coming into the Galway half. He was told to stop men too, of course. He did well. The game was trundling along at such a pace, and defences at both ends of Croke Park were being torn apart. It was not the easiest of games in which to make an impression as a substitute. But Sylvie did just enough. No doubt, the red hair helped in making sure that every ball he sent back down the field was noted. In fact, it may have been the tipping point that earned him his place on the starting fifteen against Kilkenny.

It was not a game Galway were expected to win. Three years earlier, the county had reached the All-Ireland Minor final for the first time since 1958. They lost to Cork by sixteen points, even though they had classy hurlers out on the field, Iggy Clarke and Joe McDonagh amongst them, as well as PJ Molloy, while a tough fella, though a little on the small side, was in at full-forward. His name was Ciaran Fitzgerald, and he'd remain just as tough for the next fifteen years on the rugby fields of Ireland, England and France, and as far away as New Zealand and Australia. In 1971, the Galway minors were dealt a right thrashing by Cork in the All-Ireland semi-final. It was a sorry 4-13 to 1-4 by the end and, twelve months later, things did not get much better. In the semi-final, again, Kilkenny scored seven goals against them. This time the final scoreline was a miserable 7-9 to 2-8. So, in no shape or form, were Galway expected to win, or even get close, to Kilkenny in the 1973 All-Ireland minor final.

Farrell, being the youngest of the Galway men on the sideline, was expected to do most of the running, and taking himself around the whole field if necessary. Fifteen minutes before the ball was thrown in, he saw Kilkenny's hugely respected figurehead, Paddy Grace, walking in his direction. Farrell braced himself for a business-like few words, but Grace did all of the talking. And Farrell barely got out a "Thanks, Paddy" at the end of it.

"They'll be telling you where you can and can't go," Grace warned him, turning his head slightly in the direction of a handful of Croke Park's hardiest of match stewards who were huddled a short distance away.

"I'm telling you, do what you have to do!" continued Grace.

"Young man, coach your team." said the Kilkenny man. Turning away from Farrell, he added, "… and good luck!"

Galway had all the luck they could have asked for that afternoon, in the spills of rain, and on a pitch that demanded fast-thinking and extra bravery from every young man out there. Then their luck ran out.

Sylvie Linnane started in the middle of the field with Ger Holian from Athenry, who, at 17 years of age, had already grown into a huge man. He was twice the size of Sylvie, but they worked well together. The whole team played well in the first half, despite starting slowly. Kilkenny's first score of the game, just like their last score, was a goal, with their full-forward Seanie O'Brien getting both of them. The Kilkenny No.14, a James Stephens lad with a rare first touch, would end the game with four goals to his name. Whether it was a good idea or not for Galway to play their young goalie, who'd broken two of his toes in training the previous week, was a debate which would liven up later. But, at half time, even though it had taken a fair while to find their feet, Farrell was happy on the sideline. They only trailed by that one goal. It was 1-4 to 0-4.

On the restart, Galway levelled it. Holian tore through the centre of the Kilkenny defence for the third or fourth time, but this time passed the ball off to Fred Power who hit the back of the net. The game was on. Suddenly, Paddy Grace had his Kilkenny selectors running all over the place, blindly ignoring the complaining stewards. Farrell observed the flurry of activity. There was no need to be over-anxious. Kilkenny were worried. He could see that but, before he knew it, O'Brien doubled overhead on an in-coming free for his second goal. Midway through the half, the teams were still level.

O'Brien's third goal put Kilkenny a point up, 3-5 to 2-6. Sylvie was in the thick of everything. The first half had been a blur. Everything that had happened over the previous 24 hours had been a blur; getting the train up from Galway, getting the bus out to Malahide to the magnificent and huge Grand Hotel, getting their own rooms for the night. It was heady, exciting stuff for all of the young Galway men. It was hard to keep calm, and it was necessary for them to keep reminding themselves that they had a game at the end of their great adventure. An All-Ireland final.

As Galway powered on, getting closer and closer to the final whistle, Sylvie was finally doing himself justice. He felt at home in the huge stadium. He had stopped listening to the roar of the crowd. There was no more looking around him. He was holding the middle of the field; Holian was rampaging through the Kilkenny defence, and one more such big run down the middle, with his strong legs eating up the ground, had earned Tynagh's Gerry Burke a half a chance in the large square. There were three Kilkenny defenders tight around Burke, but he was a big man for a young boy, and he used his weight advantage to make enough room for himself to get his stick on the ball and give Galway the lead. Burke had goaled. And he quickly clipped over a point minutes later. Galway were two points up. It was 3-7 to 3-5.

There was less than three minutes to go. Then there was just two minutes, and Farrell knew that his team never looked stronger. In the middle of the field, Sylvie Linnane never felt stronger at any point in the entire game. Word had reached him that there was only a minute left. Another, last-gasp Kilkenny attack down the left side of the Galway defence was stopped in its tracks. The ball went out over the sideline. It was a cut to Galway. The game was up, surely, thought Sylvie as he looked up at the giant clock over the Canal End of the ground. Castlegar's Tom Murphy took the cut at the ball. Somehow, and something nobody had ever seen Murphy do in his young life, the ball sliced off his stick and went over the same sideline, five yards further up the field.

Kilkenny substitute, Sean Purcell from Mooncoin, gathered the ball. He quickly looked towards the packed Galway goalmouth, and instinctively slapped the ball across the field instead, to Seanie O'Brien. His fourth goal won the All-Ireland title for Kilkenny. It was 4-5 to 3-7. The referee's whistle sounded as Kiltormer's Frank Larkin struck the ball with the last puck-out of the game.

Sylvie was in a daze. Everyone was. Cyril Farrell walked amongst his players, shaking their hands, and hugging them. He told them they'd be back, but, of course, more than half of them would never play for Galway in Croke Park again. Sylvie knew he did alright. He had a real battle with Joe Hennessy for the last twenty minutes of the game. It was, in fact, the most exhilarating duel he'd ever had on a hurling field. Hennessy was a bloody good hurler, he knew that for sure by the end of the game. At the same time, Sylvie knew just as well, that Hennessy had been given his stomach-full of it, and some more. But, they'd lost. The final scoreline was the bottom line. Nothing else mattered that evening, or the next few days. They'd lost. Worse still, they'd thrown it away. History would repeat itself in 2003 when his son, Tadhg took to the field with the Galway minor team that was beaten by one point, by Kilkenny, 2-15 to 2-16, in the All-Ireland minor final of that year.

Sylvie would be one of the Galway players walking off the field in Croke Park that sorry afternoon in 1973 who would be back, he'd play centre back in 1974, when Galway met Kilkenny again, and never looked like winning.

. . .

Margaret Nolan said 'Yes'.

She had been asked out onto the dance floor by the boy she had noticed over half an hour earlier. She knew his name was Sylviea and she had already noticed that he could dance. He could do the jive, and a foxtrot or a waltz, and he had an energy and expertise that was something to watch. Every bone in his body seemed to be at work as he was out there on the floor. Margaret thought to herself that he looked a regular Fred Astaire. They had only been out in the centre of the floor for a few minutes when she knew that Sylvie Linnane could actually dance her off her feet.

The Classic Ballroom in Gort town was a place for some serious dancing. Whatever occurred between a young couple before or after the dancing had started, was an entirely different matter and proposition. Many great romances were born within its walls, and many came to a tearful end there as well. The ballroom was a splendid sight during a set dance, and any kind of set, Lancers or Connemara. That was in the early '50s but, in the '60s, all of the best-loved showbands in the country started turning up in Gort, and put on a big night in Albert and Noel Mullins' place. They all came. Gene Stuart, The Indians, Roly Daniels, Big Tom and The Mainliners, Larry Cunningham and Ray Lynam.

In Gort, a generation earlier, Sonny Mullins was the sort of man who wore many hats. He was a farmer and a butcher to begin with but, as the years passed and opportunity presented itself in Gort, Sonny Mullins also became equally well-known as a builder and an auctioneer. He owned a garage in the town. He did good business as an undertaker. And then there was The Classic, which became the apple in Sonny Mullins' eye, and, for thirty years, The Classic lived the life of Reilly. Though, like so many great ballrooms of romance all over Ireland, time was called on it, too. The building was eventually demolished and a petrol pump built on the famous old site that had sent so many hearts into overdrive.

When The Classic was being built on the Ennis Road, local folk were not sure what Sonny was doing, or what he was going to present to them next. And he liked to keep them guessing. He said nothing. But, once the maple floor was laid, Sonny had the biggest smile of any man in Gort. He had a ready audience at his fingertips. They thronged into The Classic from the very beginning and, indeed, some young couples left just as fast, heading to Sonny's hay shed and, if the utmost discretion was needed, then the coffin store was a probable destination. If there was no room left in either location, then back gardens and porches up and down the street were a final resort.

Margaret Nolan stood on the left-hand side of the ballroom with all the girls. From the main entrance door, the girls always took up their positions to the left, and the young men and the fast-growing boys would hold up on the mineral bar side of the room. The lads knew that, after they left the dance floor, if a girl accepted a bottle of orange from the bar, then at the very least a commitment for the remainder of the evening was expected. If the orange was declined, the boy's hopes were well shot. The girls were tricky. Sometimes a jerk of the head was the easiest way to invite a girl onto the dance floor. Or the slow extension of a hand. It was best not to be too direct in case a harsh refusal followed. The boys had to be on their toes, and not just on the dance floor. A boy with a bike outside The Classic was under more pressure than a young man with any class of a car, and if the boy left his right trouser leg crinkled, after stuffing it inside his sock as he cycled to The Classic, his hopes of landing the right lassie were entirely dependent upon his ability to light up the dance floor.

Sylvie Linnane had no car. But he could dance alright. From the first night she saw him on the floor, Margaret Nolan knew that he likely came from a family that cleared the furniture on the kitchen floor out of the way more than one night of each week. She would indeed discover, in the months that followed, that all of the Linnane family were renowned for their dancing skills, but none more so than her future husband who, throughout their courtship, and the length of their marriage, would constantly be in demand at social events as a prized dancing partner.

Sylvie would never change. Through their married life, and through Sylvie's hurling career, a dance floor was seldom ignored for very long. If he could dance, a man could forget many of his worries out on the floor. After

All-Ireland finals won, and All-Ireland finals lost, Sylvie Linnane would spend more time out on the dance floor than any other Galway hurler.

After the tough, painful defeat in the 1986 All-Ireland final, Margaret had left her husband on the dance floor late in the night. She was tired. And she needed air. Margaret walked out onto one of the balconies at the Grand Hotel in Malahide, which the Galway team had booked for its post-match meal and possible celebration. She was standing there, next to a rail for a few seconds, when she thought she heard someone in the shadows behind her. When she looked around she saw a man sitting on the ground, his head buried against his chest. He was crying softly, but with deep and wrenching sobs.

One of Sylvie's teammates, in the hours after the game, was still struggling to come to terms with the crushing blow and his own personal loss. Margaret looked down at him, and she felt her heart breaking all over again. Then she looked behind, through the open doors which led from the ballroom onto the balcony and, there, in the middle of the floor, she could see her husband. He was dancing, and, in his own way, trying to deal with what had occurred earlier in the day. She knew his heart was crushed just as badly as anyone else's, and she knew that when Sylvie woke the next morning, that the horrible, frantic realisation that everything had been lost 24 hours earlier and could never be regained, would hit him afresh, and leave him shaken and sorrowful.

For days, the defeat and the regrets attached to it would keep a grip on Sylvie Linnane, day and night. Sylvie knew that, and his wife knew it, too. But, the night of the All-Ireland final defeat, Sylvie would dance. All night long, that Sunday night and Monday morning in September, Sylvie Linnane danced.

CHAPTER
7

One month after Galway minors were sent packing from the All-Ireland semi-final by Kilkenny, Sylvie Linnane had the honour of leading Gort to a county Championship win at last. It was plain enough sailing that September, 1974, as Gort scored three points in the first five minutes and, by the time the rain had stopped and the sun came out at Duggan Park in Ballinasloe, Gort were on their way to a commanding 2-9 to 2-2 victory over Turloughmore.

Midway through the first half, as the drizzle developed into some fairly heavy showers, Turlough looked ready to make a fight of it. After a good save by Tony Monaghhan, the Gort defence was not able to get the ball cleared and Pat Fahy banged it to the net for Turlough. The scores were level, but Sylvie cleaned up around the middle for the ten minutes before half time and won enough ball to see to it that Gort led 0-7 to 1-1 at the end of the first half. Gerry Flaherty scored their first goal three minutes after the restart, and three minutes later, when a Christy Monaghan shot dropped short into the Turlough square, it was Flaherty who was again quick as a light in smacking the ball home. It was all over by then.

The club, and the whole town, found it a sweet win. Everybody had waited for so long for a win that would shut up, not only some doubtful souls in their own parish, but which would be acknowledged and reckoned with by some of the other parishes that considered themselves the hoi polloi of Galway hurling. At its most basic level, it was about earning a bit more respect. And giving Gort's own lads increased levels of self-respect. That too.

Gort had won the Under-14 South Board title back in 1953 and, that year, the minor team also won the South Board title, and the minors would continue to be No.1 in the south of the county for the next seven years. But, becoming county champions was beyond them. That was until 1957, when they won the county minor title for the first time and held onto their crown for three successive years. It was a magnificent achievement for the club but, in the Linnane household, there was also a degree of sadness that Micheal, and Johnny, and their boys now living their lives in London, were not at home to help and be part of such a fantastic achievement.

Reclaiming the Galway minor title in 1974 soon allowed the club to set its sights on bigger things. With Sylvie Linnane, Gerry P. Fahy, John Nolan and Kevin Fahy proving they were amongst the best young hurlers in the whole county, Gort suddenly looked a whole lot stronger at senior level. They reached the final stages of the county senior League in 1978 and '79, and lost out to Kinvara in the Championship semi-final in 1979 as well.

Gort were on the move for sure, and, in 1980, they won the county Under-21 Championship for the first time, seeing off Meelick-Eyrecourt in Tynagh. In 1981, it was decided that Sylvie Linnane, now one of the oldest of the new breed of ambitious Gort hurlers, should captain the team.

• • •

In the early summer of 1974, as Sylvie Linnane was toing and froing to London, Margaret Nolan, one of the twin daughters of Mick Nolan and Mary Joe Connors, was a busy young girl herself.

Margaret was nearly always on the go and, on the family farm, the six Nolan children had enough work cut out for them by their parents. The two boys in the family, John and Michael, got the giant slice each, but Theresa and Catherine always had their chores lined up for them, and the twin girls, who were the youngest, got it a little easier in comparison. Margaret and Mary were born that same day and hour, but they could not have been more different in appearance and temperament. But they were closer than most siblings, as is often the case with twins.

In the summer of '74, the pair of them decided that they needed to earn some serious money between them during their school holidays. There were enough hands doing what needed to be done at home, so Margaret and Mary enrolled themselves in a 'Silver Service' course for six weeks in the local technical school and, by the end of it, the two of them were proper little waitresses, with their scrolls to prove it to potential employers. They had set themselves up for good summer work for a few years to come, but, better than that, their waitressing careers were about to start at the very top. Margaret and Mary found themselves working in Ashford Castle.

It looked perfect, and their mother, in a rare moment of weakness, allowed her heart to get the better of her when her two girls spotted the prettiest platform sandals made of denim in Treston's shoe store in Gort, and thought immediately that they had to have them. They went off to Cong with their new sandals in their bags. Neither Margaret nor Mary were certain what a commis waitress actually had to do, but they quickly found out as they carried trays of perfectly beautiful food up one big flight of stairs and carried the same tray with empty plates back down the stairs. In between, they served the tray to more fancily dressed waitresses who walked the floor of the immaculate dining room in the castle. At the end of their first week, their feet had been cut off them. The new sandals were a disaster. A bigger disaster loomed after their first month in the castle was almost complete. Their Grandad Connors passed away. But when the two girls asked to go home to attend the funeral, they were told absolutely not. Margaret and Mary packed their bags and the two of them spirited themselves away first thing the following morning.

After Grandad Connors was mourned, the two girls wondered what the rest of the summer would hold for them. The pair resolved that there was nothing to be done but to return to Ashford Castle and ask for their jobs back. Remarkably, Margaret and Mary received a warmer reception than they imagined might await them and, after a lengthy and robust discussion, they were told that they could have their jobs as commis waitresses back, but, not in Mayo. They were dispatched to a sister hotel in Kerry, and spent the remainder of their summer carrying trays at the Waterville Lake Hotel.

In Mayo and Kerry that summer, in 1974, Margaret Nolan was far from heart-broken to be away from home, and neither did she spend any great amount of time pining at the thought of Sylvie Linnane making a new home, and potentially a new life, for himself in London. She hoped he might come back home to Galway, however, and she was much happier than she had expected to be when she heard the news of his return. But, the only time Margaret actually got to see Sylvie that summer was on a television set in the hotel in Waterville, when she stole away from her serving chores for an hour and watched him play in the All-Ireland minor semi-final against Kilkenny.

Margaret was ready to go steady, when she returned home to Galway. It was Sylvie who was waiting at home in Gort, back home for good, his days in London long over and half-forgotten. Five years later they would be married. Margaret was not yet twenty years old, Sylvie was two years older. They were on the maple dance floor in The Classic, dancing energetically to Elvis Presley's 'Blue Suede Shoes' when Sylvie popped the question.

As she had, all those years earlier in the same ballroom, Margaret Nolan answered, "Yes!"

Margaret and Sylvie, in truth, had met some time before their Classic Ballroom adventures began, though they had had an inauspicious beginning to their relationship. They had actually come to blows on that first occasion. But, luckily, Mary Joe Nolan and Celia Linnane were present and immediately separated the volatile pair.

Margaret had been four years old, and Sylvie six. Their mothers had taken them to the Health Centre in Gort that morning.

Margaret was busy with a box of toys in the corner of the room when Sylvie walked over to her. There was nothing said, until Sylvie grabbed the wooden horse Margaret had been playing with, and which Margaret intended playing with again. Sylvie would not give the horse up. Margaret grabbed the horse. Sylvie grabbed Margaret and the horse. All hell was about to break loose, when Margaret and Sylvie were quickly grabbed by their arms and escorted out of the corner. Sitting back on her mother's knee, Margaret Nolan took another look at the boy, and never forgot his face, or all that red hair which surrounded it.

• • •

Three times in the '70s, Gort were turned back at the semi-final stage of the Galway senior hurling Championship. Killimordaly in 1970, Turloughmore in 1972, and Kinvara in 1979 had blocked Gort's entry onto the greatest stage in the county, and the opportunity of proving themselves, without question, the greatest team in Galway. It was 47 years since 15 men from Gort had paraded around the field at the start of a county final, when Mick Linnane was amongst them. But, on Sunday, October 25, 1981, Sylvie Linnane said the final few words to the team in the dressing room, in Kenny Park, Athenry, and led Gort out to face Castlegar, and to face the Connollys in the Championship semi-final.

Gort were three points down at half time.

Castlegar were All-Ireland champions the year before. They'd beaten Ballycastle McQuillans to make some serious history for the parish and for Galway, and they were warmest of favourites all week long, no matter what parish a man visited, no matter what home or church or public house. With those three points in their favour, and with a controversial goal also about to come their way at a crucial point in the second half, every conversation that had taken place about the game for the preceding seven days, outside of the parish of Gort, appeared to have the course of the game and its final verdict accurately nailed down.

The first half had been tough, and dour, and such a battle also favoured the team that was well used to winning battles that were fought up close. When Gort did get a chance for a big score, either their finishing was off early on that afternoon or else Tommy Grogan in the Castlegar goal manfully stood in their way. Midway through the second half, Kevin Fahy took off on a bustling solo run down the middle of the Castlegar half and, despite losing possession on his way through, managed to flick the ball to John Crehan. He passed quickly to full-forward Michael Cahill, who goaled, giving Gort their biggest break all day. But, with the county final staring them in the face, that break was almost immediately cancelled out.

There was a right scramble in the Gort goalmouth and, after Martin O'Shea had a great chance bravely blocked down, Jimmy Francis finished the ball to the net. The referee, Tom Lenihan, from Carnmore, raced in to the scene of the crime. There, he had a good chat with his umpires. Most people in Duggan Park, including the members of the Press, who occupied the best seats in the house, considered that Gort's goalkeeper, Tony Monaghan, had been roughly tackled in his small square. A free out looked like a fair decision. But Lenihan allowed the goal to stand.

The mighty John Connolly had opened the day's scoring. Connolly was Sylvie's man, but John Connolly was also the man who had ruled the hurling fields of the county for so long. He was as massively respected as much as he was feared. All the Connollys, who made up one-third of the Castlegar team, were outstanding hurlers, and, on the sideline Micheal Linnane, who was in charge of Gort, knew that Sylvie would not be able to give John Connolly, and John Connolly alone, his undivided attention. Before the 60 minutes were up, Sylvie would have played in four different positions on the field. Most of the time he was marking a Connolly, and he reduced the number of Connolly brothers out on the field when he rattled into Gerry Connolly with a fiercely bracing, but fair, shoulder which the referee agreed to be the case even as Gerry Connolly was helped off the field.

But, to start with, Sylvie's first big job of the afternoon was to hold John Connolly at centre-forward for Castlegar. The game was six minutes old when John Connolly had opened the day's scoring with his first point. Connolly would finish his day with three points from play and three more from frees. Sylvie Linnane could not be everywhere, even his own brother on the sideline knew that.

Pearse Piggott won the ball in the middle of the field, and raced the whole way to the 21-yard line to open Gort's account and, midway through the half, Gerry Lally pointed from a free to make it 0-2 apiece. It was the sort of game in which a point had the value of a goal, and was celebrated as such by the rival supporters. Castlegar led 0-7 to 0-4 at half time. John Connolly had taken over the free-taking duties from his brother, Joe, and also landed an outrageous score from 60 yards out during play, which might have knocked the stuffing out of Gort if it had come late in the game. However, with Gerry Lally and Colie Rock getting on top in the middle of the field immediately after the restart, and with Lally knocking over a good point fast enough, Gort were right in it and within sight of a surprise victory. Six minutes into the second half, Lally also pointed a '65' to leave one point between the teams. A

Mattie Murphy point brought the teams level.

The game had opened up, and both teams began to throw off their shackles. Neither team looked like they feared losing anymore. After John Crehan risked life and limb to win the ball, Gerry Linnane got the point that put Gort in front.

Suddenly, Gort were flying. Lally hit over two frees and Cahill scored his goal. Gort were six points up, and it looked more like sixteen points for a couple of minutes at least – until Jimmy Francis' disputed goal brought the difference right back to three points. One goal separated the teams. John Connolly shot over a point from a tough free. He also clipped over another point from play, after Sylvie gathered a quick puck-out from his goalkeeper and looked to clear the ball down to the opposite end of the field. Connolly blocked Sylvie's clearance, and scored.

Sylvie made up for that straight away, when his shot from the left sailed over the Castlegar crossbar. Lally put Gort back three in front. There were two minutes left. With seconds remaining, Castlegar worked the ball slowly up the field. Gort had men back, everywhere. There was no room for a shot at goal, but, right on full-time the referee awarded Castlegar a 21-yard free.

John Connolly aimed knee-high. Tony Monaghan saved the ball, and emerged from a forest of tangling, desperate players, and cleared. The referee blew the final whistle.

• • •

It was the proudest day, and the greatest year, in the living memory of the vast majority of people in the parish of Gort, when their senior team finally brought home the Galway senior Championship crown, in the late autumn of 1981. Though, like the semi-final win over crusty old Castlegar, the final itself was a tense, long drawn-out affair that needed two games before dividing Gort from Kiltormer.

The first day, the teams were level, 2-8 to 0-11, and it was just as close in the replay. Gort, however, once again grabbed a most valuable brace of goals. They won 2-6 to 0-8 on another tense, nervy day when defences laid down the law at both ends of the field.

However, there was an extra sweet, and emotional, twist that came with that victory for many of the Linnane households. In March, 1982, Gort defeated Tooreen in the Connacht final, 8-13 to 0-3, and in the All-Ireland quarter-final Gort had the pleasure of entertaining St Gabriel's of London in Ballinasloe. That was as hotly contested a game as Micheal Linnane, Sylvie Linnane, and every Linnane who had ever lined out for St Gabriel's, knew it would be. It was 4-12 to 0-9 at the end of a memorable afternoon and evening for the London champions and, in particular, the Linnane family.

Two weeks later, the Gort team was asked the sternest questions it had ever been asked, when they travelled down to the home of Kilkenny hurling to take on James Stephens in the All-Ireland semi-final. Gort threw themselves into it, and they had the Kilkenny champions in all sorts of trouble early on. It looked quite possible that, after waiting 47 years to make it to a Galway final, Gort would be in an All-Ireland final within a further six months. John Crehan, Gerry Lally and Pearse Piggott all had points in the opening six minutes. It was 0-3 to 0-0 on the scoreboard at the town end of the old ground. After eighteen minutes, The Village had drawn level, 0-4 each, and a goal from John Joe Cullen just before half time gave them a lead of 1-6 to 0-7. Gort, however, had given their all. Billy Walton scored five points without reply in the third quarter of the game and, in the final quarter, Gort looked, and looked again and again, for the goal that might have given them a lifeline.

It never came. The journey home was longer than anyone in the parish of Gort who had set out that morning could ever have imagined. Victory in the Galway final seemed a long and distant memory. A fresh draw for the 1982 Galway senior Championship had already been made. Gort had never thought it possible to be so intensely disappointed in the month of April, with a whole new Championship about to start.

The club had only a couple of weeks to hide away that sadness.

CHAPTER
8

The 1981 Galway title had not been won without some harsh comment and condemnation. The two games against Kiltormer had unearthed a number of controversial incidents that neither Gort nor their opponents were particularly proud of and, for Gort in particular, the magnificence of their long-sought victory, after 47 mostly sorrowful years, was tinged with some annoyance that they had not received the fullest of credit from every corner of the county. It didn't help that 1982 brought nothing but disappointment, first in the spring when James Stephens had been too powerful in the All-Ireland semi-final, and then in the late summer when Gort never got into their full stride in the defence of their precious county title. Kiltormer won the Championship in '82. Kiltormer, indeed, looked the real thing as champions, having narrowly lost out in '81 and then making certain of their No.1 position the following year.

Word got back to Gort, on a regular basis, that their detractors suggested that maybe, just maybe, they had been a lucky team in 1981. The words 'flash' and 'pan' were used in the same sentence more than once. That hurt. It also fuelled a desire to make 1983 a year beyond reproach. In the semi-final in '83, Gort made fast and tidy work of Sarsfields, and waited for Kiltormer. There was unfinished business to see who was the best team in Galway after all.

In the other semi-final, Castlegar and Kiltormer, always tough and brilliant rivals when they found themselves together on a hurling field, left Gort waiting. It needed two enthralling games to decide the winner. Gort had to wait three weeks for the county final in St Brendan's Park, in Athenry. Finally, the opportunity had arrived to prove to every single man, woman and child in the whole county that they were made of the stuff of true champions. But they had to prove their worth against Castlegar, and Castlegar had the little matter of some sweet revenge for their semi-final defeat two years before to attend to, on that Sunday afternoon, on October 23, 1983.

An attendance of 6,500 dropped a round total of £12,000 into the pockets of the Galway county board. The conditions were good and dry, and there was little wind to trouble the keenest marksmen on either side, and not enough that it could be used as an excuse by the teams.

Gort built their wall the length of the half-back line, and dared Castlegar to pass. There, Michael Brennan, Pearse Piggott and Sylvie Linnane took their positions. Piggott would mark John Connolly. Sylvie would take Joe Connolly. There was no doubt in the mind of the swollen attendance that the 1983 final would be won or lost by what transpired on that very line. Within two minutes, Piggott – never the shyest man in Gort, or in the whole county – made the first big statement of the day.

He raced far up the field and, as he came into scoring distance, the ball was brilliantly balanced on his hurl. Piggott, in one sweeping movement, struck the ball over the bar and charged back to the wall Gort needed building on their half-back line. John Connolly was facing a rare day. That was already obvious, but, as the game progressed, the great old man of Galway found out that he was in one of the occasional games in his life where absolutely nothing came easy. Piggott never gave him an inch. By the end, John Connolly had been overpowered. He looked rattled. In the 38th minute of the second half, when Castlegar needed a goal from a 21-yard free, and Connolly himself was set up to make it a rasper, the ball somehow did not fully rise for him, and the most decorated hurler in the county had to quickly save the situation by taking his point. Five minutes from the end, from the penalty spot with at least two goals now needed, Connolly struck the ball hard and high, but too high, and it sailed well over the bar once again.

Piggott was supreme. Sylvie was just as lively and, in the earliest and most tenacious moments in the whole game, when men were crowding in on rucks, he repeatedly emerged with the ball in his hand and ended any doubts anyone had about which team might be the hungriest on the day. Sylvie Linnane's natural aggression, and willingness to take any hit from any quarter or side, was going to have to be matched by the men from Castlegar. That was not going to be easily done. On the other side of the line, Michael Brennan was also in no mood to give Joe Grealish a sniff at it and, by the end of his day's work, Brennan had held his man scoreless.

Behind them, John Nolan had Gerry Connolly to attend to, and the Gort full-back kept his man to a point from a free, and, knowing that his opponent had two broken bones beneath the heavy strapping on one hand, Nolan doubled the pressure any time the ball came in between them. Michael Cahill and Colie Rock also ruled the middle of the field in the first half, and, all told, Castlegar looked a defeated team by the end of the opening thirty minutes, even though Gort only held a three points lead, 1-4 to 0-4. The goal had come in the 13th minute, and fortunate it was too, as Gerry Lally topped his free from fifty-five yards out, but Brian Brennan met it on the bounce to send it to the bottom left corner of the net from six yards out. Castlegar had only two points from John and Joe Connolly, John taking the best score of the half from forty yards out in the 20th minute, and Joe snapping over a score from twenty yards four minutes later. But Gort looked in total control, even though the scoreboard did not tell such a tale. A spectacular turnaround was needed from Castlegar in the second half. Either that, or the backside would have to inexplicably fall out of Gort's thundering performance.

Gerry Lally pointed from a '70' three minutes into the second half. When Gerry Connolly was stretched off the field in the 40th minute, John Connolly made a mess of the resulting 21-yard free. One minute later, despite having a divot tossed in his direction by an opponent, Lally again struck the ball over the bar from seventy yards out. And, one minute after that, Mattie Murphy drifted fifty yards out and scored; with fifteen minutes remaining Gort led 1-10 to 0-5.

John Connolly's low shot was not cleared by John Commins, and Joe, although on the ground himself, knocked the ball into the net. Castlegar had brought it back to five points, but, three minutes later, Gerry Linnane poked the ball into an empty net after Castlegar's keeper, Tommy Grogan, badly misjudged the flight of the ball and batted it down into no-man's land in his own square. It was back to eight, and Lally immediately pointed a 35-yard free to make it nine. The final scoreline would show Gort winning their fifth county title by a slim enough 2-12 to 3-6 but, in truth, it was a win that was more than worthy of a six points, or nine points, difference between the teams. There had only been one team in it, from start to finish. Gort had almost all of the power, and almost all of the most maddening resolve. Nobody could doubt that for one second. They had won in style. They were the finest of champions. More than that, they had won two Championships inside a 24-month period, and hurling folk in Galway could see that Gort looked set to become the dominant force in the county for some years to come.

• • •

Six years after their first son had been born, Margaret and Sylvie Linnane were preparing for a second baby in the house. It was 1984, and a mild spring day in April, when Margaret knew that the baby was on the way. The baby's due date was July. Before either of them knew it, Sylvie was driving Margaret to Portiuncula Hospital, in Ballinasloe, with a hastily packed bag in the rear seat of their car.

Their second son, who would be named Darragh, was born almost ten weeks early. When Margaret first held Darragh in her hands, he weighed just under three pounds. But there was little opportunity to hold him for very long, as the baby spent the first four weeks of his life in the intensive care unit of the hospital. There were two other children in the unit, each of them bigger than Margaret and Sylvie's son, and one of whom would, sadly, not survive. But Darragh Linnane was a fighter. Surprisingly, he had no problems with his breathing. With each passing week, he gained in strength, though not necessarily in weight. He had a fine head of hair, even though he'd been premature, but he had no nails on his fingers. And there was a coat of downy hair covering his back, which was also quite normal for a baby that had come into the world some months before his time. Finally, the doctors felt that the baby would perhaps thrive that little bit more if he came into contact with his own family every hour of every day. Margaret was assured that there was no risk of infection from one of his own.

It was safe to bring Darragh home.

It was close to the end of May, and the baby was indeed doing well. The day was so nice that Margaret decided that she'd go for a walk with him. She headed for her mother's house. Her little baby boy was still so tiny that Margaret, on advice from hospital staff, was dressing him in doll's clothing. He had the weakest, quietest cry. And, the baby never made a sound when he was snatched off the sofa in the front room of the Nolan house. Margaret had left the room to get the baby's change bag. Her mother, Mary Joe, was in the kitchen making some tea.

When Margaret came back into the room she had left less than a minute earlier, her baby was gone. She stared at the sofa where she had left him. He was too small to have fallen off onto the floor. He wasn't anywhere on the ground or anywhere in the room as Margaret, frantically, looked in all of the most unlikely and foolish of places. Finally, in absolute desperation, which had now taken complete hold of her, she rushed to the window and looked up and down outside.

Across the road, far off in the distance, she saw her mother's beautiful collie, Lassie, running across the field. It had been a stray animal but it was a real beauty from day one when the Nolan's took her in. Margaret could see something in the dog's mouth.

Lassie was a friendly, gentle dog, Margaret knew that. But, the dog would be forever grabbing any little kittens she came across in the house, or out in the yard. The dog had been neutered shortly after she was found but her dormant maternal instincts continually came to the fore when there were any weak kittens, making their tiny hopeful cries, around the place. She'd grab them and race off with them but they never came to any harm. Now, as she stared hard out the window, still frozen with terror, she was sure that she could see Lassie with her baby in her mouth. Something … something life-like was dangling from the dog's mouth, as she trotted purposefully up the field.

The dog gripped Margaret's little baby by his baby-grow suit. As they raced outside, Mary Joe urgently warned her daughter not to shout at the dog. Margaret was in complete emotional turmoil, but she listened to her mother and when she got to the gate she called, as softly as she could, for

Lassie. She called again, a little louder. The dog stopped, and looked back.

Margaret called again, too loudly.

She took a deep breath.

"Lassie... Lassie... Lassie ... come here girl," she heard herself calling gently, and trying to take more deep breaths at the same time, to suppress her desire to scream out at the dog.

Lassie turned and started walking back to Mary Joe and Margaret. She took her time, the baby still dangling beneath her chin. But Lassie had the suit tightly clenched between her teeth.

"Good girl, good girl, Lassie. Here you come, girl." Mary Joe was too traumatised to speak. But Lassie began running home. When the dog reached the two women, she immediately laid the baby at Margaret's feet.

The district nurse, about fifteen minutes later, arrived unexpectedly to check on baby Darragh's progress and when informed of the walk she expressed her stern disapproval at taking a premature baby outdoors so soon.

"Who knows what could have happened?" the nurse admonished Margaret. Margaret thought it best not to mention anything about what had just occurred with the dog.

When the baby was born in hospital in Ballinasloe, Margaret and Sylvie were surprised and delighted that the staff had very quickly suggested that they take a photograph of Darragh with his proud parents. Sylvie thought it a nice touch by them. Margaret was also none the wiser. It would be some weeks later, upon enquiring, that she was told by one of the nurses that they had feared the baby would not survive. A family photo had been of the utmost importance, and far more important than Margaret and Sylvie had ever realised.

Darragh's weight had to be constantly monitored in those first few weeks and months. Margaret would look at the nurse working the scales in the family kitchen, and see her putting three one-pound bags of sugar on one side and her little baby on the other.

• • •

It was decided to find out, over a single weekend, which was the greatest hurling team from any parish in the country. The All-Ireland Championship was to be decided on the weekend of April 14 and 15, 1984. Gort had beaten Tooreen, 3-13 to 1-5, in the Connacht final two weeks after finishing off Castlegar so comprehensively in their county final. On Saturday, April 14, Gort were due to meet a Midleton team that included no less than seven Cork senior hurlers. It was going to take a mighty effort. Sylvie's job was to go toe-to-toe with John Fenton, the stylish playmaker in the heart of the Midleton team. Win that, and Gort might be in an All-Ireland final, most likely against Ballyhale Shamrocks.

The Kilkenny champions got their full of it from Antrim's Ballycastle McQuillans in their semi-final, finishing up 3-14 to 2-10 winners, but that day in Limerick the real battle was between Gort and Midleton. Gort won by four points at the end of a nail-biting sixty minutes. It was 1-11 to 2-4. Sylvie Linnane was much too powerful for John Fenton in the most crucial battle, but every last man on the Gort team had given it his all, in order to make it onto the All-Ireland final stage. The stage for that final was in Birr, the following day.

Gort and Ballyhale fought for every ball, almost to a standstill, and the All-Ireland final ended in a draw, 1-10 apiece. Efforts to entice both teams to play extra-time fell on deaf ears. Both were happy to live and fight another day, and after a long and tiring weekend, it was probably the fairest decision as well. Shamrocks could have snatched it at the very end, but Kevin Fennelly's shot in the final seconds was just off target. Gort breathed a sigh of relief, and were the happier of the two teams to troop off the field.

Gort, too, had enough chances to win the game. They shot 17 wides, a horrendously high total, but a figure that also tells the story of the dominance the Galway champions enjoyed for long spells in the middle-third of the field. Ten minutes into the second half, Gort looked to have all the momentum. They were three points in front. They were showing the greater dash, and the greater determination under each dropping ball. At that stage, Shamrocks threw on the injured Liam Fennelly, and the very presence of one of the game's supreme poachers suitably distracted Gort. Within a couple of minutes, they were a point down. Shortly after that they were down to 14 men, after full-back John Nolan had brought down Kevin Fennelly with a high tackle. The same man sent the resultant free over the bar. Shamrocks were two to the good. But the game continued to bounce back and forth, and Gort, crucially, went back in front after a high centre from Sylvie was finished to the net by Mattie Murphy.

It would have been a shame for either team to lose.

Without any extra time, the replay would have to wait, however. A congested fixtures schedule held the game back for almost two months, and it was not until June 3 that Gort and Ballyhale took to the field in Thurles to finally decide the best hurling club in Ireland.

The seven Fennelly brothers would never enjoy themselves more, or play better together, than the afternoon of the All-Ireland final replay in Semple Stadium. Gort had the wind at their backs in the first half, but found themselves scoreless and, worse still, three points down, after the opening ten minutes. Their finishing touches never improved sufficiently thereafter. Ballyhale also used their experience in the replay to telling effect. Gort were looking to win a first All-Ireland, whereas the Shamrocks were in their third national final since 1979 and had already been champions once. They settled into the replay and looked intent upon getting the job done. The Fennellys looked perfectly at home. Gort had worked their way back into the game coming up to half time, and the sides were level, 0-4 apiece, when the Kilkenny champions pounced for a goal that turned out to be the game-winner. Ger Fennelly shot home that goal in the 27th minute.

Sylvie was picked right corner-back for the replay, directed to keep tight on Liam Fennelly, and that he did. The most decorated member of the Fennelly clan was held scoreless, and was replaced before the end. Shamrocks held a 1-5 to 0-4 advantage at the change. In the second half they tagged on three points without a reply from Gort, and the game, effectively, was at an end midway through the second half, though Gort kept plugging away and the switching of Pearse Piggott into attack helped create more chances. But the decisive score, a goal, never came.

All of the Ballyhale scores, on a gut-wrenching day for Gort, were scored by the Fennellys.

CHAPTER
9

Some Sunday evenings, Sylvie Linnane likes to go to Tom Mullins' rustic old pub in Gort for his pint. Tom Mullins' family also has an undertaking business next door, and locals like to tell one another that a man would need to have 'one foot in the grave' to drink in Mullins' pub. That's a little unfair, but the place can be quiet, even when Tom is serving up good pints and his select clientele are enjoying some good conversation.

Even on a Sunday evening after the biggest hurling and football games of the year have been on television, the establishment can be desperately quiet. That's the way Sylvie likes it. He knows the dozen regulars and they know him, and there's never any great worry of too many other people looking to bother them with either endless, or mindless, chatter.

Sylvie had always liked his peace and quiet.

Throughout his career and, indeed, through the two long decades that have passed since he last played for Galway, there has never been a time when he has purposely sought the limelight. He would never have had to wander very far. Sylvie, possibly, was the single strongest iconic figure who best represented all that was good, and all that was as hard as nails, about the Galway team that played its heart out in seven All-Ireland finals in ten seasons.

The man Margaret Linnane married has always had two qualities stronger than any others – Sylvie has always liked hard work, and he has always been in good humour. Each underpins the man.

He has never missed a day's work in his life. Apart, of course, from the necessity of spending an entire Monday travelling slowly home from Dublin to Gort after an All-Ireland final. Seven times he has made that journey. Seven Mondays have been missed. But no other days: not the Tuesday or the Wednesday. Sylvie Linnane has never let a drinking session get in the way of a day's work. And that's not just because he has spent the longest period of his working life contracting his machinery to Galway County Council, and doing his duty to keep the roads of Galway in the best possible shape. Sylvie has always liked work.

In the early years of their marriage, Margaret would see Sylvie working right up to the last minute before it was time to collect his kit bag and hurls and head off to training. Even when training was hardest, in the late spring, a full day's work was still to be completed. One day, the Linnane's had borrowed a tractor to visit the bog. Hours were spent loading the trailer with bags of turf, but the thing got stuck. The tractor was stuck solid. The remainder of the day was spent carrying dozens and dozens of bags and getting them home to the shed. Sylvie only stopped for a quick bite to eat – a sandwich and a pot of tea. His arms were falling off him by the time daylight was finally waning, and Margaret wondered would he still go to training that evening. He offered her a quizzical look when she asked the question.

At games, she'd hear people shout awful things at her husband. Awful, hurtful, slanderous things, especially at club games when parishes were getting stuck into one another and the dander was up amongst the players and supporters on both sides, and the Galway jersey was temporarily forgotten.

Sylvie would never take anything that was said, or done, to heart. It was just the game. His love for the game and his happiness at playing the game mattered more to him than a fiery incident that might arise on the field, or things he might hear. In the field in Ballindereen one evening, tempers were well and truly frayed and one elderly gentleman, who was standing close to Margaret Linnane, was in an extremely agitated state. The single greatest cause of this agitation was Sylvie Linnane. Margaret knew the man quite well. He was a nice, quiet man, but that evening in Ballindereen he was hardly recognizable, such was the metamorphosis that had taken place as the game progressed in Gort's favour. He was vexed, and Margaret wondered would the poor man live to see the end of the game. Shortly after half time, the ball crossed the sideline, just a couple of yards in front of the man who was kneeling.

Sylvie Linnane had been up in front of a disciplinary committee in Croke Park just a few days earlier, but the table of wise and elderly GAA men ordained that Sylvie had been sinned against, just as much as he had sinned.

"LINNANE!" roared the elderly man.

"We all know you got off lightly yesterday. TOO LIGHTLY! They should have done ye, LINNANE, they should have … JAILED YE!"

Sylvie had placed the ball on the ground and had walked back to take a look at it. But, before he cut the ball, he turned around. He looked the man in the eye. And there was a smile on Sylvie's face.

"You be quiet there, old man," said Sylvie, quietly, without everyone on that side of the ground hearing him. But he wasn't finished:

"BEFORE YOU DO YOURSELF AN INJURY!"

The group of supporters either side of the demented man roared with laughter. Sylvie was still smiling. Eventually, even the old man himself began to chuckle, as he moved further down the line.

When the time came for him to stand on the sideline himself, or stand his ground outside the wire, Sylvie never said very much. And when the time came for him to watch his sons play for Gort, he also kept his head. He never liked being known as the 'hard man' of Galway hurling. It was a label that attached itself to him, and he would have preferred if it hadn't. He never saw himself as a hard man. He always saw hurling as being a naturally hard game, and it didn't take a 'hard man' to play the game well. Once a game was over, Sylvie believed in immediately leaving all hostilities behind, and he always enjoyed meeting up with his opponents.

He'd talk about an upcoming game, when his sons might want to talk, which was seldom enough. Otherwise, Sylvie was content to have his lads find their own way as hurlers.

Hurling folk in Galway, and throughout the country, may have thought him different, thought him tougher and naturally more aggressive and far more intent upon enjoying the massive physicality of the game, than most men who were lucky to call themselves countymen. But Sylvie Linnane never understood that, he never encouraged it. And whenever a friend or a stranger grabbed him by the arm and sought to talk about past games, and the big hits given and received, Sylvie never much enjoyed those conversations. He liked to keep those conversations short. He never saw himself any different.

Sometimes, with some of the things they might say, people had a habit of disappointing him.

On the Monday evening, after the Galway team bus had arrived in Ballinasloe and emptied itself of the 1987 All-Ireland champions, Sylvie Linnane had stood on the makeshift stage and looked down at the thousands of delighted faces. For once that day, Margaret Linnane was by her husband's side. On the long, celebratory journey home, the wives and girlfriends of the players were on a second bus, right behind the team bus. In Ballinasloe, the wives and girlfriends joined the heroes on stage, to share the greatest moment in their hurling lives, and witness the unbelievable. The speeches and the singing finally ended and it was time for everyone to get back on their buses and continue their journey into deepest Galway.

Sylvie was leaving the stage when Margaret grabbed him by the arm and pointed at a man who was only a couple of yards away, and who'd been fighting his way through the crowds for ten or fifteen minutes. He was calling up at Sylvie. The man had a little girl in his arms, who could not have been more than two or three years old, and, though his progress in getting to the stage had been slow, he was almost there and he wanted Sylvie.

Margaret asked Sylvie to wait a minute longer for the man and his daughter. Finally, he gushed with satisfaction at arriving in front of Sylvie, but he didn't look to shake Sylvie's hand.

"Sylvie…! I want you to kiss my little girl," he exclaimed.

"I want her to be able to say she was kissed by the toughest man in Ireland!"

Sylvie Linnane obliged.

"It would have been better," Sylvie said to his wife, as they walked away, "to hear he wanted her kissed by one of the greatest hurlers in Ireland!"

• • •

Twenty-one-year-old Sylvie Og Linnane wore the No.8 jersey on the Gort team that won the Galway county title on Sunday, November 6, 2011. He was one of six sons to wear the green and white that day, whose fathers had worn the same jerseys when the parish claimed the title in 1983. Twenty-eight years had passed without a county win. It was a long passage of time, which contained more heartbreak and ever-deepening frustration than anything else. The dominance Gort had threatened to hold over Galway hurling, after their victories in 1981 and '83, had never materialised. Instead, there was a long string of quarter-final defeats, and a very occasional semi-final appearance. There was only one final. Fifteen times, in total, Gort had a good summer under their belt, but found themselves coming up short.

In this quarter of a century, Kiltormer, Sarsfields, Athenry and Portumna each produced dynasties that were powerful to behold. Each, in turn, dealt with the Gort challenge decisively.

In 2008, Gort had actually reached the final. Portumna awaited them, and the champions were in the process of winning five titles in a mesmerising seven years. Defeating Gort by 1-18 to 2-7 was simply part of that same process. Before the game, that autumn, the Galway county board thought it a suitable idea to honour the Gort team of 1983-84, and actually got Sylvie and the other fathers, and the remainder of their colleagues from that winning dressing room, out onto the field before the game and wave to the crowd. By the time the game had ended, Sylvie and mostly everyone in Gort realised that it was not the best of ideas to celebrate a piece of parish history, not when a young Gort team was attempting to focus on making their own history.

Mattie Murphy was the team manager in 2011. He had helped guide the Gort team since the players were gossuns. Murphy, Josie Harte, Joe Regan, Sylvie Linnane and Gerry Lally, amongst others, had all taken turns in guiding the lads up through the underage ranks. On the first Sunday in November, Gort faced Clarinbridge. There were 9,000 people, just over or just under, to see Gort take on the reigning All-Ireland champions in Pearse Stadium.

Gort, typically, raced into a commanding lead. They were 0-6 to 0-1 in front after 12 minutes and, in perfect conditions a five-point lead looked massive. Sean Forde had got their first after just thirty seconds. Gerry Quinn got four of those points. Aidan Harte was also on target, and two further points by Quinn and Ollie Fahy by the 21st minute, increased Gort's lead to 0-8 to 0-2. Clarinbridge had struggled to get into their stride, but finally they began to click in the ten minutes before half time and it was 0-9 to 0-6 at the break. Gort ploughed on in the second half, however, and it was 0-12 to 0-7 after thirty-six minutes, with Quinn hitting two more.

Two points from play from Alan Kerins left just a single goal between the teams entering the final quarter, and all of Gort's hard work over the preceding forty-five minutes was up in the air as the game came trundling towards the finishing line. When Gort 'keeper Peter Cummins stopped a long-range effort from Eoin Forde from going over the bar, Billy Lane nipped in to finish the ball to the net for Clarinbridge. The teams were level, 1-11 to 0-14. The champions lost a man when Eoin Forde received a second yellow card after fifty minutes, but they remained composed and never took a step back. With four minutes remaining, Stephen Forde edged them in front.

In the final sixty seconds of normal time, Harte levelled the game once again. Team captain Andy Coen showed his mettle to land a free from seventy yards to put Gort one up. In the dying seconds of added time, Harte scored his fifth point of the day, to finish off a 0-17 to 1-12 victory.

Gort had stormed home.

The following February, Gort never found their feet against Coolderry in the All-Ireland semi-final in Limerick's Gaelic Grounds. The Offaly and Leinster champions had one goal in the first half, and two more in the second half, and Gort were chasing the game down with points to the bitter end. It was 3-16 to 0-17 at the final whistle. There were no complaints.

• • •

Sylvie did not speak to Sylvie Og for very long after either game. After the victory and after the defeat, he shook Sylvie Og's hand, and told him he had done well. Once a game was over and done with, he never saw the need to discuss what had just happened with any of his sons, or his daughter, after any game in which they played. They know their father believes in them. They know how proud he is of all his children. But they also know that he has never been one for heart-to-hearts. In the Linnane household, heart-to-hearts have always been left to Margaret, and Margaret speaks for Sylvie.

His own father never fussed unduly over Sylvie's career, and Sylvie always believed that, whatever transpired on the hurling field, a man has to play his own game. The same goes for his sons.

Win or lose, every second Sunday, they must make their own way as hurlers. They know Sylvie loves them. They know he would do anything for them at any time, but they also know that he will never get in their way. It breaks his heart when he sees them disappointed after losing a game. At times like that, however, Sylvie Linnane lets them know all too quickly that playing the game is more important than either winning or losing. Win or lose, the hard work which a man puts into his game is usually the same.

Winner or loser!

It's not only about medals, he's told many a man that, and he has laid that belief in front of his own sons as well. A stranger touring in Galway called to the Linnane door one day. He asked to see Sylvie's medals.

They were left on the table in front of the visitor. And he eyed the three All-Ireland winning medals with greater interest than any of the others.

"Are they really gold, Sylvie?" he asked, finally.

Sylvie was sitting across the table from his visitor. He looked down at the medals, which he had not taken up into his own hands in ten or twenty years.

"To tell you the truth," Sylvie replied, "they're nearly all sweat."

A box of medals does not tell the story of Sylvie Linnane's career, and neither will they tell the full story of the hurling careers of his sons. There are other, more accurate, ways of measuring and valuing a single hurling life. And there are other reminders.

• • •

Sylvie Linnane has not one finger left on either hand that can be straightened out. They were all broken, at one time or another, on some hurling field or other, and usually a field far, far away from Croke Park. Each finger reminds him of a different slap, or indeed a nasty hit, he may have received. All of them were broken long before he caught his right hand, foolishly, in the steering wheel of the battered old tractor he had always kept at the back of his sheds.

His sons call it a fossil of a machine.

Sylvie tells them it was the first of its kind, a tractor with real power-steering, if a man had power enough in his hands to manhandle or steer the ancient thing in any direction! And Sylvie, one fine day, was proving to himself that he had the power in his hands and arms to steer the blessed thing, when he did the damage to his right hand.

The hands of a 54-year-old man were X-rayed in the Regional Hospital in Galway, after Margaret had driven her husband there that same evening. When the American doctor on duty finally got the X-rays up on the board to examine the potential damage to the patient's right hand, he had no idea he was about to look at the hands of a 54-year-old hurler.

The X-rays had been taking an age, and Sylvie asked Margaret to go and check what on earth was keeping them. The doctor was looking at the bones in her husband's right hand when Margaret Linnane peered around the doorway.

"The wrist is not broken, at any rate," the American confirmed to the junior doctor at his side.

"But … my Gawd! Look at this guy's fingers!" he exclaimed.

"What happened to that HAND?" the American asked.

The question was left in the air for a few seconds. Finally, the young Irish doctor helpfully offered an explanation.

"I'd say … " came the matter-of-fact reply, "you're looking at a hurler."

PART THREE
Making of a Legend

CHAPTER
10

Cyril Farrell was manager of the Galway senior hurling team. It was his first night to be surrounded by his players. Finally, they were Farrell's players. They were also the property, at least for the foreseeable future, of Bernie O'Connor and 'Inky' Flaherty, who were Farrell's selectors. It was a late October evening, in 1979. Two months earlier, Galway had lost the All-Ireland final to Kilkenny by seven points, a defeat that cut Farrell deeper than most, even though he had no greater reason than anybody else in the county to take it personally.

The usually loud and always commanding figure of Babs Keating had been team coach for the '79 championship. The living Tipperary legend had five men carefully chosen to help him select the Galway team, Sean Conroy, Bernie O'Connor, Michael Howley, PJ Qualter and Paddy Egan.

Cyril Farrell was the team trainer. He could have his say in who was going well, and who wasn't going so well, but he was not, officially, in the inner circle.

Farrell was thirty years old. He had watched greatly respected men guide the county, and look to do their very best for Galway. Babs had been the main man in 1977. Joe McGrath was the man in '78, and Babs had come back for another long summer in '79. Now it was his turn. The team was in his control. As he waited to speak to them for the first time as their team boss, in an age when a 'manager' was called a 'coach', and a 'coach' was never referred to as a 'team boss', Farrell knew that there were big decisions to be made.

Great and wise men had been in charge of the team in the preceding years, and there were some great hurlers in the room waiting for him to speak. Amongst them John Connolly, the finest hurler Galway had produced in over a generation, and a man who was some years older than Cyril Farrell.

Others were, more or less, the same age as their new coach. Niall McInerney, Sean Silke, Frank Burke and PJ Molloy were also big names. So, too, were Iggy Clarke and Joe McDonagh. All of them were at the height of their hurling careers, or as close to the top as they ever expected to be, and all of them had All Star awards. Connolly had two of them. And Farrell knew that the massive, brick-like figure of Castlegar's John Connolly was still seen by everybody in Galway as the starting point for the new team that the new team coach would attempt to build after the gut-wrenching loss to Kilkenny. John Connolly saw that as clearly as any man.

John Connolly also saw the No.6 jersey as his. That's what he wanted, and he would be sorely disappointed at being dispatched anywhere else on the field. But Cyril Farrell already knew that he didn't want John Connolly as his centre-back. Farrell would play him there in his first competitive game, when the National League recommenced the following month, and less than 2,000 Galway supporters were bothered to turn up in Pearse Stadium to see them gain the tiniest morsel of revenge over half a Kilkenny team. It was a brutally dark November afternoon and the rain had been bucketing down from early morning. But the match went ahead. Galway won 0-9 to 0-7. John Connolly did well at No.6, but Cyril Farrell had no intention whatsoever of leaving him there. Connolly had been the one true leader of the team in the middle of the field in the All-Ireland final defeats to Kilkenny in 1975 and '79. Farrell didn't want him in the backs. He wanted him up front. In the front line, and John Connolly would indeed wear the No.14 shirt in the 1980 and '81 All-Ireland finals.

Farrell knew what he wanted. To one side of Connolly in his first game he had chosen Sylvie Linnane. He wanted more cut and thrust. He wanted a harder core to the Galway team. He saw that in Linnane, and he saw it as well in Jimmy Cooney. Twelve months earlier, and many months before the

1979 All-Ireland final, Farrell had told Babs what he saw. Babs and Farrell met up twice each week in Dublin to head off to training together. It was always a journey that was in danger of bordering on the dull side, as their route became punctuated by the same 'slow-coach' villages and towns every single blessed evening. But the conversation between the two men was never punctuated by very long periods of silence. They filled each other's ears with talk of hurling, and racing, and then more hurling.

Farrell informed him more than once that Sylvie Linnane was going unbelievably well. He told Babs, and any of the others who gave him an ear, that Sylvie should be on the team. In the weeks leading into the All-Ireland semi-final, and then the final, Farrell had been refereeing the matches in training, while Babs and the selectors stood on the sideline, and Linnane and Cooney were the two wing backs on the 'B' team. The two of them were naturally harder than most other ordinary, mortal Galway hurlers. Too many lads on the team that would be selected for the All-Ireland final were outstanding hurlers, and polished, no doubt about it. Linnane and Cooney, however, were two who were different.

Linnane had that something else. But he also had as much natural skill as John Connolly. In the second half of the decade, when the Galway team had Joe Cooney as the finest jewel in its ranks, Cyril Farrell still believed that Sylvie Linnane was the most naturally gifted hurler in the county. Left, or right, it didn't matter to Linnane. The ball was always welcomed back by him, like an old friend.

On that first evening when he spoke to the Galway players for the first time as their team coach, Cyril Farrell also told Sylvie Linnane what he truly believed. He spotted Sylvie, who had arrived early, and before he spoke to the players he walked over to him, casually, his hands in his pockets. They'd been friends since 1973, when Cyril had taken Galway so close to the All-Ireland minor title.

"You should not be wearing that tracksuit." Cyril said, matter-of-factly, as he arrived in front of Sylvie.

Sylvie looked surprised, which was unlike the fiery, confident young man who was usually quick enough to speak his mind, on behalf of Gort or Galway.

"It's cold out there," Sylvie replied, after a full two seconds.

It was fairly freezing that night in Athenry, alright.

"I'm not talking about the weather," said Farrell. "I'm talking about Galway. You should not be in a Galway tracksuit!"

Sylvie Linnane was not slow to continue the conversation, or move it on a pace. He gave Farrell a good look at that strong, stubborn chin of his.

"You give me a chance. Anywhere," said Sylvie, "and I'll keep my place on your team."

• • •

The first time Sylvie Linnane saw John Connolly, in the flesh, all dressed up as a mighty Galway hurler, was in 1971. Galway were taking on Tipperary, in Birr, in some sort of challenge game. Sylvie got a lift with the Connaughtons. The Connaughtons were first cousins to the Linnanes, and Sylvie and his brothers were frequent visitors during the summer holidays. Mickey Connaughton was also a Galway selector.

That same Sunday afternoon, the first time Sylvie Linnane saw John Connolly, was also the first occasion on which he got to look at Galway with his own eyes. Better still, he was on the sideline for the whole game.

He was amazed.

More than anything else, even as he stood there on the sideline, he felt close to being overpowered by the noise and the raw physical intensity of what was happening just yards in front of his nose. Men ran like giants that afternoon. Nobody held back. And, when they smashed into one another, as they did repeatedly and with a fearsome relish, Sylvie was amazed that men were not being killed, or being dragged off the field every few minutes broken in two. He was awestruck by what he saw, and a little frightened. But, mostly, he was thrilled to the bone.

The only things that came to a bad ending that same afternoon were hurling sticks, and several of them. In the second half, Ballinderry's Michael McTigue, who was battling his heart out in the corner of the Galway defence, threw his stick in the direction of the sideline and let a roar out of him for a another one.

Sylvie ran to the discarded implement. He took it up into his hands. It was cracked down the middle and looked useless, but he held onto it. He brought it home that evening. A right bit of strapping made it not entirely useless. It was good for a few more months.

More than that, it was a prized leftover from a game he never wanted to forget, all summer long.

• • •

When his time came to wear the Galway jersey, as a sixteen-year-old, Sylvie Linnane had Cyril Farrell as his first coach. Farrell did his damnedest with the team in 1973 to win the All-Ireland minor title, when they were sickened by Kilkenny's late goal, and the following year Sylvie was Farrell's centre-back when Galway never even got close to Kilkenny in the semi-final.

Sylvie's three years with the county's Under-21s flew by. The promise of the 1973 minor team went unfulfilled, but, in his final year in the underage ranks, Sylvie Linnane's name also appeared for the first time on a county senior selection. It was the start of a four-years trek in which he sought to nail down his starting place on the team. But without too much luck.

When the GAA authorities, for some strange reason, decided to haul both Wexford and Galway down to Pairc Ui Chaoimh for the All-Ireland semi-final in 1976, Sylvie was part of the squad, and could rightly claim the title of 'first sub', though he was never made to feel like a very distinguished member of the Galway party. Galway drew with Wexford on August 15. It was 2-23 to 5-14 in the end, in a game celebrated as something of a classic of the time, but, with Tony Doran's giant paw always available in the middle of Galway's large square, more trouble brewed in the replay. Wexford scored three more goals seven days later, 3-14 to 2-14, and while Sylve Linnane got himself game time in both games, he was finding himself on more losing teams than winning teams every time he wore a Galway jersey.

There was one nice victory in 1976, however. Galway made a good run at the Oireachtas Tournament, and, in October they had three points to spare over Cork in the final, winning 1-15 to 2-9.

At the end of the year, the team even had a night out to celebrate their win over Cork. The players were called up, one by one, to collect their medals. Team first and then the substitutes. Sylvie was the first of the subs to march up to the stage and receive his little round of applause. When he got back to the table, however, there was a little surprise waiting. Someone asked to see his medal, and Sylvie handed the box down the table.

"There's nothing here, Sylvie." came the voice to his right.

"Do you have the medal in your pocket already?" someone else laughed. Sylvie asked for the box back. There was nothing there, not a glint of any metal of any description.

"Someone must have forgotten to put it in." Sylvie suggested. But, a moment later Tony Breheny, at the same table, said that his box was empty as well. Then Larry Byrne came back from the stage and, sure enough, there was another empty box.

There had only been 15 Oireachtas medals, and a decision had been made not to buy any more. Sylvie Linnane was not pleased. Actually, he felt insulted. Before going home that same evening he told more than one county board official that they could keep their box, and they could hand it to the next man who was fool enough to walk up on stage to receive it.

He decided, that same night, that he wanted nothing more to do with the Galway team. And he did not change his mind for twelve months. Neither did he miss the games. Gort, he thought, was more than enough for him, and he enjoyed every day of 1977. Despite an exhibition of points scoring from PJ Molloy, Galway lost the All-Ireland semi-final to Cork by five points. But the Galway team did not appear to miss Sylvie Linnane, and all Sylvie really missed that year was the craic, and the chat and the laugh with the lads from all the other parishes when they sat down in the Galway dressing room together.

It was left to Sean Silke to talk Sylvie round.

That he did at the start of the following year. Sylvie was in the field one evening, training with Gort, when Silke pulled into the ground. He was working in Shannon, and passing through on his way to county training in Athenry. Sylvie Linnane had all the time in the world for Sean Silke.

He looked up to him as a something of a hero. He also knew him to be a true gentleman. And they'd been travelling to games together the year before Sylvie said enough was enough. Silke would do the driving, and also in the car would be Finbarr Gantley, Pierce Piggott, and the team's masseur, Willie Bennett. The five of them saw themselves as a bit of a gang. The car and the lively discussions they'd have on their way to training and to games – when they'd right the wrongs of the world, after first of all righting the wrongs of Galway hurling – were as brilliant as any game of hurling a man might get to play. But Silke was the centre of it all. Sylvie loved the way Silke could strike the ball off either side. He loved his strength. He was a magnificent man for any team to have in the centre of its defence, and Sylvie always thought that if Sean Silke had widened his shoulders that bit more, he would have been one of the greatest centre backs who had ever played the game of hurling.

"Are you coming in with me?" asked Silke, that evening when he pulled his car into the GAA grounds in Gort.

There was no way Sylvie Linnane could tell Sean Silke what to do with himself. There was no way he could say no to such a man.

• • •

Sylvie was back in the car with the boys, and back in the Galway camp. But, on the Galway team itself, he remained a bit of a wandering minstrel. He got a few League games in 1978, and while hopes were high in the county for the Championship, a first half in the All-Ireland semi-final, which ended with Kilkenny in front by 3-11 to 2-6, finally concluded on a 4-20 to 4-13 scoreline. There was no place on the starting fifteen that belonged to Sylvie for very long, and it was the same in '79. Sean Silke was in the middle of the half-back line, with Joe McDonagh on one side, and Iggy Clarke on the other, and none of the three looked like they had any intention of playing anywhere else.

Sylvie definitely eyed one of the wing-back positions. He also loved playing anywhere up the centre of the field. But, mostly, even though he prided himself as one of best defenders in the county, Sylvie Linnane had to settle for odd jobs down the other end of the field, usually looking to unsettle or beat defenders from other counties. He played against some of the best, Wexford's Mick Jacob, and Clare's Ger Loughnane, and from each and every one of them he made it his business to learn a little bit more about the art of being a great defender.

When he was on the field, they also had him taking frees more often than not. Sylvie had a good eye. He put up some decent scores. But, every time he played in the forwards, he felt he was at the wrong end of the field.

In the backs, he had the whole field in front of him, spread out like a brilliant large canvas. He could see everything that was happening and, just as importantly, guess what was about to happen next. Sylvie, in his heart, knew that he was not born to be a forward, and he also knew well enough that he might struggle to hold onto one of the forward jerseys if a really fast lad, or a really big lad, or one of those natural hurlers who had played in the forwards all of his life, came around the corner and sat himself down in the dressing room.

He also knew what those defenders on other teams were thinking when they took their first look at him. They'd see him running onto the field, coming in as a second-half substitute, and they'd notice straight away that he was that bit on the small side. Every defender he ever played against thought it was his job, if not his birthright, to lay down the law to a man Sylvie's size. He knew what was in their heads and he'd wait for them to try. He never minded the knocks he got as a forward. Usually, he invited the vast majority of those same knocks, as he made it his business to get a good hit in on his man as soon as possible. Better to test them early. That way, Sylvie knew what to expect later on. And, when a big hit came his way, Sylvie always accepted it. He welcomed them, and let his man know that he welcomed them.

The early spring of 1979 brought some hope to Galway, as Offaly and Limerick were dispatched in the quarter-final and semi-final of the National League. That hope hit the wall in the final against Tipperary. Actually, the wall caved in on top of the entire Galway team, and even though the message was sent out that day that Joe McDonagh was no full-back, there was no man on the team who could look Joe in the face and say a single word. Tipp won 3-15 to 0-8. Babs Keating was not a happy man, and, as he walked out the Ennis Road in Limerick after the game, the Galway manager was getting it in both ears, from both Galway and Tipperary supporters.

In the All-Ireland quarter-final, the team was still wobbling on its legs. Laois were four points up well into the second half, and it took a goal from PJ Molloy, from a free, to settle everybody down. Galway won, 1-23 to 3-10, and earned the right to take their place in the semi-final against a Cork team intent on making it four All-Ireland titles in a row. Not too many teams envied Galway that right.

Sylvie got his run against Laois, coming on for Joe Greaney, and settling into the half-back line beside Sean Silke and Jimmy Cooney. He was left on the bench for the semi-final. Actually, he was huddled into the tiny dug-out beneath the Cusack Stand, with twenty other substitutes and officials and helpers, all standing or sitting in a space tailor-made for no more than ten grown men. At times, there appeared to be as many people in the Galway dugout as there were in the whole ground. Less than 12,000 people chose to attend the All-Ireland semi-final. But, in a near-empty Croke Park, Galway sailed into a six-point lead after twenty-five minutes and, roughly, that amount of daylight remained between the teams right to the finish, when Galway were still 2-14 to 1-13 in front.

In the 1979 All-Ireland final on a damp old afternoon, Galway led by 1-8 to 1-6 after forty-eight minutes, when a Noel Lane goal appeared to leave Kilkenny badly shaken. But the Leinster champions picked themselves up, shook themselves down, and proceeded to score the same again, another goal and six points before the final whistle. Galway did not manage anything more. It was 2-12 to 1-8 in the end. An all-round disaster, really! Both Kilkenny goals were long-range efforts, one of them directly from a '70', and, in the Green Isle Hotel on the Naas Road leading west from the city later in the evening, as the team and their supporters tried without much success to eat very much and resorted to quickly drowning their sorrows, there were mini-tragedies at both ends of the field to toast. Seamus Shinnors, in the Galway goal, was to blame for both goals, but John Connolly was to blame for a missed penalty, which Noel Skehan saved without too much fuss, and there was also a total of eleven wides in the first half, which apportioned even further blame on a wide variety of Galway forwards, one midfielder, and two defenders.

• • •

The following day, Sylvie had a drink with Seamus Shinnors. It was the last time he would ever talk to the man, and it was also the last time he would ever see the man until, one day, almost 20 years later, he saw Shinnors out of the corner of his eye as they walked into Croke Park and they said a quick hello and goodbye to one another. Babs Keating exited after the 1979 All-Ireland final defeat. Cyril Farrell remained, and he stayed on the condition that he could build a team he wanted to build and build it a way he wanted to build it. The County Board granted Farrell all the power he requested. There would be changes in the next twelve months.

But, that Monday after the All-Ireland final defeat, Sylvie could see that Shinnors was in a bad way. Too many people, for Sylvie Linnane's liking, were already giving the goalkeeper a hard time. Sylvie didn't want to hear any of that talk. And people had long forgotten that Shinnors had made more than one brilliant save in the semi-final, to get Galway to the final in the first place.

"Fuck it, Sylvie. I went up for the ball and ... next thing ..." explained Shinnors. "the two legs, they went out from under me."

Sylvie hated seeing any man hurting like Shinnors was hurting that Sunday and Monday. All-Ireland final defeats always cut deep, and deeper than anyone imagined they could. It was wrong to also put a knife into a man.

Sylvie had come onto the field in the final after forty minutes. He came in for Bernie Ford in the forwards. He knew already that the game was going against Galway. Everyone knew that. Too many things were going wrong. There were too many missed chances, and there were other things. Joe McDonagh looked a sick man. He was physically weak on the field, and it was foolish to leave him on Chunky O'Brien. The classy Kilkenny marksman would score 1-4 by the end of the game. But, as Kilkenny did all the scoring in the final quarter, Galway continued to rifle in ball after ball into PJ Molloy's corner. Molloy was having an off-day with his frees, and the rest of his game was suffering as a result, but Sylvie, as he readied himself to run onto the field in place of Bernie Ford, was told by Babs to hit the ball into Molloy's corner.

John Henderson was dominating that corner. Sylvie could see that, and knew that everybody else on the field could see it too. But Galway continued, steadfastly, stubbornly, to target the same bloody corner. Meanwhile, in the other corner, Finbarr Gantley didn't get half enough opportunities to really test Fan Larkin. Sylvie knew that Gantley was strong enough to win his ball. Gantley was stronger than most people ever realised, but, foolishly, he stuck to his orders from the sideline, same as everyone else. There were goals in Gantley! Sylvie knew he would look to go through Larkin and go for his goal, but Finbarr Gantley remained largely ignored.

Sylvie Linnane had Nicky Brennan on his tail in the final. The future president of the GAA was a classy sort of hurler, and more that sort than the usual brazen Kilkenny defender who fancied himself as a tough man. Brennan was a naturally brilliant hurler, though Sylvie did his job when he came in. In fact, he did that job too well, and too faithfully.

• • •

While he knew that the tactics that held fast for the duration of the 1979 All-Ireland final were wrong, Sylvie believed that Babs Keating was a right good coach. Babs always knew what he wanted, and he had no trouble telling a man what that was. Babs was always hard with his words, and he was always honest. And the man's brain nearly always amazed Sylvie Linnane.

Babs knew so much, and Sylvie knew he had so much to learn from him. Every tiny little detail, right down to the innocence of a line ball. Babs would let Sylvie and others know where they should be standing for a type of ball, and where they should not be standing. There was the man's brain. There was the main's sheer presence. When he talked, everyone in the dressing room or everyone out on the field listened, and listened in a way they would not always listen to a coach. That Babs confidence, that energy he gave a team, that fullest of self-belief. Sylvie Linnane felt that Galway lost a great man the day they lost Babs Keating.

Cyril Farrell was a very different man.

Sylvie Linnane, the same as every other hurler in the Galway squad, was prepared to give Farrell the time he needed. However, unknown to them, Cyril Farrell did not believe that he needed that much time at all. Nobody really knew what was inside Farrell's head. The good news for Sylvie Linnane was that he was one of the hurlers definitely in that head. Farrell could see that Sylvie liked presenting himself as a tough, uncompromising, devil-may-care type of character, but Farrell also knew there was so much more to him than that. There was depth to the man and a fierce passion.

Farrell could see that Sylvie Linnane wanted it. Why else would he nearly always be the first man at training? Why would he never miss a night? Why would all of his training gear be close to immaculately prepared?

And, as the years passed under Cyril Farrell's watch in Galway, Sylvie Linnane never changed. Sylvie would never say anything but Farrell knew that his corner back was going for long runs in the early hours of the morning on the railway tracks near his home, that Sylvie was keeping an eye on the calendar, and waiting for Farrell's call back to full squad training.

A good few of the lads also waited for that call, as Galway went in search of a second All-Ireland title in the mid-80s. And Farrell would see it in Sylvie Linnane straight away. The first few nights back in training, he'd be dancing fit. He'd be flying: moving his feet like a professional fighter, left, right, in perfect balance, always magnificently and finely balanced on the balls of his feet. Sylvie was never going to be one of the lads at the back of the pack. Neither was he going to be one of the lads in a heap at the side of the field, throwing up his early dinner or his guts.

Farrell always believed that Sylvie Linnane was as hard as nails, and as fine a hurler as Galway had ever produced, and that he was also a winner. He hated losing at every little thing, at five-a-side soccer, at darts, at squash. Farrell knew that he could play Sylvie anywhere, and he would give it everything. In a future season, he would throw Sylvie in at centre forward against Offaly in a league game with nothing much at stake, and Sylvie Linnane would score ten or eleven points. Was it thirteen points? Farrell stopped counting that afternoon. But it was in the thick of his defence, however, that Cyril Farrell saw a position for Sylvie in that very first year that he was appointed Galway coach.

• • •

Farrell had the team in good physical shape in 1979, when he was team trainer. However, it was the mindset of the team, more than anything else, that he believed needed to change, needed to be sharpened and definitely hardened. That was the No.1 item on Cyril Farrell's list.

As the son of a farmer and publican, from Woodford, and as a hurler with Tommy Larkin's who had helped out in the winning of one county title, but only got the barest sniff at getting on the county team, Cyril Farrell did not know any better than the next man exactly why Galway had achieved so little.

But Farrell's life would bring him to places, and to meet people, who would definitely help him understand.

Farrell had worked in Dublin after leaving secondary school. But the tragic loss of his father brought him home to Galway. It was a normal enough July day in 1968, the day his father died in a tragic fall from a tractor about a mile from the Farrell home. They were travelling to the bog to bring home some turf. Mick Regan was driving the tractor, and Cyril was in the trailer with his uncle, Brian. His father was sitting on the mudguard, beside Mick, and they were passing a cigarette to one another when the tractor hit a hump on the road. Before anyone knew it, Cyril's father had slipped down in front of the back wheel. He died before Cyril's eyes. He was only fifty-three years old.

Cyril knew he needed to come back from Dublin for good and, when he did, he thought about going to University. Soon enough he signed on as a mature student at University College Galway. It was there, surrounded by hurlers he knew, and meeting and playing with outstanding hurlers from so many other counties, that Cyril Farrell not only began a journey that would lead him to become a teacher and, eventually, a school principal in St Raphael's College in Loughrea, but it was also there in UCG that he commenced his first early days of growing into one of the most outstanding and gifted managers in the modern history of the GAA.

First things first, he saw that young men from other counties were no different to young men from Galway. As hurlers, they had the same weaknesses and strengths, similar doubts, similar inhibitions, and all of them had the exact same capacity to improve and, better than that, in UCG Cyril Farrell saw young Galway hurlers develop just as fast into confident, ambitious sportsmen.

Farrell saw no good reason why Galway should be second-best. Only the GAA's history books determined that that was the case, and suggested that it would remain so for some time to come. Farrell knew that the 1950s had been cruel for the county. The epic battle with Cork in 1953, the tough loss to Wexford in the '55 final, and the more disheartening day against Tipp in the '58 final. He also knew that the ten-year experiment of including Galway in the Munster championship from 1959 had gone as close as anything ever could to wiping the county completely off the hurling map in the country.

Cyril Farrell was only twenty three years old, and still had his head filled with the adventures and possibilities in UCG, when he was invited to begin his inter-county coaching career in 1973 and work with the Galway minors. The sickening defeats down through all the years that had passed were no more than old war stories to him. He had no reason to be afraid. Neither did he have any good reason to dim down his personal ambition, or the instinct he might build into a team that he had at his fingertips. Seven years later, when he held the Galway senior team in his hands, Cyril Farrell had not changed very much, if at all. In between, Farrell had brought the county Under-21s to the All-Ireland final, in 1978, where they met Tipp. And Farrell's lads beat Tipperary, and did so in a replay, to prove on the double that fifteen Galway hurlers could be just as good, and maybe a little better, than any fifteen hurlers from any county in Ireland.

• • •

Farrell's first game as Galway coach was a two-point win over Kilkenny. His second game was a 21-point defeat by Limerick.

Limerick got hold of them in the Gaelic Grounds that afternoon. In truth, the giant figure of Joe McKenna at full-forward got hold of Galway, and the rest of the Limerick crew backed him up. The scoreboard at half time was 4-6 to 0-1. Full time was 6-8 to 0-5. Ten months later, Galway would play their last game of the 1979-80 season also against Limerick when the two teams would meet in the All-Ireland final.

McKenna had scored three goals in the game. He made hay against Conor Hayes from the start to the finish. The humiliation started with the Galway full back, but it included everyone on the field. And, on the sideline, Farrell ate his humble pie as well. Though, as he did, he took more mental notes than he did for any game of hurling he had ever watched in his life.

The squad was back, to start off a whole new year in 1980, on January 6. There was a thick frost covering the ground. Farrell couldn't wait. He ran the legs off the whole lot of them in Fahy's Field. And, when they got to play ball, Farrell ensured that there were sliotars by the multitude, behind both goals and dotted down each sideline. Farrell wanted everything in training to happen fast, just as it would in a championship game, even faster in most cases.

The Railway Cup was his first target.

Galway had not won the competition since 1947. So far back that 'Inky' Flaherty, his older and wiser selector, had been on the team. The year started off with a three-point win over Offaly. A week later, Connacht beat a right good Leinster team in the semi-final of the Railway Cup. The game was a bit of a battle, and it tipped into extra time, before Farrell's lads walked off the field, tired and very sore, with a 1-13 to 1-10 victory. Sylvie Linnane did not get to walk off the field, however. And neither did Leinster's Joe Hennessy.

Sylvie and Hennessy had thrown themselves into the heat of a surprising battle more wholeheartedly than any other pairing on the field. And, once they commenced their white-hot individual contest for every single ball that dropped anywhere near them, there was no stopping it. Not until the referee ordered the two of them off the field in the second half.

The referee had no choice. By then, the argy-bargy between Sylvie and Hennessy had long ended. Their sticks had been dropped to the ground. Punches were being thrown. Most of them were wild. And the vast majority of them were missing but, no doubt about, Sylvie and Hennessy were trying as best they could to take the heads off one another. Sylvie had landed two or three of them. He'd received as many back.

The following Sunday there was a ten-point loss to Cork in the league. But Galway nailed down a place in the quarter-finals of the league with a six-point win over Clare in Ballinasloe two weeks later. On St Patrick's Day, the Railway Cup final had the afternoon to itself, and it was also staged in the relative splendour of Croke Park, which suited Cyril Farrell down to the ground. He wanted it to be a big day in the history of Galway hurling. The team needed to start winning, and there was no better place to win than the fine old home of the GAA. In 1979, Galway had been forced to lick the envelope closed on a year, which included defeat in the All-Ireland senior and All-Ireland Under-21 finals, in addition to defeat in the Railway Cup.

More than winning, Farrell wanted his team to stop losing.

The appeal that Croke Park offered on a Sunday afternoon in the middle of March was fairly diminished by sheets of a viciously icy rain. The crowd totalled 7,351 and very few of them had come by car or train from anywhere in Munster. Sean Silke scored a goal from a '70' after 10 minutes. Meanwhile, at the other end, Munster, with a forward division brimful of wonderful stickmen, including Joe McKenna, Jimmy Barry Murphy, Ray Cummins and Mossy Walshe, could not score from any distance early on. Iggy Clarke was unbeatable in the half-back line, and, by the end of the game not much was getting past him, or Sylvie on the other wing. Silke was supreme between them, and his goal, fortunate as it was, proved the winning of the game. The thirty-three-year wait for Connacht was over. Galway held onto a 1-5 to 0-7 win. Joe Connolly made the quick trip up the steps of the Hogan Stand to grab the cup, and while he was up there he thought it a good idea to tell the few people who remained in the ground that he would be back in September to collect the MacCarthy Cup as well.

The league ended faster than Farrell hoped, and left Galway with another summer that started too early and stretched on forever, with too few games. It had taken two games to get by Waterford in the league quarter-finals, and, in the semi-final, Cork were too good. There was a goal in it at the end, 1-12 to 0-12. Farrell's first season was moving at a fair pace, and one more big defeat and it would all be over in Year One.

Seamus Shinnors had been replaced by big Mike Conneely in the Galway goalmouth. Conneely had been demoted from the No.1 jersey twelve months earlier after he had conceded three goals in the last five minutes against Clare in a league game in February. Farrell still felt that his team was safer with 'Big Mike'. If only he could do something about Mike's confidence. And if only he could do something about Mike's puck-outs. 'Big Mike' did not have a big puck-out. In fact, they were often terrible things to behold. He seldom took the same number of steps before striking the ball. And his follow through was half-hearted.

There was nothing to be done but start thirty-year-old Mike Conneely off on a training course on how to puck the ball out, and that's what Farrell did, keeping his goalkeeper back for an hour, sometimes two hours, after training sessions, and telling him to keep hitting ball after ball, until the arms were falling off the goalkeeper. Farrell would be out in the middle of the field, where he had dotted dozens of flags as targets for 'Big Mike'. By mid-summer of 1980, Farrell and Mike were happy. The coach was happier still that his lads, especially the older crew, had taken to his insistence that every second ball should be hand-passed out of defence. No more belting the thing down the field every single time and hoping to regain possession. Galway spent the summer holding the ball. And, when the ball was rained down the field, John Connolly was there, in the full-forward position, to give the team every chance of holding onto possession. Connolly hated the sight of the No.14 jersey as much as Farrell knew he would. Connolly did not hide his feelings in conversations with his young coach, but the coach was not for turning. Anyhow, Connolly had other things on his mind for the first half of the year as Castlegar had marched to an All-Ireland club title, which they took by defeating Ballycastle, in Navan of all places. Sean Silke was doing everything Farrell required of a centre back, and, by the time John Connolly got his head cleared of club duties, Farrell's plans for the rest of the year had been well and truly ironed out for everyone to see.

Kildare did not put up much of a fight in the All-Ireland quarter-final. They were beaten 5-15 to 1-11 and, once again, Croke Park had a hollow sound to it as only 3,688 supporters turned up. They saw Galway put up a big score, but they also saw the winners hit 15 wides in the first half, and add another nine to that number by the end of the day. Though, in Leinster, interesting things were happening. Offaly had actually defeated Kilkenny in the provincial final. As Galway were due to meet the Leinster champions in the All-Ireland semi-final, Farrell was in Croke Park, with 'Inky' and Bernie O'Connor, taking it all in as the winds of change blew over the grand old stadium. There were only 9,500 people in the ground for the Leinster final, and that number was reached at a push. Everyone else missed a real thriller. The final scoreline rested at 3-17 to 5-10. Offaly had reached the big time, but the team and its supporters had still a lot to learn.

Conor Hayes was in Holland when the semi-final came around. He had smashed his thumb earlier in the summer, and had decided to put work before sitting idly to one side watching the team seek a place in the All-Ireland final again. Farrell had to ring the changes. Niall McInerney was put in at full back. Seamus Coen went into the corner of the defence. Paschal Ryan stepped into a midfield spot to replace Steve Mahon who was struggling to find his true form. But Farrell would find himself having to make further rearrangements, once the game began, sooner than he would have liked. Iggy Clarke smashed his shoulder and had to be carted off. And Sylvie got himself sent off once again.

• • •

It was one of those days, and the difficulties were further compounded by the fact that 'Big Mike' was having a bad time as well. Iggy had been playing brilliantly when he was injured. Sylvie was not having quite the same stormer, but he was still having one of his best games of the entire year when he was dismissed from the field. Farrell's first sub for either defensive position was Joe McDonagh, but that was also a problem. The day was drizzly, and McDonagh had his contact lenses in!

Sylvie had been having a duel with Pat Carroll – who would die at such a young age so shortly after when he fought a brave fight against illness – that might best be described as ding-dong. As worst it would have been described as a bit savage. But, in reality, both men were going at it fair and square, and holding nothing back. Sylvie didn't think there was anything to complain about. Neither did Carroll. He liked playing against Pat Carroll. He was a hard, tough man, but he was an honest hurler. There was nothing sly about him. He had great hands, and he had strong legs, so it was best not to let him get the ball in the first place. Suddenly, a slap with the stick, accidently struck Sylvie over his ear and brought him to his knees momentarily as the Galway medical team worked on him. His head was bandaged up, and play resumed. Afterwards, the same cut would require nine stitches before the wound was firmly closed.

The ball had been dropping down between them. Carroll pulled a bit wildly, and hit Sylvie's head and missed the ball completely. Neither man wore a helmet. So, the damage was going to be maximised, and there was lots of blood on display by the time referee JJ Landers from Waterford arrived on the scene.

Sylvie Linnane had nothing against helmets, or the men who might choose to wear one. But he couldn't, and every time he ever tried, the sweat would come out of him by the bucket-full.

Sylvie was on the ground, when the referee looked down at him.

'He pulled on my head!" Sylvie shouted up at Landers.

The referee took another look at him.

"You should have been wearing a helmet!" Landers replied, as the blood started to pump out of the wound.

Sylvie was sore and groggy, and he was also getting mad as hell. The words from the referee maddened him more than anything, more than the belt from Pat Carroll.

"What are you talking about!" roared Sylvie, as the referee walked away, unsympathetically. The next thing Sylvie remembered was he saw Pat Carroll racing up the wing. His man was coming up the line with the ball. Sylvie went to charge him over the line. And he did. He sent Carroll flying. And he was happy with himself. He'd hit Carroll with his body and pushed his hurl against his chest. He'd hit him with everything, but it had been a fair challenge. Hundreds of times, Sylvie had made that challenge, successfully, job done and no word about it. Indeed, apart from the blow to Sylvie's head, the game had been virtually clean as a whistle all through, and the referee only saw fit to award nineteen frees in total (seven of them to Galway).

Carroll was now down on the ground, however. And the Offaly officials started to make a hullabaloo over the tackle. Sylvie thought Carroll was making a meal of it, so he didn't think of walking away from the scene, or making himself scarce. He did nothing wrong. So he stood his ground.

But not for long, because JJ Landers arrived on the scene once more, and gave Sylvie his marching orders. In years to come it would be called a red card. In August of 1980, the referee just asked Sylvie Linnane his name, for the second time, after having already booked him in the first half, and told him he was 'off'.

"Off, off," said JJ Landers, as he pointed Sylvie in the direction of the Galway dugout.

Sylvie walked.

Nobody said anything to him when he reached the sideline, and looked to sit down somewhere, anywhere. Everyone was busy. The game was fifty-two minutes old.

• • •

With thirteen minutes left on the clock, Galway were nine points in front. Sylvie was able to take a deep breath on the sideline. It looked like he had not actually ruined everything for the team, and helped in no small measure to lead Cyril Farrell, in his first season, to a fairly calamitous defeat. Two goals from John Connolly, and one each from Noel Lane and Bernie Ford, helped Galway to get to where they were with time running out fast.

Then Brendan Bermingham goaled for Offaly. Then Mark Corrigan also found the net, though how the ball from fifty yards out spun past Mike Conneely was anyone's guess. Offaly kept coming. All Galway could do was defend. There were only two points in it, 4-9 to 3-10, when the referee finally brought the game to an end. Offaly were unhappy. They claimed the game still had about a minute remaining, and they fancied their chances of getting one more match-winning goal.

Sylvie sat back in the dressing room with the rest of the lads. He was relieved, but still sore as hell with the referee. And his head was pounding, harder than ever, now that the game was over. And he wondered: What would the referee write down in his match report? What would the men in suits in Croke Park's offices think?

He didn't know, as he unlaced his boots, and searched for his towel in the bag underneath his seat, if he'd even get to play in the All-Ireland final. Just then, Padraig Horan walked into the room to speak on behalf of the Offaly team.

Horan was living in Limerick that summer. He knew what people in that county were thinking, and he duly informed everyone in the Galway camp that every last man, woman and child in Limerick thought that they had the beating of Galway and Offaly, put together, in the All-Ireland final.

"But if you go in hard… and keep at it," concluded Horan, "I think you'll beat them!"

CHAPTER
11

Iggy Clarke was gone for the 1980 All-Ireland final. Long gone. The evening of Galway's victory over Offaly, he was operated on in the Mater Hospital in Dublin in an attempt to correct the severe ligament damage to his shoulder. Clarke had been in the greatest form of his hurling life.

That was one wing-back gone, and there was a widespread fear in the county that the man on the other wing might also be missing for the final. The newspapermen who watched the same game as referee JJ Landers were not sparing Sylvie Linnane in their assessments of his tackle on Pat Carroll. It was classified as 'wild' in some newspapers. Others termed it 'dangerous'. If the men on the 'Activities Committee' in Croke Park, who were to sit in judgment on him, were reading the same newspapers Sylvie was reading, then he fully believed that he might be in big trouble.

Hurling folk around the country were reminded in the days that followed the semi-final, that it was Sylvie's second time to be sent to the line in 1980. After the first sending off in the Railway Cup, he had received a minimum two-weeks suspension. If JJ Landers wrote in his match report that Sylvie was dismissed from the field for 'dangerous' play then another two-weeks suspension, from the evening of the semi-final, would apply. But, if the referee had the word 'striking' in his report, then the punishment would be much stiffer.

• • •

The days were long as Sylvie awaited his fate.

But, as usual, he never brought the game home with him, and he never let a victory or a defeat get in the way of a day's work. Nor would he allow it to tamper with the happiness in his own family home. That was Sylvie's way.

He was worried sick at the thought of missing the final game of the year. There was a gnawing heaviness, continually, in the bottom of his stomach, but he would do anything not to show even a hint of the doubts and fears that were a gathering force inside him. Better to present a smile, he always felt. After all, it was still only a game, and he tried his best to remind himself of that.

In his mother-in-law's one afternoon, he decided to go a step further. It was his turn to have a little fun at Mary Joe Nolan's expense. They usually took turns looking to catch one another out, and, on the Tuesday before the final, Sylvie could see that Mary Joe was altogether fussed over the number of visitors who had been calling, both announced and unannounced, to the house. People from any county, and occasionally from any continent, usually far-flung cousins, were calling in and staying.

When he got home, Sylvie picked up the phone and called Mary Joe. He opened up in his finest American accent, which was usually a fairly decent effort, and introduced himself to his mother-in-law as a second cousin from Ohio who was in Ireland, and was looking to call in.

"Just to say hello," Sylvie added. "And, sure, we might stay a couple of nights … my good wife … the five kids … that sound ok, Mary Joe?"

Mary Joe Nolan told her Ohio cousin that that would be just fine and she'd be pleased to see them later that evening. Sylvie thought no more about his little prank.

He got caught up, working at the back of his house for the rest of the afternoon. He never thought again about the conversation, which had left his head completely. All he could think about was the game, and the verdict. Waiting for the verdict on his suspension was the worst part of the whole thing. Every single hour dragged its backside.

That evening, Margaret wanted to go back to her mother's. Sylvie tagged along. When they got to the Nolan house, they saw one of Margaret's sisters disappearing through the back door with a mattress. Inside, in the kitchen, there was pandemonium. Pots and pans were piled to the left of the sink. Two big bags of food, full to the brim, were plonked in the centre of the kitchen table.

"We've no time to talk," said Mary Joe. "No time, no time. Cousins! The whole way from Ohio arriving any second, brazen as you like. And they're staying!"

Sylvie walked up to Mary Joe and stopped her in her tracks. He held her by the two shoulders and, in his best American accent, and even better than it had sounded over the telephone, explained that he and the wife and the five kids had changed their minds and would not be coming to Galway after all.

Mary Joe Nolan smiled, initially from the sheer relief, but that smile of Sylvie's mother-in-law's was, already, turning mischievous.

Sylvie was in her back garden the next day.

Mary Joe had the radio on and was the first to hear the news that Sylvie Linnane had been cleared to play in the All-Ireland final. The Activities Committee of the GAA had settled on two weeks. Sylvie was a free man.

Mary Joe raced out the back door and painted her face with a massive sense of disappointment as she marched purposely in the direction of her son in-law. Sylvie could sense that she had something to tell him.

"Aw, Sylvie! Aw, Sylvie!" said Mary Joe. "You've got two months. I'm so sorry, Sylvie."

Sylvie's stomach churned more heavily than it had churned in days. He stopped in his tracks. He felt cold with the disappointment. The only words he had heard from Mary Joe's mouth were 'two months'.

"Is that the way?" said Sylvie, quietly. "That's that, so!" he added.

Then Mary Joe Nolan broke into a smile and laughed her greatest laugh, before immediately apologising to Sylvie for breaking his heart.

"No, it's not," said Mary Joe, happily, "you've got two weeks!"

• • •

Sylvie Linnane had received the minimum suspension. The men on the Activities Committee had privately considered that a man who had a gash on the side of his head, which required nine stitches, could not have been entirely to blame for what had happened on the field.

Sylvie had the okay.

But it was a close-run thing. And, for the remainder of his career, Sylvie knew that after the events and the great fuss of 1980, that he was a hurler walking thinner ice than most other defenders. He knew that referees were watching him.

Not every referee, but the vast majority of them. There was no doubt about it, referees were calling out his name and number, and calling him over, for the littlest things. Other defenders, at both ends of the field might be flaying their men, but if Sylvie so much as stepped on someone's toe, he was the first to getting a telling off.

It was something he decided to ignore.

Referees may be looking at him, but there was no point worrying about them. And there was no point in standing off tackles either. Do that, and he'd find himself back on the sideline, without any referee sending him in that direction. Sylvie decided to do a few things.

He decided to let the referee do his job. He decided to do his own job. And, if the man he was marking on any given day purposely decided to create a bit of a scene, or start a little skirmish, in front of a referee, then Sylvie could only hope that the reputation that had been built up around him did not do him in in the coldest blood. But, more than anything, he decided after 1980 not to hold back, and to continue to play the game he had played since he held his first hurl in his fist.

The 1980 season was the first time he had ever been sent off in his life, for club or county. Only at the tail-end of his playing days for Gort did he get his first, and last set of marching orders, in a game with Loughrea. He had never been some sort of especially 'hard man' on the field. Giving an opponent 'timber' had never been his speciality.

And, until he played his last game for Galway, and his very last game for Gort, he always believed that hurling was a man's game, that you should never be afraid of any man, that you should never take prisoners, that an acceptable level of aggression always sent out the fairest and clearest message, and that whatever happened on the field you try to walk off happy with your performance if you lose, and happier still if you win.

Things would always happen, out there, which could not be anticipated of course. Like the first time he ran onto the field as a substitute, against Kilkenny and ran into Frank Cummins. Sylvie bounced off Cummins' hip bone. It was the hardest hit he had ever got in his life. He imagined that only a man who had been kicked by a horse could feel as he felt, trying to run off the challenge and strike the next ball. Cummins put hurling out of young Sylvie Linnane's head for ten or fifteen minutes. Other times, now and then, he might have to contend with an opponent coming at him in a tackle with the handle of his hurl. Usually, however, he'd see them coming. He'd know what sort of man would be prepared to use the handle of his hurl. And he'd be more than ready for him.

Sylvie always liked marking the lads who thought they were tough and wanted to prove it. At a very early stage in his career, he came to the conclusion that any man on a hurling field who had to act tough most likely did not have a tough bone in his entire body.

Talking was also something that didn't interest him. He smiled a lot. He loved to smile at opponents, when things were going well, and most especially when things were looking bad for Galway. But, talking was never a large part of the Sylvie Linnane repertoire. It was better not to say anything. And it was better not to answer back. Though Sylvie Linnane would end his playing career with one of the most memorable utterances on a GAA field attributed to him. It came in the dying minutes of the 1988 All-Ireland final.

Sylvie heard Nicky English ask the referee how much time was left, as the game inched out of Tipperary's grasp. And Sylvie, before the referee could say anything, butted in. "You've got 12 months, Nicky!"

• • •

Cyril Farrell picked up the phone in Bernie O'Connor's house and said he wanted to speak to Conor Hayes. It was the day after the semi-final victory over Offaly, and Farrell's full back was working in Amsterdam. By the end of the same week, Hayes was training with the team.

With Hayes back, and with Sylvie cleared to play, Farrell was able to put his team for the final back together. McInerney had done well against Offaly. Hayes did a nice job for Farrell at corner back on the All-Ireland winning Under-21 team. And Farrell didn't fancy Hayes coming back into the squad, and going straight back out against Joe McKenna, who had run over him a couple of times in the League game earlier in the year. More than that, McKenna would be confident of doing further damage against Hayes.

Sylvie did not give Hayes's return a second's thought. All of the lads were delighted to see him back. He had as much right to an All-Ireland medal as any one of them and, if he was fit, as much right to be back on the team. Hayes was a cool one, Sylvie always thought. He could walk onto the field at any time, it seemed, and fit in anywhere. Hayes always minded himself between games, and he had a confidence that Sylvie would have liked to have for himself. And he had such great hands. Besides, Sylvie had his own game to think about. He wasn't worried. He knew what he had to do and he knew how he wanted to play. He'd be marking one of the Fitzmaurice brothers, Paudie – who, like Iggy Clarke, was also a priest – on the Limerick team, and he'd need to keep him scoreless. And that's what Sylvie Linnane did in the 1980 All-Ireland final. But, just before half time, Limerick switched Brian Carroll on to Sylvie. Carroll was a tougher customer entirely. Sylvie limited him to a single point in the second half.

McKenna was the inspirational figure for Limerick. He was their giant. Limerick had Ollie O'Connor and Eamonn Cregan in opposite corners of the attack. Farrell knew he only wanted one man on McKenna, and that was Niall McInerney, or, simply, 'Mac'.

'Mac' was the cutest defender in Galway. He would be able to move McKenna all around the place, and annoy him, and talk to him, telling him little things, reminding him that it had been too long since he'd scored, too long since he'd even got the ball in his hand. Such were the powers of 'Mac'.

Filling out the rest of the team was harder. It would be a big job to fill Iggy Clarke's boots, and Farrell had a choice between Gerry Glynn, Joe McDonagh and Seamus Coen. But it was not just the Galway half-back line that dominated Farrell's thinking. He was just as concerned about the Limerick half-back line, as it was from there that so much of the ball landed in on top of Joe McKenna came from the stick of Limerick captain, Sean

Foley. Foley had to be stopped, and driven back at every opportunity.

Farrell knew that Galway were close. Two or three of the correct decisions and the run of nine losing All-Ireland finals, since Galway last came out on top in 1923, would be at an end.

The team stayed in the Clarence Hotel, halfway up the quays between the Phoenix Park and O'Connell Bridge, the night before the match. It was a bad choice, and all of Farrell's meticulous thinking about every last position on the field seemed to be in jeopardy at 5am when he joined Bernie O'Connor and went downstairs to plead with other hotel patrons to go to their beds and stop making such an almighty ruckus. For the rest of the morning, and early afternoon, things still refused to go as smoothly as the Galway coach would have liked.

When they got to Croke Park and made their way through the cheering fans, keeping their heads down, trying their best not to be lifted up high into the air by the electrifying atmosphere that poured over the entire stadium, Galway found themselves in the wrong dressing room. 'Big Mike' had marched into the first dressing room he found, and immediately sat down in his favourite corner, and the rest of the team were not far behind him. Except Croke Park's ever-exact stewards in their green coats arrived to tell Galway that they were in the wrong room. 'Big Mike' was not for moving.

"It hardly makes any difference Mike." Farrell advised him.

They moved down the corridor. When they came out of the correct dressing room an hour later, and started warming up on the pitch, a wild swing of a hurley caught Noel Lane over one eye. Lane had to be brought back inside, and stitched up.

Farrell was a relieved man when the game finally started. Everyone was happy to finally just play the game they had been waiting for, for weeks. Nobody was happier than Sylvie. He wanted to put the semi-final behind him, and the great confusion and nervousness of the days that immediately followed it, as far behind him as possible. But nobody in Galway dreamed of getting the All-Ireland final off to a start that far exceeded anyone's dreams. It was 2-1 to 0-0 after 10 minutes.

Bernie Ford had done what he always did best, and nipped in and kicked a goal to begin things. Joe Connolly pointed a free to show that he had his eye in for the big day in front of him, and then PJ Molloy was upended, but refused to stay down or stop playing, and as others looked around them he kept going and shot to the net.

Quick as a flash, Limerick scored a goal at the other end. Cregan had beaten Hayes to a few balls, and it was clear that he was taking time to settle, which he would do in due course, but not before Cregan grabbed his goal to lift Limerick out of their slumber. The remainder of the half went to plan, which was all that Farrell and Galway could ask for, and Frank Burke, especially, was doing the exact job requested of him on Sean Foley. It was 2-7 to 1-5 at half time.

Twice, Galway had led by seven points – at the beginning of the game, and again 10 minutes into the second half when the lead was 2-10 to 1-6. Limerick never dropped their heads, however, and, with a full nine minutes to go the gap between the teams was down to just two points. Joe McKenna had scored a goal in the 52nd minute, and in the 61st minute Cregan took his second goal coolly from a penalty. Galway won because of their precious start, and also because, in between Limerick's two goals in the second half, Forde scored three points that were as valuable as they were brilliantly taken. Forde could have eased Galway's agony further in the dying minutes but, from the edge of the large square, he found himself with a great goal chance but mishit his shot.

That miss looked as though it would be costly, when, a minute later McKenna broke through. 'Big Mike' made a fantastic save, catching the ball on the line and sweeping it away to safety. Moments earlier, a rare mistake from McInerney had left Cregan inside and he sought out an unmarked McKenna, but Hayes pounced to intercept the final, deadly pass.

The pressure doubled up on every single Galway man in those final hectic minutes. Sylvie willed referee, Noel O'Donoghue, from Dublin, to blow the final whistle. He tried not to, but once, and then twice, then three times and four times, he had glanced at the giant clock over the Canal End of the ground. He knew that at about 'five to five', when the big hand touched upon that last mark on the clock, that the referee would surely be fit to blow. He could hear nothing from the sideline. There wasn't panic, but things were becoming a little manic on the pitch.

Galway would lose the second half by 2-4 to 0-8. The whirlwind start had made the greatest difference. And the whirlwind recommenced as soon as the final whistle sounded. Sylvie found himself halfway up the steps of the Hogan Stand listening to a Galway captain speaking to the whole country. The MacCarthy Cup was in Joe Connolly's hand. And when Sylvie looked behind him, a throng of celebrating supporters had filled the huge field with one large maroon mass.

Sylvie had never expected to see such a sight. Even when he had closed his eyes and tried to imagine Connolly lifting the magnificent cup over his head, he always failed to capture what would be occurring on the field. And so many of the faces were faces he knew. His brothers had reached him out on the field shortly after the final whistle. He also knew Margaret was out there, somewhere.

He could see neighbours. And others, lads from other parishes he had played against and fought against, and now they were all cheering and shouting. People were going mad with delight.

He looked over at John Connolly, who was at the side of the presentation rostrum. Sylvie looked at the happiness and sheer relief that was spread across the face of the greatest hurler in Galway's history. It then dawned on him, suddenly, that he never thought he would see John Connolly standing and celebrating in a ground in which so many magnificent hurlers from so many counties had celebrated so often. It seemed, almost, as if it was their birth-right. More than anyone, it was John Connolly's finest hour. No Galway man deserved it more.

It was a sight Sylvie thought he would never see. Neither had he ever imagined one of his own teammates taking up the microphone on such an occasion, and filling the old ground with a brilliantly emotional rendition of 'The West's Awake'.

That was Joe McDonagh in his finest voice.

• • •

Only many hours later, when it was all over, and the team and their family and friends were dining in the Grand Hotel in Malahide, did it hit Sylvie

Linnane, like a great clumsy slap on the side of the jaw, how much he would have loved to have his father, Mick Linnane in Croke Park that afternoon.

His mother was there, and his brothers and sisters, but the quiet man, who had died three years earlier, who had done so much for him, and who had taught him right from wrong, and who had just as quietly allowed him to become the hurler he had become, was hugely missing. How he wished to spend one minute with his father, to have just one short conversation. Without it, and as brilliant and magical as every single minute of that Sunday night was, and every minute of the earliest hours of Monday morning, Sylvie Linnane knew that the most important man of all was missing.

Without him, what had happened was not complete. But then, Sylvie imagined, would Mick Linnane have been there? Of course, he wouldn't. He would have stayed at home in Kilmacduagh. Croke Park, the game itself, the noise and the clamour, and the agonising final minutes and seconds before Galway were finally announced as All-Ireland champions, all of that would have been too much for Mick Linnane.

The old man would be at home, thought Sylvie.

Their short conversation would have had to wait until Monday night, or maybe even Tuesday morning. And Sylvie would still have had that to look forward to, the greatest and happiest conversation he would ever get to have with his father.

• • •

While the bus journey home on Monday from Dublin to Eyre Square was long and arduous – with one bus carrying the players being closely followed by a second bus transporting wives and girlfriends, slowly making their way west – it was also the most amazing and wonderful 12 hours that Sylvie and Margaret Linnane had ever experienced in their lives..

At so many points along the road, Sylvie found it a wonder that people were not being killed, especially the little children who were sucked tightly to the side of the bus.

When the light of the day began to recede, the bonfires were lit. The faces all around the bus glowed, and the heat from the fire penetrated the steel and glass of the buses. Old men held their caps in their hands, and waved them respectfully as the buses passed on the long homeward journey. Tears flowed down faces, old and young. The further west they inched, the more people shook off all of their inhibitions and shouted and cried. The team had come through Kilbeggan, and Moate, and everywhere people celebrated, and not all of them Galway people, not until they arrived into Athlone, and the first formal stop on the slow, triumphant march home. Crossing the Shannon brought a lump, finally, to more than one throat in the front bus. Grown men in that bus also shed a tear.

The buses and convoy of cars slowed even more as they drove the last few miles through Roscommon county to the Galway border. People were banging the sides of the bus. Grown men had children on their shoulders and their faces were being pressed against the windows. Ballinasloe was slower still. Farrell and all of his players had to work their way through the crowds and climb a makeshift stage. The first of dozens of speeches, by Farrell, and by selected players from different parishes, began, and continued, from parish to town, from Kilrickle to Loughrea. And finally, finally … finally … finally … into Eyre Square, where the giant arms of the people of Galway patiently awaited their heroes.

• • •

It was an ungodly hour of the morning when the team finally arrived at the 'home' of Galway GAA, the Sacre Coeur Hotel, in Salthill, and had the chance to get something to eat. Everyone was starving, and everyone was tired, and close to being out on their feet. The garda escort, which had worked as best it could all day long, was now doing much more serious business. It was time for everyone to eat, and then hit their beds for a few hours at least.

In his inside jacket pocket, Sylvie had the tickets for the hotel function. Nobody was going to ask Sylvie Linnane for a ticket, but, Margaret Linnane thought that she might suddenly be in a long line of Galway supporters trying to persuade the men on the doors that she really was Sylvie Linnane's wife – and needed to get inside the hotel!

Sylvie was of a mind to get into the hotel as quickly as possible. As usual, people were pulling at his arms as he squeezed his way through, and lashing out to touch him and the rest of the players ganged up in front of him and behind him. In Eyre Square, things had got a little too 'bumpy', and someone, accidently, had slapped him on the side of the head as they attempted to reach out and toss his hair.

The cut on the side of his head, from the semi-final, had reopened. It started to bleed, and Sylvie's handkerchief was a bloodied mess. He wanted to get inside the hotel as quickly as possible. Margaret, meanwhile, was shouting at him, and trying to grab his attention. She could barely move amongst the bodies heaving back and forth between the buses and the doors of the hotel. Finally, she made a desperate attempt to reach out at her husband.

Sylvie was not having any more of that.

He'd been grabbed and mauled enough for one day in his life, and he yanked himself away from the hand that had grabbed a hold of the back of his jacket. Margaret gave out a yelp, in sudden pain.

There was a shooting sensation in her hand. After getting out of her bed, later that same morning, she would quickly discover that two of her fingers had been broken. Sylvie had never looked back as he had squirmed and pushed his way to the front doors of the Sacre Coeur. When Margaret showed him her hand, at breakfast, her fingers already turning black, he wondered what had happened to her.

"What... how... who on earth did that?" he asked his wife.

CHAPTER
12

The new All-Ireland champions presented themselves to an American audience on both the East and West coasts. At JFK Airport, in New York, there was a rousing reception. Staying in the Statler Hotel, which had a bird's eye view of a shooting incident across the street where two men had been shot dead twenty-four hours earlier, the excitement and amusement, and great novelty, of living the 'high life' as a hurling team awoke everyone in the Galway party to exactly what they had achieved the previous September. The life of All-Ireland champions had its benefits. By the end of the trip, nobody in the party wanted to give up on that life.

A Noel Lane goal was enough for Galway to defeat the All Stars on a rock-hard ground in Gaelic Park. The second game of the tour was in Chicago, the third in LA. On the flight from JFK to Chicago's O'Hare Airport, the stewardess had a special word of welcome for 'His Excellency the Lord Mayor of Bullaun, Mr Jimmy Cooney.' The poor girl made a right mouthful of 'Bullaun', but got close at her fourth attempt. Even the 114 storeys of the Sears Tower, at that time the tallest building in the whole world, were at the team's feet on their very first day in 'The Windy City'.

Disneyland was top of the list of priorities in LA. Sylvie and Margaret got to meet Ralph Waite, who was enjoying world-wide fame as John Walton Senior in 'The Waltons', and, at a country and western night they saw, but didn't get to speak with, an even more famous actor, Larry Hagman, better known in a total of 130 countries as JR Ewing in the most popular TV series ever made, 'Dallas'.

Everywhere, Galway folk splashed out to give the team the biggest welcome they could muster. The best night of the tour was at the Glendora House, in Chicago, where the banquet was lavish, the drink flowed, and the music was lively. Joe McDonagh sang his heart out. Sylvie danced. And each time they lined out against the All Stars, every single member of the Galway squad was kindly, and formally, reminded just how far he had travelled in his hurling career. It didn't matter that, also in Chicago, they played the All Stars in the grounds of the local Argo High School, which was too small for 30 men to play a game of hurling, and which had floodlights that made the sliotar quite invisible for large portions of the evening.

A Mrs Nicolai, who hosted the travelling party in LA, invited everyone to a fancy restaurant. In fact, she was taking them to a steak house but she convinced Sylvie that dress was strictly formal and so Sylvie wore the only tie he possessed in his suitcase. As soon as he sat down at the table, a waitress appeared in front of him and started ringing a bell as loudly as she could. She dipped her other hand into the pocket of her blue apron and pulled out a pair of scissors. Before Sylvie could stop her, she cut his tie in half.

The remains of the tie were pinned to one of the rafters as the rest of his so-called best friends on the team quickly removed their own neckwear during the lightning assault on one of their own. Suitably embarrassed, Sylvie declined to make a run at the 'cowboy steak' that weighed in at over two pounds and, instead, chose one of the 'cowgirls', a less substantial cut. He didn't want to be the centre of attention at the end of the evening as well as the beginning.

The tour was go, go, go! There was sight-seeing, and shopping, and eating and drinking. And usually a function to round everything off, every day and night; four hours of sleep was a luxury, five hours a rarity. For the last four days of the tour, Sylvie went down with food poisoning, and needed Niall McInerney's wife, Dr Mary, to serve up tablets and administer injections to try to get him back on his feet for the final game, and the fight home.

On the last night in LA, Bishop Eamon Casey held the team in his embrace, literally, at a function in their Holday Inn, where he entertained the new All-Ireland champions with a selection of his favourite songs. The journey home from LA was something else. They flew over the Grand Canyon, and viewed Las Vegas beneath them. The names of so many amazing landmarks in the country were trotted out to them, as well as historic events and amazing cities.

Sylvie, same as every other man around him on the long flight home, vowed that there would have to be a second All-Ireland title. Immediately.

There was no going back now.

• • •

Offaly were waiting for their opportunity. The team was also growing stronger, almost with every month that passed, between losing to Galway in the 1980 All-Ireland semi-final and reaching the final of the National League the following spring. Kilkenny's Dermot Healy was changing the face of Offaly hurling, and he was also, swiftly, giving the county a whole different attitude to winning and losing. They had won their first Leinster title. They had run Galway to two points in the All-Ireland semi-final and, amazingly, after a memorable schemozzle with Clare in Tulla in December of 1979, they were ordered to play all of their League games the following season away from home.

That did not deter Offaly from winning more games than they lost. In Thurles, in the League final in May, Offaly won the toss, but decided to play against the wind in the first half. It was a costly decision. They were 2-3 to 0-0 down after ten minutes. For the remainder of the game they outscored Cork, 2-8 to 1-8, but there was no way back after their brutal start.

Galway had the chance to see exactly what Offaly were about in 1981, because, on the 'undercard' of the League final in Thurles that same day, Cyril Farrell had to put the new All-Ireland champions out against Wexford in a relegation play-off. Galway won by three points. After winning just two out of six games in the regular League, it was at least good to win, but Farrell knew that he still had a fair job to do to get his players' minds exactly right after a six-month period when All-Ireland celebrations looked that they might never tail off.

In the middle of the field, Sylvie had enjoyed a partnership with Steve Mahon through most of the League. He enjoyed the freedom. But there was something missing in the Galway team, a bite, a real finishing thrust, and the decision of thirty-three-year-old John Connolly to announce his retirement, immediately after the All-Ireland final, was being sorely felt on the cusp of the summer of '81. Connolly had come back training with Castlegar in the spring. The next step was to get him back with Galway. Frank Canning had been used in the No.14 jersey in the League, and he seemed to have a handy knack for scoring goals when they team needed them most, but, mentally and physically, Galway were clearly a lesser team without the eldest Connolly.

Finbarr Gantley manned the full-forward post in the All-Ireland quarter-final against an Antrim team who had mowed down all in front of them when winning the All-Ireland B Championship, scoring 14 goals and 74 points in the process. Sylvie was back on the right wing of the defence, with Silke and Clarke for company. Antrim, as had been forewarned, put up a big score in front of a paltry number of 4,315 people in Croke Park. They scored 3-11. Galway's total was 6-23. It was the best and worst of preparation for a semi-final meeting with a Limerick team that was still feeling sore about losing the All-Ireland in September.

Limerick, in contrast, were already hitting their best form, after taking two games to see off Tipperary, and then take Clare in the Munster final by a handy enough six points. In the semi-final, Limerick decided to lay into Galway. Galway returned the compliment.

It was a day when pulling remained on the wild side from start to finish. And, after nine minutes, Sean Foley was sent off for an accidental foul on PJ Molloy. That should have been the signal for Galway to move up a gear. It never happened, however. In a fascinating afternoon, in which four penalties were awarded, and not one was smashed to the net, Limerick continued to make most of the running, and that despite being reduced to thirteen men when Joe Connolly and Jimmy Carroll had to walk disconsolately to the sideline, their arms wrapped over one another's shoulders, after being dismissed for an impromptu wrestling match.

Cregan pointed with the first penalty of the day. Noel Lane drove the second penalty wide, which was added to the team's twelve wides in the first half alone. The biggest miss of the day turned out to be Eamon Cregan's penalty ten minutes into the second half, at a time when Galway trailed by 0-9 to 1-3. The fourth penalty was also pointed, this time by Joe Connolly.

Just before that fourth penalty, Sylvie spurred the team onto a higher level when he raced forward and shot brilliantly over the bar. But Galway never once led in the game and, true to the afternoon's character, it took a late pointed free from Finbarr Gantley to tie the teams up, on 1-8 to 0-11, and earn the champions a replay.

Frank Burke had been clearly missed due to injury. But the team was still crying out for John Connolly's presence, not only to lend his giant hand to the effort of defending the All-Ireland title, but to serve as a huge distraction for the opposition defence. Before he left Croke Park, Cyril Farrell found Connolly in the ground, and spoke to him. And, before ending their chat, Connolly promised to be at training in Athenry that same week. He had booked his holidays for Wexford the next day, but, in an instant, his stay in the south-east was cancelled.

Farrell knew they'd been lucky. Inky Flaherty told newspapermen he was absolutely delighted with the draw. Captain Sean Silke hoped the hard struggle would get the lethargy out of the team's system. No doubt about it, Galway had lived to fight another day, and, in their dressing room, as the players showered and dressed, PJ Molloy puffed away on a cigarette and chose to ignore the fourteen stitches that had been inserted in two facial wounds.

It had been that sort of afternoon.

• • •

The GAA was fast out of the traps to slap a three-month suspension on Sean Foley. He was gone for the semi-final replay, and the final if Limerick were to advance. Joe Connolly and Jimmy Carroll were okay to play, after their little wrestling match, but a great number of neutral observers felt that Foley had been dealt a serious injustice, as he had seemed to be swinging at Molloy's stick and not his head. Further problems for Limerick came in the shape of injuries to Dom Punch and Pat Herbert and, during the course of the replay, they would also lose Michael Grimes after thirty minutes and, nine minutes into the second half, Leonard Enright was also gone. But Limerick did not back down. They were 1-15 to 2-8 in front when Enright was forced to depart, and that lead could have been bigger, but the fifth penalty awarded in the prolonged contest between the two teams, also did not deliver a goal as Enright failed to hit the back of the net.

Joe Connolly came to Galway's rescue. He scored 2-7 on the day, and Cyril Farrell needed every one of those scores, as his lads finished up winning 4-16 to 2-17. Galway hurling supporters, who helped make up the majority of the 42,666 attendance, had a third All-Ireland final in a row ahead of them, but they had every reason to worry about the form of their team. Limerick had been hard to break down, and it took a PJ Molloy goal to break the heart of their mighty defence. After that, John Connolly came out to centre-forward and Joe Connolly went inside. Gaps appeared everywhere for Galway after that. Joe Connolly grabbed a marvellous point from long range. He then smacked home a goal. Bernie Forde took a point. Joe Connolly knocked over another point. Noel Lane pointed. Joe Connolly got two more. Steve Mahon came forward to score. And the Limerick dam was well and truly broken.

At the other end of the field, Niall McInerney was locked tight to Joe McKenna. At the end of the two games, he had held the powerful full-forward to just six points. There were no goals from the mighty McKenna.

Watching it all unfold, and looking calm and strangely composed, was Offaly coach Dermot Healy. He said he was happy to have seen the two games. He actually admitted that most of the questions he had in his head were answered during the course of the 140 minutes. Healy duly named an unchanged team for the final, which included Liam Currams in the middle of the field, as he went in search of an historic All-Ireland football and hurling double. Currams was also due to line out at half back on Eugene McGee's football team against Kerry, who were heading for their four-in-a-row.

Farrell also decided to go with the same team in the defence of the All-Ireland title. He kept faith with Sean Silke in the middle of the half back line, even though the team captain had been out of sorts in the semi-final replay and was replaced by Pearse Piggott. John Connolly was given the No.14 jersey. On the substitutes' bench, Farrell also had aces up his sleeve in Joe McDonagh and Brendan Lynskey, and also Conor Hayes who was fighting to regain full fitness after injuring his back against Antrim in the quarter-final.

Thirteen of the Galway players who had lined out the previous September were back for more. The only change in the defence was Iggy Clarke, while Finbarr Gantley was in for Frank Burke, who, like John Connolly, had retired after the final in 1980, but was also drafted back by Farrell in the late summer. The bookmakers, all over the country, had Galway odds-on favourites to do an historic double. The two games were deemed to have stablised Galway and given them greater momentum, as they advanced to the final. Also, Galway had all of their strongest players hitting their best form, and that included Sylvie Linnane who, after the long battle against Limerick, was duly awarded with the B + I GAA 'Personality of the Month' for August.

There was simple agreement amongst GAA fans: the All-Ireland final was Galway's to lose.

• • •

"It's fairly wet back here, Finbarr!"

Willie Bennett, had been picked up by Finbarr Gantley, as usual, before collecting Sylvie Linnane. Sean Silke was already in the passenger's seat. The gang were in the best of form as they counted down the days to the All-Ireland final. However, Gantley was the rogue in the pack, if ever there was one, though all four men liked to play the part of the rogue if they got half a chance. This particular evening, a week before the final, with Farrell tapering everything down in training and with the players relieved at arriving into the final week of the season, the mood and the craic in every car heading for training was mighty.

When Gantley arrived at Willie Bennett's, he noticed that Willie was wearing a fine, new suit. Silke and Bennett never saw Willie looking so well-dressed, but they said nothing to him as he happily jumped into the back of the car with a big smile on his face.

The seat was wet. In fact, it was wet and sticky, as well as having a fair smell. Bennett manoeuvred himself about as best he could, but failed utterly to find a dry patch. When he informed the driver of his situation, Gantley threw his head back and laughed.

"Had a calf in there an hour ago, Willie. You'll be fine there, Willie," added Gantley, "and so will Linnane."

Everyone in the Galway hurling camp, and everyone in every car, felt good about life in the first week of September, 1981.

. . .

The 1981 All-Ireland hurling final had a character and a demented personality all of its own. It's no wonder, it also had a finish that was secretly hidden away from everyone in the ground, and knocked everyone, Offaly and Galway supporters alike, off their feet.

Galway looked strong from the very start. But they played like a team that had a set of invisible chains holding them back, refusing to allow them to break free and lift their whole performance to a far higher level. Nevertheless, Galway had scored 13 times in the first half. They led 0-13 to 1-4. It should have been a nine-point lead, but referee Frank Murphy amazed practically every last soul inside Croke Park when he disallowed a John Connolly goal ten minutes before the break. Murphy determined that Offaly goalkeeper, Damien Martin, had been fouled before Connolly hooked the ball over the goal-line.

Sylvie saw nothing wrong with the goal from where he was standing. Nobody did. If anything, Sylvie took a long look as the goal was scored, to make sure that the referee had not decided to give a penalty. To Sylvie, it looked as if Damien Martin had definitely fouled John Connolly. Sylvie also thought that Connolly should have buried the ball earlier, before the Offaly 'keeper came anywhere near him.

Galway's control was close to total. In their defence, everyone was dominating their immediate opponents. Sylvie had Mark Corrigan to contend with, and the game was going exactly as Sylvie had planned, and hoped, it would go. The first half could not have gone any better, in fact. And, when Steve Mahon burst through into space, they found themselves seven points in front and, perhaps, about to coast home. However, Galway would score just one more point before the final whistle. And, when it was all over, when Johnny Flaherty palmed the ball to the net to score one of the most controversial goals in the modern history of the game and put Offaly three points in front in the dying seconds, Farrell and his players had nobody to blame but themselves.

Though, staring at a 2-12 to 0-15 loss, which scarcely looked believable, there was a desire to apportion blame. There was certainly an urgent need amongst Galway supporters to find out what had gone so disastrously wrong.

Flaherty was the easiest of targets. Most people vowed that he had thrown the ball into the net as Niall McInerney tried to bottle him up. But the game should have been closed out long before Flaherty got that last ball into his hand. Galway had sat down. Galway had relaxed. Galway grew over-confident at the start of the second half. These were all perfectly legitimate thoughts. However, word also went out that there had been an almighty bust-up between John Connolly and Farrell at half time, that Farrell had been trying to take Connolly out of the game, and Connolly was refusing to go. Most people chose to believe that to be the case, even though there was not a word of truth in it.

Sylvie, like everyone else, spent days nursing the belief that Galway had thrown the All-Ireland final away. Frank Murphy had been hard on them in his decisions, he had no doubt about that, but anytime he thought too long about the referee he usually stopped himself looking for someone outside the Galway team to blame. There had been fourteen wides from play in the second half alone. The more he dwelt on what happened, the more he regretted the amount of ball which he, and everyone else, had seemed to be hitting down the throat of the long, muscular figure of Pat Delaney in the Offaly half-back line. Ball after ball had rained down on Delaney, and he accepted almost every one of them as a special gift from someone on high.

Sylvie couldn't understand why Cyril Farrell and the lads on the sideline had watched Delaney win so much possession over the head of PJ Molloy. In that vital 15 minutes period in the second half, in which Offaly turned the tables on their opponents, it was surely time to get Frank Burke onto Delaney, or Joe Connolly, someone bigger than Molloy, someone who could look to stop Delaney in his tracks?

Delaney's victories in the air, and his repeated charges forward, propelled the entire Offaly team into a game-winning position. But, as he looked to put the defeat behind him in those painful few days and weeks after the final, Sylvie also came to the realisation that, perhaps, it was simply Offaly's time.

Up and down the Offaly team there were men who had waited all their lives for the chance of winning an All-Ireland title, and most of them were outstanding hurlers, every bit as good as Galway, and every bit as deserving of making the last-gasp breakthrough, starting with Damien Martin. The Offaly 'keeper had waited a lifetime to win a Leinster Championship medal, and when he got that in 1979, he decided to retire, finally. He held on. He got a second Leinster medal, and Damien Martin had been there when Offaly won their first All-Ireland. How could any Galway man moan or give out about losing a game to such a man, or the men directly in front of him, Eugene Coughlan or Pat Fleury, Aidan Fogarty or Ger Coughlan?

Sylvie could not do that.

Galway had not been ruthless enough in killing off the game, and leaving Offaly for dead, when they had the chance of doing exactly that. That's why Galway had been beaten, Sylvie Linnane resolved. Galway were new to being All-Ireland champions, and they were not tough enough, not nearly greedy enough, to hold onto their All-Ireland title and let no man or no team come within a yard of taking it from them.

That's why they had lost their All-Ireland title. It was nothing to do with a fluky, or illegal goal for Offaly. In truth, Sylvie, unlike so many people in Galway, always believed that Johnny Flaherty's goal was perfectly good.

He had watched the ball going from Delaney to Bermingham to Flaherty, and there wasn't a damn thing wrong with it in Sylvie's estimation. He'd been keeping his eye on Corrigan. He was waiting for Corrigan to move, and had decided in those hectic final moments not to give Mark Corrigan as much as an inch of room. Should he have gone to meet Bermingham?

As he thought about it, all that week, he knew that he should probably have risked it, and left Corrigan. He would have left a wide gap behind him but it would have been the right thing to do – perhaps.

He could have stopped Bermingham. He could have brought him down, and Offaly would have had to try to concoct something miraculous from the resultant free. There would have been no final pass to Jonny Flaherty, no overhead flick of the ball, no goal, no All-Ireland title left in tatters.

CHAPTER
13

On Friday, August 10, 1984, *The Connacht Tribune* declared that there was no longer any hope for the Galway hurling team. In fact, the newspaper made it known to its readers that the team was already six feet under.

There seemed no doubt about that.

The previous Sunday, Offaly had polished off their former arch enemy by 14 points in the All-Ireland semi-final. It finished 4-15 to 1-10. 'Galway Hurling is Dead and Buried', was the headline on Michael Glynn's report of the game from Semple Stadium.

"Galway hurling died on Sunday – having been in a critical condition for some time," wrote Glynn. "The passing away was relatively un-mourned, however, with the feeling persisting that the demise was partly self-inflicted.

"Whatever the cause, there was more life in the proverbial doornail – and certainly that inanimate object has rarely endured a pounding of the type that Offaly doled out with such relish in Thurles on Sunday."

On the same page, like a 'Wanted' notice posted in a village square, Tom Rooney's reflections were headlined, 'New Breed of Hurler is Now Required'.

"The story of Galway hurling since the historic victory of 1980 is a sad one," wrote Rooney. "That great day was the beginning of a deadly decline.

"It is time to use a more investigative criteria for selecting talent for the county. Even more important in today's competitive environment are individual qualities, such as application and character. The two qualities have been missing for a while in Galway teams. The level of fitness in the quarter-final against Westmeath, admittedly on a day of intense heat, was doubtful and it just wasn't good enough on Sunday."

However, on the very same page, John McIntyre wrote, pertinently, of the forthcoming All-Ireland Under-21 semi-final against Tipperary, when Galway were defending the title, and the task of rebuilding the county's senior team. Names were trotted out. Seven of the lads from the victorious 1983 team were still available to the Under-21s, Tommy Coen, Pete Finnerty, Tony Keady, Michael Costello, Michael Coleman, Michael McGrath and Eanna Ryan.

Ollie Kilkenny's name was mentioned, and Sean Treacy's, and McIntyre was also able to reassure the Galway hurling public – on a subject on which they would need reassurance for several years to come – that, "speculation that Keady would not be available for the Championship has proved unfounded as the Killimordaly player has been flown back from the United States for the occasion. Keady's return is certainly a boost to Galway's hopes."

• • •

At the beginning of 1982, the Galway players had made it known to Cyril Farrell that they had enough of him.

In the months following the bitter loss in the 1981 All-Ireland final, some of the older players had started grumbling. And, over the Christmas and New Year period, the unhappiness within the squad reared its head fully. Finally, before January was over, Cyril and his two selectors for the year ahead, Bernie O'Connor and Mick Curtin, turned up for a meeting with the players. Thirty players were asked to attend. Only 21 were present, but a vote was taken on the appointment of a new coach, and preferably a man from outside the county. It was 14-7 for a new man. Sylvie Linnane voted for Cyril Farrell to stay.

A few nights later, however, the Galway Hurling Board held a special meeting and made it known, in no uncertain terms, that a new coach would not be appointed to replace Cyril Farrell.

At that same meeting, Farrell had earlier announced his resignation. He

Mick Linnane from Ballynastaig and Celia Diviney shortly after their marriage.

Sylvie Linnane's eldest brother Patrick and his sister Sheila on the day of their 'double wedding', with Sylvie the first boy in short trousers on the left of the photo; and the Linnane home in Kilmacduagh (below).

Micheal Linnane on one of his summer holidays in Salthill when back home from London, with his little brother, Sylvie, playing peek-a-boo.

Six of the Linnane children at National School in 1966 (from left) Carmel, Sylvie, Anne, Gerry, Bernie and Martin; and making hay is Gerry in the front, with Carmel, Martin, Sylvie and their father, Mick Linnane.

Margaret Nolan and Sylvie Linnane at a Gort GAA club dinner dance, in the mid-1970s.

Seven Linnane brothers guard Margaret and Sylvie on their wedding day (from left) Martin, Gerry, Micheal, Johnny, Brendan, Patrick and Colie; and, below, the family party (back) Bernie, Johnny, Martin, Gerry, Micheal, Magaret and Sylvie, Patrick, Anne, Colie and Brendan, and (front) Mary, Sheila, Mick, Celia and Carmel.

The happy couple with their wedding cake and (below) Margaret's twin sister, Mary, with Margaret and Sylvie outside the church.

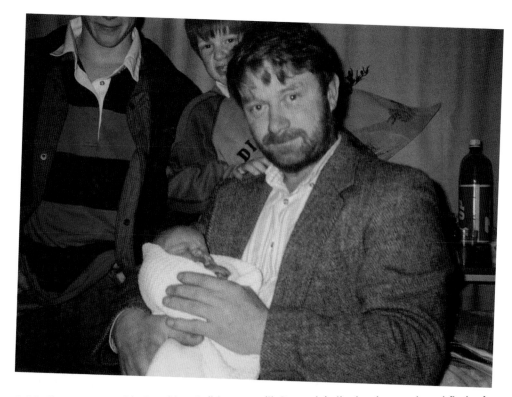

Sylvie Linnane nurses his daughter, Aoibheann, with Darragh in the background, and (below) on her graduation day Margaret holds Aoibheann with Sylvie, Darragh, Sylvie Og, Shane and Tadgh.

Margaret and Sylvie with their eldest son, Shane, on his graduation day, and (below) Darragh plays with Lassie at the Nolan home.

Sylvie receives the 1981 Galway Sports Star of the Year award from Galway Mayor and future President, Michael D. Higgins (top); Sylvie and Margaret with his first All Star award in 1985 (centre), and on holiday in Rome with Sylvie Og and Aoibheann.

Sylvie's mother, Celia, with her grand-daughter Mary (Martin's daughter) who died tragically while abroad on holiday in 2008.

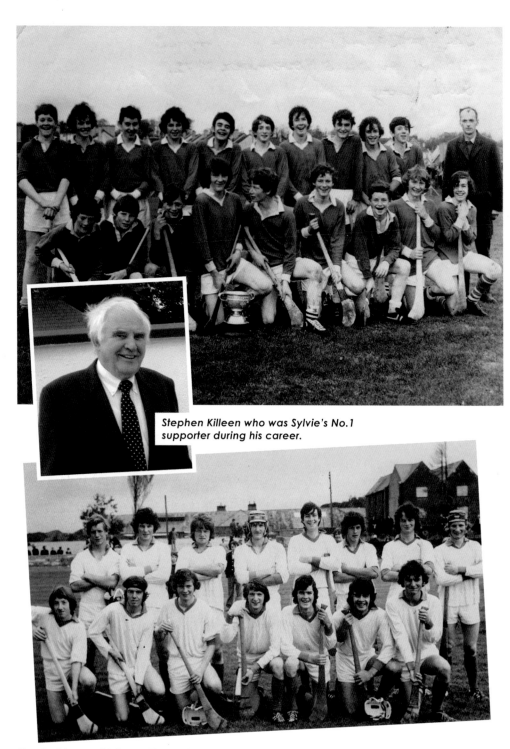

Stephen Killeen who was Sylvie's No.1 supporter during his career.

The Gort team which won the Under 16 Galway final, with Sylvie in the middle of the front row talking to his future brother-in-law John Nolan, while another brother-in-law Michael Nolan is second from the right on the front row; Sylvie is third from left on the back row (below) on the Gort minor team which won the county title in 1974, with John Nolan on his left and Michael Nolan on the right of the back row.

Sylvie and his brother-in-law, John Nolan, photographed in 1979 had to wait for their county titles.

The Gort team (above) which won the Galway Senior hurling title in 1981 and (below) the Gort team which recaptured the county crown in 1983.

Sylvie with Martin Staunton of Kiltormer in the county quarter-final (top), Sylvie and his eldest son Shane (middle) after their victory in the game, and the Gort team (below) with Shane second from right on the front row, and Sylvie in the middle of the row with Sylvie Og at his knee.

Darragh and Tadgh with their father after Gort's magnificent County final win in 2011; and (below) Darragh's girlfriend, Niamh, and Margaret join in the celebrations.

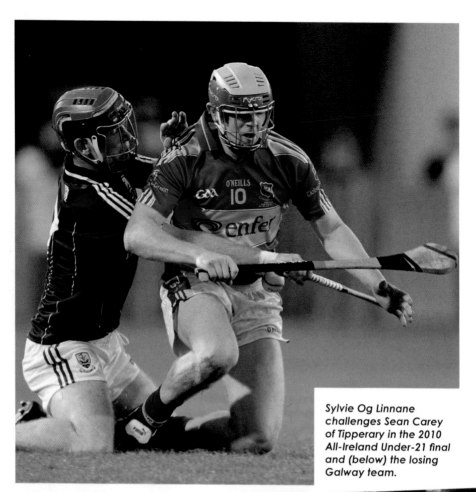

Sylvie Og Linnane challenges Sean Carey of Tipperary in the 2010 All-Ireland Under-21 final and (below) the losing Galway team.

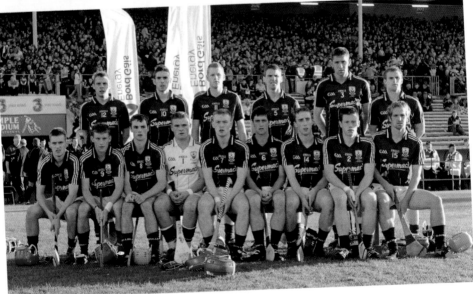

told the delegates that, if the players wanted a new coach that they should be given one, but he explained that he would be unable to work within a new management team. O'Connor also offered his resignation as a selector and, quickly, Farrell, O'Connor and Curtin withdrew for a private discussion as the board sought to get its head around what needed to be done.

By the end of the evening, the three agreed to abide by the wishes of the board. "We are all prepared to operate as we were elected to do," stated Farrell, adding, "and we'll do it our way."

The 1981-82 National League campaign was halfway through as Farrell and his senior players had their honest chat. It had started off with a stormy game in Birr, when Galway went to the home of the new All-Ireland champions in October and both teams were in an uncivil mood. Galway won by 13 points. And they would meet Offaly again, in a play-off in the League the following spring, when a 1-11 to 1-7 victory in Limerick was to be celebrated, but, at the same time, two successive wins over Offaly in a six-month period only further stoked the regret of losing their All-Ireland crown to their neighbours the previous September. An unhappy, and unsatisfactory, National League campaign finally ended with a quarter-final defeat to Kilkenny, 1-11 to 1-6.

Sylvie Linnane was not in the best of form himself. He had spent more time in the forward line than in defence in the League, lining out at centre forward with Bernie Forde on one side and Pearse Piggott on the other, but, by March, and the defeat by Kilkenny, he was back on the right wing of Farrell's team. Conor Hayes had injured his back once again, this time playing a game of squash, and Farrell made a late decision in pulling Sylvie back. And he loved being back in his own territory but, after a brilliant block-down on Richie Power's shot at goal from twenty-five yards out, Sylvie ended up taking the blame for Kilkenny's goal in the 20th minute. Having blocked down Power, Sylvie was surrounded by Kilkenny forwards and he couldn't get the ball into his hands. Instead of whipping the ball out of the way, he looked one final time to get it into his hands, but Kieran Brennan flicked it from him to Billy Fitzpatrick and he beat Tommy Grogan in the Galway goal with an unstoppable shot.

Galway were out of the League, and Sylvie was soon out of the Championship. A groin injury that simply would not go away, and which did not receive the utmost care and attention from Sylvie, ruled him out for the whole summer.

Galway dispatched Antrim in the quarter-final, but a wide range of retirements and injuries left Farrell selecting a very different looking Galway team for the semi-final against Kilkenny. Frank Larkin was in goal. Hayes was centre-back, Ollie Kilkenny was on his left, while Piggott was centre-forward, and Brendan Lynskey was in at full-forward. After everything that had transpired, Farrell had not done everything 'his way', as he had promised everyone he would when the Hurling Board offered him its unanimous backing earlier in the year. Against Kilkenny, as he had done all year, he let the players decide which direction they wanted to play if they won the toss.

Galway won the toss. The players opted to play into the wind against Kilkenny, and that was a mistake that left Farrell kicking himself for the remainder of the half. Galway had a new team, and they needed a good start, but Kilkenny were 2-11 to 1-3 in front by half time, and the game, effectively, was long over before the second half even began.

Farrell decided, quickly enough, that it was time to move on. He was teaching in Dublin, and leaving the city for the journey to Athenry needed a daily departure time of no later than 4pm. It was always the early hours of the following morning when he got back home, and into his bed.

It was time to hand the team to someone else.

• • •

In 1983, former Hurling Board secretary, Frank Corcoran, took over the Galway job from Farrell. A year later, Bernie O'Connor took over the job from Corcoran. And, twelve months after that, Farrell would be back.

It was a time of change, and some turmoil, for everyone associated with the Galway team. And it was hard to watch.

For Sylvie Linnane, however, the early '80s were also some of the best years of his hurling life. Gort had ended their long wait for a senior hurling crown in 1981, and they had regained their title in 1983. And, in between, at a team meeting, he was named captain of the Galway team by the players.

It was a huge honour, of course, but, unfortunately, 1983 was not the most memorable year to be a Galway hurler. There were new faces on the sideline, and there were new faces on the field as well as lads came to the conclusion that the good years were over, and might not return for a long time. Mistakes were being made in team selections. Training was not getting the fullest attention of all the players. Some defeats really hurt, and, all told, there was no sense that Galway were a team with an immediate future that held any real hope of winning anything.

It came down to taking it one Sunday at a time.

And, the 1982-83 League commenced with such a Sunday, when Sylvie led his team out onto O'Connor Park in Tullamore for another battle and a half with Offaly. The problem that November afternoon was that the 'battle' did not end when referee, George Ryan sounded the final whistle. In fact, it really only began at that point as an estimated 500 supporters invaded the pitch.

The distance from the pitch to the dressing rooms was 60 yards, but it appeared more like half a mile as threats began to be issued to Galway players, and punches started to be thrown. Frank Corcoran was struck on the head with a stone. When the team finally made it off the pitch, gardai on duty locked the gates to the dressing room and warned them to stay inside until they got further word that it was safe to come out again. Sylvie and his teammates stayed inside for forty-five minutes.

The gardai were reinforced by Offaly officials, and some Offaly players, when the time came to make their way to the car park across the road from O'Connor Park. There were still over a hundred unhappy Offaly hurling supporters outside the ground. But, apart from some shouting, and one or two roars, nothing else developed. A garda sergeant then led a line of Galway players from the car park as they walked towards the centre of the town, and the team hotel where a hot meal was on the table and was going cold.

It was time to tend to the wounds.

Pat Carroll and Joachim Kelly were already on their way to hospital. Kelly and Padraig Horan had been booked during the game, as were Pearse Piggott and Sylvie. For his troubles, the new Galway captain had a gash on his forehead, sustained during the game and not after the game, which required several stitches. He had watched his team give a might effort, and once again see off Offaly, winning 1-13 to 0-7.

• • •

Sylvie was not one for long team speeches in the dressing room. And in a year of highs and lows, and there were more of the latter after that November afternoon in Tullamore, he preferred to let his performances inspire those around him. That was the case in the spring, when he led Connacht to a Railway Cup title, with victories over Munster and Leinster.

On St Patrick's Day, in Croke Park, Sylvie looked up at the steps leading up to the presentation area on the Hogan Stand.

He then looked over at Joe Connolly. Sylvie didn't fancy having to make a speech. Besides, he had not got a word of Irish prepared. He looked over at Connolly again.

"Will you go up?" he asked.

Connolly shook his head.

"No, you've got to go on up," said Sylvie. "I've got no Irish, you'll do the best job!"

Joe Connolly just shook his head again.

"Are you going to go up or not?" said Sylvie.

"I'm not!" said Connolly, now slowly chuckling to himself. "You're captain, it's your job!"

Sylvie uttered a few more words of displeasure to Connolly and the remainder of his teammates who were proving to be just as unhelpful. He walked up the steps of the Hogan Stand. The speech was short. In the Galway dressing room, minutes later, it was agreed that Sylvie Linnane had made the shortest, and fastest, speech ever made by a captain in Croke Park.

"That's the last time I'm doing that!" Sylvie replied.

And so it was.

• • •

Galway put out an experimental team against Antrim in July, in the quarter-final of the Championship. They won handsomely, 3-22 to 2-5. There were more changes for the semi-final against Cork the following month. Pearse Piggott was dropped and replaced at centre back by Steve Mahon. With

Mahon dropping back, Michael Connolly and Iggy Clarke were chosen in the middle of the field. Frank Burke was recalled to the team. On the Cork team, John Buckley was switched from defence to the half forward line, especially to deal with Sylvie.

Buckley was a much bigger man, and a tough customer to boot, and Sylvie had his hands full all afternoon. He kept his man to one point. And he raced forward to slip over a point himself. But there was nothing Sylvie, or anyone else in the Galway defence, could do about a Cork forward line that sizzled from the very start, and slapped up 5-14, with Jimmy Barry Murphy and Tomas Mulcahy planting the pick of the goals into the back of the Galway net in the second half. Galway had been given their goal on a plate inside the first minute, when Ger Cunningham failed to catch a harmless lob and Noel Lane found the ball at his feet. There were ten points in it at the end, as the Cork full-forward line contributed the full sum of four goals and three points in their 5-14 to 1-16 win.

Kilkenny scored a two-point victory over Cork in the 1983 All-Ireland final, but, by the end of September, Galway had a new man in charge of their immediate fortunes. On a 25-22 vote, Bernie O'Connor defeated Frank Corcoran for the position. Corcoran and 'Inky' Flaherty were named as his co-selectors.

• • •

The 1983-84 League saw Galway playing half-decently, and well enough to gain a play-off place in March against All-Ireland champions, Kilkenny. O'Connor saw his team keep things tight in the first half in the Gaelic Grounds in Limerick, but only two pointed frees were reward for the team's efforts after the break. Ten of Kilkenny's points, in their 1-14 to 1-7 victory, came from frees also, which told the tale of exactly how badly the Galway defence struggled throughout. The longer the game went on, the more powerful and unassailable was the Kilkenny half-back line of Joe Hennessy, Ger Henderson and Paddy Prendergast, while Frank Cummins in the middle of the field was nothing short of masterly from beginning to end.

In the heart of the Galway team, there was nobody to touch those four.

In fact, there were definite question marks by the very end, as to whether this particular Galway team possessed a heart at all.

During the course of 1984, good days were nearly always followed by bad days but, occasionally, bad days gave life to days that were surprisingly good. Consistency was a problem. So, too, was team discipline. However, after the disappointment of losing to Kilkenny, Galway held onto their place in the top division in the League, when they went back to Limerick and dealt out an expert 6-12 to 1-11 demolition job of Waterford. Finbarr Gantley, at full-forward, got a hat-trick. So, too, did Joe Connolly. Ollie Kilkenny was everywhere in the middle of the field.

For every step forward in the spring, there were three or four steps backwards. Ollie Kilkenny and Aidan Staunton withdrew from the squad, wishing to concentrate on club hurling until the start of the Championship, and captain, PJ Molloy, unhappy with his form, handed in the role of captain. Conor Hayes would later step into the role. The team was also without a fitness coach, as Jim Wall's period in charge of training ended after the League. John Connolly, and Cyril Farrell, both declined the offer of replacing Wall. And, for a time, Galway were also without a manager, as Bernie O'Connor and Inky Flaherty temporarily resigned after a heated and critical Hurling Board meeting in March, and people wondered, for a few days, would Farrell or Connolly be taking over as manager.

Two goals from David Kilcoyne, just before half time, gave Westmeath the lead in the All-Ireland quarter-final. There were only 4,559 people in Birr, and, with Gantley and Clarke retiring with nasty injuries, a surprise looked on the cards. Molloy replaced Gantley and quickly missed with a penalty. It was level at half time. Eventually, Galway would cut loose in the second half and win, 2-17 to 2-8. Another big meeting with Offaly in Thurles, two weeks later, now awaited a still distracted and wary Galway squad.

Offaly still held onto eleven of the team that had defeated Galway in the 1981 All-Ireland final. The additions were Liam Carroll in defence, Tom Conneely in the middle of the field, and Declan Fogarty and Joe Dooley up front. They had produced some stirring stuff in defeating Wexford in the Leinster final. Offaly were still holding their ground, but most commentators felt that Galway had lost ground, and the players officially cited by most newspapermen as going backwards in the three years were Sylvie Linnane, Conor Hayes, Sean Silke, Iggy Clarke, Michael and Joe Connolly and PJ Molloy.

Galway took the game to their opponents from the very start, as Offaly fully expected. It was hot and humid in Semple Stadium, and Galway had no choice. They had to get out in front, and that's where they were until the 17th minute when they conceded an unfortunate goal. However, Galway knuckled down to their task for the remainder of the half. Offaly got through for another easy goal just before the break. They led by five points at half time, and, five minutes into the second half, they got their third goal. Remarkably, Galway still stood their ground. There were only three points between the teams when the game reached its most crucial phase.

Then Offaly stepped everything up a gear.

Galway had nothing more to give. They were tired. They looked lost. They were a completely finished team before the game had even reached its final quarter, and, when it did Galway, more or less, slumped to the ground.

Sylvie Linnane was foremost amongst the giant Galway effort. He gave it his all, and had a particularly torrid encounter with his old pal from the late summer of 1980, the late Pat Carroll. It was a physical battle to best all physical battles all over the field, and twice Carroll had to retire to receive treatment from the Offaly medical team, and twice he reappeared to an enormous response from the huge Offaly contingent that had decamped in Thurles and made up the largest part of the disappointing attendance of 18,708.

Nothing could stop Offaly from advancing to meet Cork in the All-Ireland final, and make it a first Championship meeting of the teams in the 100 years history of the association. Offaly beat Galway by 4-15 to 1-10. Joachim Kelly was utterly dominant in the middle of the field. Up front, Padraig Horan and Joe Dooley scored four goals and five points between them.

Horan had scored the first Offaly goal, and Dooley the second and third, which put Offaly nine points in front early in the second half. A free from Molloy, and a 50-yard run and a point by Michael McGrath narrowed the gap, and then, in the twelfth minute of the half, Mahon drove a long, speculative shot into the heart of the Offaly defence and an unsighted Damien Martin could not prevent it from slipping over the line. It was 3-6 to 1-9 in the semi-final, but everything that had happened was wiped out of sight and left having little or no value by what occurred from there to the finish. Offaly would score one goal and nine points. Galway would manage one solitary point.

It was not just the intense disappointment of the last twenty minutes that left Galway folk trooping home in a sorrowful and particularly downcast convoy. There had been the glory of being All-Ireland champions in 1980. Then there had been the anguish of 1981 when an All-Ireland title had been unforgivably lost.

After that, fast, and far too furiously for anyone to fully comprehend, there were three heavy All-Ireland semi-final defeats.

Sylvie Linnane, like everyone else around him in the Galway dressing room, wondered was that it? One All-Ireland, and no more than that?

It looked like that. And, when he read in his local newspaper that the Galway team was 'dead', was 'buried', there was nothing much he could say about it. The three semi-finals had been hard to live with. There was no doubt about that.

Kilkenny had scored 2-20. Cork had scored 5-14. Offaly had scored 4-15.

Sylvie Linnane had been at the heart of a Galway defence that had conceded 11-49 in the three games, which Galway people, and hurling supporters all over Ireland, remembered. All the other games Galway had played in those three years were out of sight.

There were only three games being talked about – Kilkenny, Cork, and Offaly, and the grand total of 11-49!

By the close of 1984, Cyril Farrell was back as team manager and, almost immediately, he let Sylvie Linnane know that his future as a Galway hurler was in the full-back line. Farrell told him Galway had to stop leaking goals.

Sylvie hated the very thought of playing right corner-back.

CHAPTER
14

"If you'd had your mouth open, Hayes, you'd have caught that ball."

Conor Hayes was spluttering up blood and bits of teeth and feeling mad as hell and sorry for himself at the same time. But Sylvie Linnane wasn't having any of it. He showed no sympathy whatsoever for his full-back, in the same way he had failed, wholeheartedly, to offer up a single condolence to Hayes' predecessor in the Galway No.3 jersey, Niall McInerney, when he had also been left bloodied in another incident a couple of years earlier.

McInerney had received a very nasty cut to his head in an Oireachtas semi-final, and was sitting back in the dressing room, getting stitched up, and grimacing silently as each stitch was inserted to close the wound. There were fifteen stitches in total. *It's a fine wound*, thought Sylvie.

Sylvie had been quietly observing 'Mac' in all of his agony. But it was time to say something and when it was time for someone to dramatically break the ice and say something in the Galway dressing room, that someone was usually Sylvie Linnane.

"It's about time you got that, Mac," Sylvie announced. "You've got away with it for too long ... not a bloody scratch on you!" added Sylvie. "But, you're the same as the rest of us now."

Niall McInerney was too intent on offering up the pain to respond. That would come later. Half time was hurrying to an end and McInerney had no intention of sitting out the second half.

And Conor Hayes, when his turn came, as he washed out his mouth and opened it wide for inspection by the team doctor, was also unable to say very much to Sylvie, either. He'd been standing on the goal line, with Sylvie and John Commins, as Peter Murphy had been taking some penalties on the three men who would stand on the line for any penalty awarded against Galway.

Murphy had close to the perfect strike of a ball. He never needed to hit it ridiculously hard, but he had mastered a spin on the ball which made it difficult, if not next door to impossible, to read.

Hayes had badly misread Murphy's final penalty. It had been getting dark and they'd said they'd take a couple more. The very next ball zipped by Hayes' outstretched stick and whacked him in the mouth. More than one tooth was dislodged. Blood was flowing over his lower lip. Everyone had gone quiet. Cyril Farrell was running around looking to keep everything calm, and get things sorted. And Sylvie looked on in amusement.

He'd keep the sympathy for after, when himself and Hayes would have time for a quiet word.

• • •

Farrell was back.

Sylvie liked to call it the second coming. Farrell was back in the middle of the dressing room floor, barking out his orders and best of plans, and never too far away from him were Bernie O'Connor and Phelim Murphy, his two selectors. The mood had lifted in the camp soon as Farrell walked back in amongst the lads. Everyone wanted to make a fresh start of it, and everyone felt that they had moved on to a second life – and that, in many ways, they were lucky to get two lives. After three years of All-Ireland finals, followed by three years of brutally demoralising semi-finals, any man still on the Galway hurling team had to count himself lucky at getting one more chance at restarting something interesting.

Farrell didn't spare anyone on the training field. He was back to his wicked self, surprising everyone with particularly harsh sessions, and pushing them, breaking them down, and lifting them back up again.

Sylvie Linnane, for one, had vowed early on in his relationship with Farrell that the man would never break him down. It wouldn't happen, couldn't happen.

Never did happen.

Never will happen, Sylvie informed Farrell without saying a word, just giving him that stubborn glare when Farrell ordered more sprints or demanded another couple of laps at three-quarter pace before they called it a night.

But the craic was back to what it had been, in the room and out on the field. Any chance for some laughter was snatched at. It was needed, in order to balance the savageness that Farrell was regularly doling out, that winter and spring, at the start of the 1984–85 season.

Farrell knew that Sylvie didn't want to go back into the corner, and he could see clear as day that Sylvie Linnane saw it as some form of retreat, as some form of demotion, something that was linked to the fact that Farrell either saw him as someone with older legs or an older head. Or both. Old legs was bad, but an old head could be considered a compliment.

Either way, Sylvie didn't like the look of it, and didn't much care for the smell of it. Farrell, for several months, found it hard to convince him that he did not have the full-back line he wanted and he needed to build a new one.

"I'm the best wing-back you've got," Sylvie told him more than once.

"I need you to be the best corner-back!" Farrell replied.

It was a conversation that trundled along through the winter and spring. Farrell knew that Sylvie wanted to stay close to the middle of the field, where the action was, where he got to meet all sorts of hurlers, half-forwards with speed and power, big, rangy midfielders, and other half-backs on the opposing team who fancied breaking through Sylvie's line. Life always looked a whole lot more interesting on the Galway half-back line.

The defence of Farrell's dreams was still a year or two away.

The half-back line of Pete Finnerty, Tony Keady and Gerry McInerney was still not even in the melting pot. But the full-back line of Sylvie Linnane, Conor Hayes and Ollie Kilkenny was, indeed, under the nose of the Galway team boss. That line was slowly coming together.

Hayes was the gentleman of the threesome, and in training and challenge games he'd often be too much of a gentleman. Hayes could make some young fella, brought in for a trial, look some class of world-beater, or he might choose to clean out the young fella in double quick time. Farrell knew Hayes better than anyone. Farrell loved his style as a full-back, and his natural grace and efficiency under pressure. Farrell also loved his enormous leadership qualities. Sylvie and Ollie Kilkenny were different, but they complemented Conor Hayes perfectly.

Sylvie and Kilkenny were equally ruthless all of the time, in games, in training, always! Both of them wanted to win at all times. Kilkenny was at his very best when told to stick to a man and ruin his day. Sylvie could find the measure of any zippy corner forward just as fast, but Sylvie could also run the line better than Kilkenny. Sylvie could see what was about to happen, before Hayes or Kilkenny sensed the trouble.

It would be Sylvie's line, Farrell believed.

With six strong defenders, forming two excellent lines in that same defence, and with a free-taker who loved the ultimate responsibility and never flinched, a Galway team was capable of beating anybody. Farrell had already spent an evening with Joe Cooney and his parents, wondering if their nineteen-year-old son was happy to come onto the senior squad immediately. Twelve months later, in that same room, the first of a half a dozen All Star awards would sit proudly on the mantelpiece.

Such a team would be in the running for another All-Ireland title, and that was the skeleton of the team that Cyril Farrell sought to get onto the field as quickly as possible.

• • •

In his first match back, Farrell's new Galway met Tipperary in a League game in Ballinasloe, and had a three-point win, 2-12 to 3-7, and, by the time they played All-Ireland champions, Cork, in Midleton the following February, they had already qualified for the semi-finals of the competition. Galway also beat Cork by three points. Sylvie Linnane was left full-back. Peter Finnerty, just out of the underage ranks and strongly fancying himself as full-back, got a run in the other corner and had still to be fully informed that Farrell needed him on the front foot as a wing-back and not on the back foot as a No.3.

The League ended, however, with a bit of a shudder. Clare were going well that spring, but nobody in the Galway camp thought there was a chance of going down to them by six points in the semi-final. Another defeat loomed, in May, in the final of the Ford Open Cup, which was a newly titled version of the Centenary Cup, which had been played on an open-draw basis for hurling and football counties, to celebrate the association's proud 100 years. Tipperary beat Galway 1-13 to 1-10 in the 1985 cup final. But Farrell learned enough, especially about the need to fast track the building of his new half-back line. Steve Mahon, Michael Mooney and Ollie Kilkenny had formed the half-back line against Tipp, but by the time the All-Ireland semi-final against champions Cork came around on the first Sunday of August, the same line contained Pete Finnerty, Tony Keady and Tony Kilkenny.

Once more, the attendance in Croke Park was pitiful, with barely 8,000 people making the journey to Dublin on that August Bank Holiday weekend. The rest resolving to stay dry. It was the mother and father of all downpours early in the day, and the skies never let up as the teams took to the field. They missed an amazing game, and one in which Cork were forced to start without their poacher and play-maker in chief, Jimmy Barry Murphy, who was injured in a club football match the week before. Cork still managed to score five goals.

Galway had wanted to rattle into Cork straight away, and they tried their best to do exactly that, but, with the pitch awash in places, and with players finding it almost impossible to stop and turn without landing on their backsides, the early entertainment was closer to something from Fossetts' Circus than a championship game of hurling. When anyone pulled on the ball, water squirted in every direction.

The champions won the toss, and decided to play into the wind and rain in the first half, and, by the end of it, they were obviously immensely proud of having held Galway to a one-point lead, 1-7 to 2-3. They were happier still when Kevin Hennessy scored their third goal, latching onto a Pat Hartnett centre, not long into the second half. Nobody saw the next sixteen minutes coming. Joe Cooney made room for himself in a hesitant defence and palmed the ball to the net. Then Lane, Forde and Cooney set up Brendan Lynskey for a goal. And then, after a quick exchange between Tony Kilkenny and PJ

Molloy, Noel Lane got one of his trademark goals, and with ten minutes left Galway had an incredible advantage of ten points, 4-11 to 3-4.

Cork rallied. John Fenton scored a couple of goals, but it finished 4-12 to 5-5, a real classic of its time, which was witnessed by so few. Those old stagers who did get a lift to the game, told younger folk that it was an occasion as close to the 'Thunder and Lightning' final of 1939, as you could ever get. It was the third time in ten years that Galway had stopped a galloping Cork team in the semi-finals, and the shock victory also catapulted Farrell and his team into the role of the warmest of favourites for the final against Offaly.

• • •

Offaly were still the team of 1981, and ten of the men who had hauled that game out of Galway's arms were still around four years later. They had torn Galway apart in the 1984 semi-final, and they had enjoyed a seven-point victory over Galway in the League the previous February. They had a lot of hurling years behind them, but Offaly still had a fierce hunger, which was unleashed in the Leinster semi-final when they fought back from nine points down to snatch a draw with Kilkenny, and then beat them by six points in the replay. They had thirteen points to spare over Laois in a facile provincial final. That left Offaly, in Dermot Healy's days in charge, as having won one All-Ireland title and four Leinster titles and having contested six Leinster finals. They were a team brimful with experience and wiliness, and the team had also developed an expert nose for victory.

Galway, in comparison, had eight newcomers, including a whole new half-back line, so why were Galway so overwhelmingly strong favourites, Farrell wondered? He didn't like it.

Offaly, also had something else that Farrell could do absolutely nothing about. He knew that Healy was reminding his players, every single night at training, that everybody the length and breadth of the country fully believed that Offaly had robbed Galway in the 1981 final. Healy was telling his lads that the 1985 All-Ireland final would have enough meat on it that a victory would taste like two All-Irelands. Farrell would have loved to have that little promise in his own back pocket to make to his players.

Galway struck 20 wides in the 1985 All-Ireland final, 13 in the first half alone, by which time they trailed 1-6 to 0-7. By the end of the game, after trying to feed far too much ball into Bernie Forde, Noel Lane and PJ Molloy in their full-forward line, and receiving just one goal and one point from play in return, Farrell knew that they had only themselves to blame, once again, for allowing Offaly to lift the Liam MacCarthy Cup a second time in five years.

Offaly's crucial goal came shortly after the restart when Pat Cleary was on hand to do the damage, though Cleary's goal actually entered the Galway net off the knee of Sylvie Linnane.

Sylvie had seen, early that season, that Peter Murphy liked to bat a high ball out of his way, more often than not. Sylvie would have preferred a goalkeeper who caught the ball clean, but Murphy had his own style, and he was excellent in every other department. In the second half, Sylvie had watched the ball fall out of the sky and drop down on top of Murphy. He should have known what was going to happen next.

And, when it did happen, he blamed himself first and foremost. Only then did he think of blaming his goalkeeper. Murphy whacked the ball down and it bounced off Sylvie's knee. It was in the back of the net, and Cleary had his arms in the air, before he knew it.

Galway dug deep. With so much going against then they had to, and a Molloy goal, followed by a couple of steadying points, brought them back to within one point of Offaly with thirteen minutes left on the clock.

By then, though, Galway had really given their all.

Offaly won by 2-11 to 1-12, and losing by two points, and scoring an own goal, did not do very much to warm Sylvie Linnane to the thrills and spills of the full-back line. Sylvie understood what Farrell meant when he urged Sylvie to sweep in front of Hayes and mind the line. But Sylvie also knew that a man could look a right clown looking after a line, and not looking after his own man. Besides, his instinct remained to get back into the thick of the action further out the field.

He knew he was not right in his new position and he knew full well that Farrell's new defence was not yet fully in place, or in any way complete. Galway did not yet have six backs settled into their positions. They didn't have a strong defensive unit at work, either.

Sylvie saw a great defence as one being as tight and happy as a family. One big family. That's what Sylvie Linnane looked forward to being part of in the year ahead.

He liked playing with Hayes and he never felt he needed to cover in front of him, despite what Farrell said. In the other corner, Sylvie knew that Ollie Kilkenny was as hard as nails and seldom needed any help, either. Pete Finnerty was still young, but he was starting to come right fairly quickly. Keady was full of confidence in the middle and, the following year, Gerry McInerney would be settled into the No.7 jersey and would prove himself, pretty much overnight, to be perhaps the most exciting and dynamic Galway hurler of his generation. Sylvie would think so. The following year, also, Peter Murphy would be in goals, a strong man who liked to claim his own ball.

By the end of 1985, Sylvie realised that he was the old man of the family. It was his job to help everyone else settle into their places and feel that they had been born to that position, like John Connolly had helped him so many years earlier to feel part and parcel of the Galway dressing room.

It was Connolly, more than anyone else, who had made Sylvie Linnane feel at home as a Galway hurler.

Sylvie Linnane had grown older and wiser in one disappointing year.

CHAPTER
15

The death of Pat Carroll, at thirty years of age, cut at the Offaly hurling team right to its very core. For so many Galway hurlers, his passing was even more shocking.

Sylvie Linnane, especially, so often had gone toe-to-toe with the Coolderry forward. Both red-headed, and both incapable of backing down, their clashes had defined the altogether enthralling and, at times, bitter, relationship between the two counties.

Six years earlier, their tempestuous battle in the All-Ireland semi-final had almost wrecked Sylvie Linnane's chances of making it through to Galway's breakthrough All-Ireland success. He had been sent off for a wholehearted tackle on Carroll that the referee had deemed downright illegal. Sylvie had walked to the line in a bloodied, angry state, having received a belt from Carroll on the side of his head minutes earlier.

Every time her husband came home from a game against Offaly, Margaret Linnane would notice another finger broken or a fresh gash on his arms or head. Margaret reckoned that Sylvie had accumulated more cuts and bruises and broken bones courtesy of the Offaly hurling team, than all of the other counties in Ireland put together.

Sylvie was not complaining.

But Margaret thoroughly disliked attending games against Offaly, and hated even more not going to them and waiting for Sylvie to come home from such games.

For Sylvie, all of those games with Offaly – and the occasions in which he had to over-power Pat Carroll, or be over-powered – defined him and made him the hurler he was, more than any other number of games against any other county. Offaly were Galway's ultimate opponent.

Carroll was his greatest likeness on a hurling field.

Pat Carroll had played in all of Offaly's games in their march to the 1985 All-Ireland final, including the semi-final win over Antrim, but had to pull out of the preparations for the final, and the eventual victory over Galway, when he started experiencing the severest headaches. Seven months later he was gone.

He had left the field, feeling unwell in the game against Antrim. He was in hospital when the rest of the team brought the Liam MacCarthy Cup to his bed in September. He was the same age as Sylvie Linnane. Both had played minor in 1973 and '74. Carroll had started out in the middle of the field, but it was at left half-forward that he won an All Star award in 1980.

Pat Carroll died in St Luke's Hospital, in Dublin, on March 16, 1986. He and his wife, Mary, had one child, three-year-old Brian. For hurlers from Offaly and from Galway and from many other counties, winning and losing no longer seemed to matter for several days and weeks. Carroll had been one of the strongest breed of hurlers on the field, and one of the quietest, and most decent, of men after a game.

He was the toughest and finest opponent Sylvie Linnane had known.

• • •

But, Galway had to win. And soon. The clock was ticking.

At the end of 1985, Seamus Coen, Sylvie Linnane, Pete Finnerty, Brendan Lynskey and Joe Cooney had won All Star awards. Each was absolutely vital, and not just for the individuals who received the impressive statuettes. Galway had lost four finals in the 12 months that was ending and, unless there was some reward coming their way, some proof that the team was heading in the right direction, there was a danger that heads would drop. That was Cyril

Farrell's greatest fear.

Would his players stop believing in themselves, before he had instilled in them a real sense of destiny?

Galway needed to win something fast and, when Farrell sat down with Phelim Murphy and Bernie O'Connor at the end of the year, that was their No.1 priority for 1986. Win something, anything.

Just win.

The 1986 League title was the only target in the team's sights in the opening month of 1986, when Galway got down to the heavy work on the darkest, wettest nights of the year. They had already played four games in the 1985-86 League, beating Dublin and Cork, losing to Kilkenny, and beating Laois. Galway were joint top of Division One of the NHL when the League campaign kicked off again in February, in Loughrea, against reigning League champions, Limerick.

Sylvie Linnane was chosen at right half-forward. The absence of PJ Molloy, Bernie Forde and Noel Lane twisted the management's hand, and forced them to release Sylvie from the confines of the full-back line, but Farrell regretted doing so. And never again did the Galway manager release him from the last line of his defence.

Sylvie did okay against Limerick. He was the designated free-taker and he popped over seven of them in the sixty minutes, but, meanwhile, back at the ranch, all hell broke loose in the final quarter. It had looked like Galway were sailing to a comfortable victory when they led by 1-8 to 1-3 with time zipping by, but then their defence, inexplicably, caved in. Danny Fitzgerald, Pat McCarthy, Liam Garvey and Shane Fitzgibbon broke through for goals in quick succession. Limerick won by 5-6 to 2-10.

When Galway hosted Clare two weeks later in Ballinasloe, and nailed down a place in the play-off stages of the National League with a seven-point win, Sylvie Linnane was back where he, and his manager, agreed he belonged.

• • •

The day after Pat Carroll died, Connacht defeated Munster by 3-11 to 0-11 in the Railway Cup final in Ballinasloe. The players on both teams had read about the Offaly star's death in newspapers that same morning. There were no great celebrations that evening, though Cyril Farrell was able to mark the victory down and store it away as a very helpful reminder for his players later in the year.

One month later, Galway needed two attempts before defeating Wexford and making it to the League final, and a meeting with Kilkenny. It was another dispiriting day in Thurles. Another defeat, another final that held nothing for Farrell or his players. Kilkenny won 2-10 to 2-6. Christy Heffernan and Liam Fennelly scored first-half goals that did most of the damage, and, afterwards, Sylvie was hanging around the foyer in Hayes' Hotel, waiting to meet up with some of his family, when Paddy Prendergast and Ger Henderson passed him by.

The two Kilkenny defenders were in good spirits.

They had a small chat.

"Do ye think," said Henderson, finally, "that ye'll ever win a final?"

Sylvie said nothing.

The Kilkenny lads didn't let up. They liked Sylvie Linnane, and admired him, and that made it all the better to have a little craic at his expense. A year or so later, Sylvie would look to return the compliment.

He must have stood his ground for half an hour in the foyer of The Burlington Hotel, the day after the 1987 All-Ireland final, and waited and waited for either Prendergast or Henderson, but neither walked through the doors. He told Margaret he had to talk to two men about a dog. Sylvie then scoured the hotel for thirty minutes, but he could not find them anywhere.

He had carried a leg injury into the 1986 National League final and had to pass one of Farrell's special fitness tests before getting the thumbs-up. He got through the game with only a little difficulty and, two days later, was named as captain of the All Stars hurling team that was due to meet Offaly the following Sunday in New York, on a shortened tour.

It was a rare honour for a Galwayman. It was good for Sylvie and it was still better for Farrell, who had further evidence for his team that they were, after all, going places.

• • •

The summer of 1986 was wet, wet, wet.

And the early weeks of the summer were the longest of Sylvie's hurling life. There was the usual long, foolishly long, wait for the All-Ireland semi-final. Galway were due to meet the Leinster champions. It would be either Offaly or Kilkenny, and one more defeat was more than Farrell, or his senior players, could endure. Or, perhaps, survive. Farrell was crankier in training than Sylvie Linnane had ever remembered him. Everyone could feel the pressure.

Kilkenny, they knew, in their naturally arrogant way, would expect to beat them in the semi-final, and that massive self-belief always gave a Kilkenny team a three or four point start on Galway. Whereas, Offaly, after the opening half of the decade, now believed that they had proven themselves to be a bigger team than Galway, and more prepared for the bigger occasion. And Offaly did not want that to change anytime soon.

Farrell had so much to work out in his head.

And, on the field, he had so much to tinker with and fine tune. And, some weeks, there were not enough nights in the week to get done what Farrell felt had to be done. Then there was the waiting.

There was so much to be done, but there were no worthwhile games, only a quarter-final against Kerry, which was unlikely to tell Farrell or his team anything worthwhile. The weeks continued to crawl.

• • •

Brendan Lynskey and Steve Mahon had been in the middle of the field against Kilkenny in the League final. Ger Fennelly had destroyed the pair of them. Farrell knew that Mahon was an outstanding hurler, but he was better with the ball than sticking tight to an opponent. Lynskey was at his best when he was surging forward with the ball.

By early July, Farrell had his plan.

He was not going to play two midfielders, three half-forwards and three full-forwards against either Kilkenny or Offaly. He was also going to make maximum use of Pearse Piggott and Tony Kilkenny. Piggott had been centre-back in the League final, while Kilkenny had been on his right, and his brother,

Ollie, on his left. That was all out the window, as far as Farrell was concerned.

Finnerty, Keady and McInerney were going to be his half back line, so Farrell had options. He decided to drop Ollie Kilkenny back to the full-back line, and he decided to push Tony Kilkenny up to midfield. Tony Kilkenny and Piggott would play beside Steve Mahon in the middle of the field. Anthony Cunningham, Lynskey and Martin Naughton would form the half-forward line. And, inside them, there would only be Joe Cooney and Noel Lane. Instead of 2-3-3, Farrell was determined to play the semi-final with a 3-3-2 formation.

It would leave Galway with a formidable amount of strength, and bodies, in the middle of the field, and it would leave Cunningham and Naughton, and Cooney when he drifted out, to use their phenomenal pace to maximum advantage. Farrell's fine plan was based on a mixture of strength and explosive speed. It was also designed to confuse the opposing defence, at least for ten or fifteen minutes, which, might be time enough to do a lot of damage.

The only slight problem, for Farrell, was his own players. When he first unveiled his idea in training, most of the lads thought he was going to make a mess of things. They thought it did not make sense.

The older lads told Farrell he was wrong.

• • •

On the Tuesday before the semi-final, in Kenny Park, in Athenry, the sky was as grey as it was angry, and the field was swamp-like. Farrell huddled his players into one of the small dressing rooms and talked through every tiny morsel of his grand plan. Kilkenny had an iron grip on Galway in All-Ireland semi-finals. They led 14-5 in victories. They'd also beaten Galway in the 1975 and '79 All-Ireland finals, and they were fresh from their League win a few months earlier. Farrell explained that Kilkenny had a sense of entitlement, every time they showed up in August and September, and found Galway standing between them and their place in the All-Ireland final.

"It's time to start from scratch!" Farrell told his players. "We've got to call a stop to what's happened," he added, "and we've got to bring the odds back in our favour!"

His plan would do that.

A cluster of reporters were standing outside in the hallway, keeping well out of the rain. They were waiting for Phelim Murphy to announce the team, which he did.

"Mahon, Kilkenny, Naughton, Lynskey, Cooney, Cunningham, Piggott, Lane and that's it lads," announced Murphy.

"Piggott at full forward did you say, Phelim?" enquired one of the more senior newspapermen, curiously.

"I did, " replied Murphy, "Sure, he's a horse of a man!"

Sylvie liked Athenry. He liked to talk to supporters and, with the dressing rooms in Athenry situated behind one of the goals some distance from the field, the players had a good walk, and a trot down a small hill, with supporters all around them as they headed for the field.

He had also been told that there was another page to Farrell's game plan for the semi-final, one that involved himself and Conor Hayes. Farrell wanted them to swap positions at the very start of the game. Sylvie was to take up Liam Fennelly on the edge of the square. It was felt that Sylvie would stick to Fennelly, whereas Hayes would be inclined to pay close attention to him. The former was a safer bet for the Galway defence.

Farrell wasn't finished, even at that.

Each time he was interviewed in the countdown to the final, he reminded everyone, and especially the match referee, Terence Murray, that Kilkenny were getting away with murder in some games. In an interview on RTE the day before the final, he spoke directly to Murray, asking him to ensure that Galway would get more protection than they got in the League final. He reminded the referee that it was his job to make sure Kilkenny played the game fairly.

Farrell was betting everything.

Win, and he would be some class of hero for getting it so right on and off the field. Lose, and he would lose everything. People would be out for his blood. Kilkenny people. Galway people, too.

• • •

Everyone clicked from the very start.

Every single Galway player, from the very first minute, looked as though he knew exactly what he had to do. They had spent hours, evening after evening, fine tuning hand-passing movements, and inter-changing positions, but Farrell knew that it would take just one man to break down under the pressure of a big crowd in Semple Stadium, for the whole thing to possibly backfire.

Up front, Piggott had come out and, with Mahon and Tony Kilkenny, he was winning lots of ball around the middle of the field. The ball was also being sent in just about perfectly. Kilkenny had opened the scoring with a Ger Fennelly free. Then Joe Cooney and Harry Ryan swapped points, before, in the eighth minute Cooney placed Lane brilliantly and the Galway captain palmed the ball to the net. It was 1-5 to 0-5 after 26 minutes. Then Cooney and Anthony Cunningham combined magnificently. Cooney drove the ball through the middle, and Cunningham controlled it and coolly guided it past Kevin Fennelly in the Kilkenny goal.

At the back, Sylvie had swung wildly in the first minute, and the referee took his book out. There was no damage done. He'd connected with Liam Fennelly's ankles, but the incident heated up the game's temperature in an instant. Martin Naughton and Ger Henderson were also in the referee's book, soon enough.

Farrell looked to his right, where the Kilkenny coach, Pat Henderson, a man he'd known all his life, and someone in whom he had always held the greatest of respect, was prowling left and right, and chewing on his famous pipe.

Henderson was trying to work out what on earth was going on out there. Farrell wondered what he was thinking. But, even if he worked it all out, Henderson would be able to do nothing about Galway's half time lead of 2-7 to 0-5. Henderson was talking to his selectors, Eddie Keher, Pat Delaney and John Walsh, and ten minutes before the end of the half he had decided to pull off Paddy Prendergast and replace him with a forward, John Mulcahy.

Kilkenny still had more work to do in the second half at rearranging their forces, but Galway had finished the job before their opponents could settle into their new positions. After Fennelly stopped an effort from Lane, Cooney scored Galway's third goal. And, after two points lifted their hopes, Naughton raced through down the right and found Cooney inside with a perfectly timed pass. It was goal number four. The game was over. The Kilkenny defence had effectively been run off its feet. Galway had dominated the middle third of the field. And Liam Fennelly had been held scoreless by Sylvie Linnane. In fact, Fennelly, Pat Walsh, Christy Heffernan and Lester Ryan had all failed to score.

Galway had nine points to spare, 4-12 to 0-13, to put the seal on a perfect plan at the end of a perfect day.

• • •

It was an interesting weekend, all round. Their whirlwind display against Kilkenny had immediately slipped Galway into the role of All-Ireland title favourites. In the other semi-final, Cork had made fierce hard work of getting over Antrim, and while they had managed to score the tidy number of seven goals, they had also conceded a huge sum of 1-24 to the Ulstermen.

The same weekend as Cyril's Farrell's lads were easily getting their own way against Kilkenny for once, in Semple Stadium, discussions were also being finalised in the county about Tipperary's immediate future.

The next day, Michael 'Babs' Keating was named as the new Tipp manager, succeeding Tony Wall. The strong, bold voice of the former legendary forward would be heard on the sideline, and Babs would have Donie Nealon and Theo English there with him for company. It was a strong declaration of intent from Tipp, who had sat back while Galway and Offaly had taken to the biggest stage of all and earned themselves All-Ireland titles.

• • •

Sylvie was told that he was staying at full back for the All-Ireland final. Jimmy Barry Murphy was all his.

But Sylvie did not think that was a good idea at all. Neither did he like the idea of playing with a two-man full-forward line. Cyril Farrell had asked his team for the same again, the same performance as they gave in the semi-final, but with an extra 10 per cent thrown on top of it for good measure. Sylvie still didn't like the look of it. There was no way, he believed, that Cork were going to fall into the trap Farrell had carefully laid for Kilkenny.

Kilkenny were caught unawares. Anyway, Cork were too cute and their coach, Johnny Clifford, was as smart as an old fox. He had seen what Farrell had done to Pat Henderson, how he'd bamboozled him. There'd be no fooling Clifford. In fact, the Cork coach was the man who looked like he was pulling most of the strings the week before the final, as he singled out the brilliance of the Galway defence, and named none other than Sylvie Linnane as his favourite player on Cyril Farrell's team.

But Sylvie Linnane's immediate worry was Jimmy Barry Murphy. He felt that Barry Murphy was made for Conor Hayes. Sylvie wanted to play on Kevin Hennessy in the corner instead. He didn't like the confines, or the rigidity, of the full-back position. At full-back, he was unable to move left or right. He had to mark his piece of ground and think of one man, and one man only. Even one mistake against Barry Murphy could be disastrous.

And, if he got too tight to Barry Murphy, or if he hit him a little too hard or a little too late, he knew there'd be right trouble. In the corner, on the other hand, Sylvie knew that he could get the opportunity of sizing up Barry Murphy, once or twice at least, and get a good rattle at him.

Full-backs didn't get to do too much rattling and in an All-Ireland final, with everyone including the referee, on tenterhooks, there was no chance of even thinking about it.

• • •

"Teams win matches, managers lose them," Cyril Farrell had announced to the newspapermen, half seriously, 48 hours before the 1986 All-Ireland final. For the 24 hours after the game, Farrell was told that it was all his fault, and for days and weeks, nobody in Galway changed their minds.

Farrell's team had experienced a second, agonising All-Ireland defeat in successive years and, since the glorious Sunday in September, 1980, he had watched over Galway teams losing three finals. The walk up the hill to his home in Woodford, which overlooked the pretty village, never felt so lonely. Even amongst his own people, he felt every pair of eyes trained on his back.

But Cyril Farrell was never one to feel sorry for himself. He felt heart-broken for his players, and he was mad as hell on behalf of Brendan Lynskey whom, he felt, had received not enough protection from the referee, John F. Bailey, from Dublin, as the Cork defenders seemed to take turns at pushing him around the place.

He didn't care who knew what he thought, either.

The Games Administration Committee didn't like what he had to say, but when they called him into Croke Park for questioning, the Galway manager took that opportunity to tell the members of the committee, personally, and up close, exactly what he thought of the referee and his performance. Farrell could have apologised. He could have informed the members that he was misquoted in the press.

Instead, Cyril Farrell stood up for Lynskey, and he duly got slapped with a two months ban for his views.

However, Farrell did not believe that he had got it wrong in bringing the same game plan, which had worked a treat in the semi-final, back to the table for the All-Ireland final. Privately, he felt that his players had failed themselves. The right corner-forward position was supposed to be left unoccupied. And, if Johnny Clifford chose to tell his left corner-back, John Crowley, to stay exactly where he was marking nobody in particular, then Farrell had told his players to run with the ball and take on the Cork defence. Either that, or take their scores from further out the field.

As it turned out, John Crowley was voted 'Man of the Match' at the end of the 1986 All-Ireland final. In the noise and confusion that can be generated in the biggest game of the entire year, and with the pressure doubled on every man who had the ball in his hand, Farrell had watched his players panic. They were sending ball after ball into the Cork full-back line, and most of that same ball was landing in on top of Crowley, who was, as everyone knew he would be, all on his own.

Any ball driven to the left was also coming back out the field, as Noel Lane struggled to get on top of Denis Mulcahy. At the other end, Cork had two goals on the board early in the game. His players continued to hurry everything they were doing. And they were doing the wrong thing.

For the second half Farrell started with a traditional formation. He felt he had no choice. He didn't want to do it, and all through the second half he repeatedly told himself that he should not have changed back. But he felt the team needed a restart. And they needed to keep it simple.

As he had feared, Sylvie watched as Kevin Hennessy ran all over the place. He seemed to be scoring at will. And all Sylvie could do was watch, and at the same time kept his close watch on Jimmy Barry Murphy.

Sylvie was on the goal-line, in the fifth minute, when John Fenton stepped up to a 21-yard free. Sylvie knew that the Cork midfielder was going to go for his goal. He could see it, the way Fenton lined up. He knew it was going to come hard. He steeled himself.

Sylvie saw nothing of the ball. Nobody on the line did. The goal had Cork 1-1 to 0-1 in front. By then, Sylvie already knew that he should be out on Hennessy. Another six minutes had gone, when Hennessy swung on a perfect centre from Tomas Mulcahy. Cork led 2-3 to 0-3. The wind was at Galway's back. Lane had chosen to take every advantage when he won the toss. By half time, the teams were level, 2-4 to 0-10. Galway were still in it. Long-range points from Finnerty and Mahon had settled Galway before half time, and Naughton had raced through to score, and Tony Keady hit over two scores from placed balls a long way out.

Not everything was going right for Galway, but neither was everything going wrong. It was tight and frantic in the third quarter of the game, and one goal from either team looked like it would make all the difference.

One more from Cork and they would be well on top. One from Galway, and one big mighty effort might then be called upon to win the game.

When Galway's goals did come, they were at the tail end of the game, a penalty from John Commins and a seventieth-minute shot from PJ Molloy, and far too late to make any difference.

In the forty-ninth minute, it was Cork who had struck the most important score of the game. The goal they wanted. Tomas Mulcahy got the ball seventy yards out or more and started careering towards the Galway goals.

Sylvie waited.

The full-back could only be the last man to move, Sylvie knew that. He stood by Jimmy Barry Murphy, and watched Mulcahy race in their direction. Nobody was going out to him.

Sylvie decided to go. But then he stopped himself. Mulcahy would pop the ball over his head and Barry Murphy would have the easiest of goal chances. Better to leave it down to Mulcahy. There was still nobody racing out to him. He was closer still. All Sylvie could do was watch and hope that Mulcahy, with so much time and space, would make a complete mess of his shot.

Mulcahy shot.

The stadium erupted with noise. It was a long way back for Galway. Ten minutes from time, they were finished. Hennessy caught a high centre from Tom Cashman and split the defence before belting the ball home for his second goal.

It was 4-13 to 2-15 on the final whistle. Jimmy Barry Murphy scored the final point of the afternoon. It was his sixth All-Ireland medal. It was Cork's twenty-sixth title. Galway had come so far in 1985 and 1986, but their place in the great order of things in hurling history, never looked so low.

Or so far away.

CHAPTER
16

Cyril Farrell's two-month suspension, for his politically incorrect comments about John F. Bailey's handling of the 1986 All-Ireland final, did not end until midnight on November 21. The National Hurling League got up and running over a month earlier, with Galway due to meet All-Ireland champions, Cork, once again, in Pairc Ui Chaoimh on October 12. Farrell decided to completely ignore the suspension.

He took charge of the team, as usual, for the game against Cork, and also the Oireachtas games against Kilkenny and Offaly in the subsequent weeks, and marched up and down the sideline without a care in the world.

Nobody said a word to him.

"I thought they had you locked up?" Sylvie asked him, as he sat back in the dressing room and looked up at Farrell standing in the middle of the floor. They'd beaten Cork, and it was a small start to getting the intense disappointment of losing the big game out of their system.

"Doesn't look like it!" replied Farrell.

"Did you not get two months, boss?" asked Sylvie, mischievously, seeking to prompt a few ill-chosen words from his manager.

"I did, Sylvie, but nobody told me what I was suspended from, they didn't do that." said Farrell, with a big smile on his face.

Farrell still expected another letter in the post the following week, asking him to make a second trip up to Croke Park, to further explain himself. But, none arrived and, over the course of the next few weeks, nobody on high in the GAA world seemed to take a blind bit of notice of him.

. . .

"Where'd you get him from?"

Sylvie and Farrell were chatting again. It was late on a November evening and Galway had just completed an evening's training in the gym in Loughrea. Training had mainly consisted of a game of seven-a-side soccer, though, at times, the two teams seemed to be bordering more on the rules of rugby.

The rougher it got, the better, Farrell always thought. He knew it would keep them all amused, at least, and once he did not have the lads outside in the damp and the freezing cold, they were generally a happy camp to begin with.

That same evening, Michael Coleman, from Abbeyknockmoy, more the football end of the county, had come to training on his motorbike. He was blue with the cold when Farrell said hello to him and welcomed him.

Coleman was a new face.

The lads didn't know that much about him. And when someone was thrown into a training session, he became an instant novelty. He became the centre of attention, in fact. Everyone liked to rush to judgment on someone new.

"So ... where'd you get him from?" Sylvie had asked Farrell a second time.

Sylvie liked the games of so-called soccer. He liked to barrel into tackles, and he had the capacity of annoying nearly everyone on the opposing team. That's when Sylvie was happiest. And, if he got a man pinned against the wall, Sylvie Linnane made that man pay a fairly serious price for turning up to training in the first place.

Coleman was big and strong. He had a fair pair of legs on him. Sylvie didn't really know who he was, but he could see that the new man was intent on impressing Farrell and anyone else watching from the safety of the outside area of the gymnasium. Ten minutes into the game, Sylvie saw his opportunity.

He moved in and was about to shoulder-charge Coleman up against the wall, where he could then really test the new man's mettle, when an elbow shot back and connected with Sylvie's jaw.

Sylvie was stopped in his tracks.

He was dazed, ever so slightly, but not enough to stop him from quickly checking out whether Coleman had meant to give him the rap. But there was no evidence of Michael Coleman having even noticed that he had given Sylvie exactly what he had deserved. Sylvie was mightily impressed at that, as well.

It was usually Sylvie, of the senior players in Farrell's squad, who liked to issue a first judgment on a new man's potential value. He liked what he had seen from Michael Coleman. More men the likes of him, the better, thought Sylvie.

But Farrell was pretending to ignore him.

Farrell knew that Sylvie, fishing for information or trying to find out what was in the manager's head, would purposely question the new man's appetite, or some aspect of his physique or his hurling skills.

"Where'd you get him...?"

• • •

In the spring of 1987, Galway felt good about themselves again. The agony of losing two All-Ireland finals in quick succession had receded a little bit, though the fear of losing three All-Irelands in a row was now growing at a pace. They had qualified for the League final once again, and, on their way to that final against Clare in Thurles, they had defeated Offaly, condemning their closest of neighbours and greatest of enemies to a visit to Division Two. Just as the Championship was about to get up and running, Offaly looked down on their luck, and, further south, reigning champs, Cork, lost the services of the immaculate Jimmy Barry Murphy.

Barry Murphy had decided to retire, fourteen years after first electrifying GAA supporters as a slender, athletic nineteen-year-old in a red shirt. He had played football from 1973 until 1980, but gave up the game because of the pulling, and the constant dragging out of him by defenders. He flirted with a career in the League of Ireland but he finally called it a day with six All-Ireland medals, five of them won in the greatest of style on the hurling fields of the country.

Sylvie Linnane thought of that: Imagine winning six All-Ireland titles and making it look, relatively speaking, all so easy.

He had one to his name.

Getting that second one was becoming the dominant theme of his life, and the lives of everybody in the Galway camp.

• • •

Sylvie had missed out on the sixteen-point victory over Waterford in the League semi-final. He was out injured, and Pearse Piggott and Sean Treacy filled in the corner pockets either side of Conor Hayes. By then, Michael Coleman was in the middle of the field, alongside Steve Mahon. Anthony Cunningham was the star of the show for Galway, scoring 3-3 in the 5-16 to 1-12 thrashing.

It was a novel pairing in the final. Both Clare and Galway were competing in the League final for the sixth time, and each had won it three times; Galway's victories were evenly spread out with two decades or so separating each of them, coming in 1932, '51 and '75. With the game hurtling to a close, Galway looked as though they were going to make it back-to-back defeats in the League final, to add to their two All-Ireland final losses.

Tommy Guilfoyle was turning Conor Hayes inside out. He had scored a goal and, on another occasion, Hayes had pulled him down. From the resultant free, Clare's Gerry McInerney (Galway's Gerry McInerney was in the United States) blasted the ball to the net. Farrell knew that the team could not stomach another defeat. They were sick of losing but, the problem was, Galway were in danger of becoming sick at even the thought of losing. And that showed in the first half against Clare.

There was panic in the Galway full-back line every time the ball came deep. It wasn't the fault of Sylvie and Hayes and Piggott, not entirely. Too much room was being given to Clare in the middle-third of the field. Too many Galway men were waiting for the game to turn their way, and they were waiting for the next man in a maroon jersey to make the first move.

Then Hayes made a mighty catch.

He also fielded the next ball and made his clearance even longer, and more dramatic. Sylvie started clearing everything that came in, in front of the line.

Galway had led 2-4 to 0-7 at half time. Both goals had come against the run of play, and both were scored by Joe Cooney, who also helped himself to six points on the day. But Clare fought back to take the lead, and led 2-7 to 2-6 shortly after half time. That's when Hayes had called things to order, by taking command of the Galway defence. It was 3-12 to 3-10 as the rollercoaster of a match entered its final seconds. Then Michael Guilfoyle sent a long pass through to McInerney.

He looked sure to score the winning goal.

Johnny Callinan, Ger Loughnane and Sean Stack, the 'old men' of the Clare team, would get a rare reward in their fine careers.

The ball bounced in front of him, only yards from the Galway goal, but McInerney, somehow, took his eye off the ball and managed to top his shot. The ball bobbled towards Peter Murphy on the Galway line. He scooped it up and belted it down the field. It was over.

Galway had finally won something. And Farrell, for once, did not have to tell his players that, soon enough, their day… would come.

That speech did not get another airing. The Galway manager had seen his team win, but, more importantly, they had responded when the pressure heaped itself on the team's shoulders. Both young and old came through for Farrell. Hayes was heroic, but up front young Eanna Ryan was breathtaking in some of his instinctive movements.

He'd scored three goals against Clare earlier in the League, but did an even bigger job in the final, despite being closely guarded by the Clare defence and being held to just two points. In the middle of the field, however, Michael Coleman had a God-awful day. Nothing would go right for him. The occasion overpowered him, it seemed, and Farrell decided to should let him go. Coleman departed the squad for the next six months.

• • •

There was a freshness to every, single step the squad took in the weeks after that victory. There was such a difference between carrying a League final defeat through the quiet and difficult first couple of months of the summer and winning the damn thing! Lads were throwing themselves into training.

Farrell had never seen Sylvie more focused.

Sylvie had his ways.

He'd always be checking out opponents – just as he would like to check out the lads, young and old, on the Galway squad often enough as well. Sylvie would not think twice of even checking out the Galway manager.

He liked to find out for himself where things stood, and where everybody else stood on things at different times in the season. Farrell knew Sylvie's ways, alright. If he thought his immediate opponent wasn't up to much, Sylvie would shake hands with him at the start of the match and make sure to give his hand a good, tight squeeze, and hold it in a clench for a second longer than his opponent might have expected.

If Sylvie knew his opponent was fairly good, he'd usually offer him half a handshake, simply letting it be known that he was intent on getting down to business.

But, if he was marking someone who was bloody good, Sylvie might choose to ignore his man altogether. The message would be sent.

Farrell could see that Sylvie, in 1987, was never more serious about what he was doing. At the very beginning of the year, early on the League campaign, Galway had played Wexford. The game had ended in a draw, and it was a tame enough affair. It was one of Galway's poorer performances in the League. But, close to the end of the game, Sylvie had clattered into Tom Dempsey in a loose tackle.

The challenge did as much damage to Sylvie as it did to Dempsey. When it was all over, Farrell walked Sylvie off the pitch, checking that he was okay. He had known that the challenge may even have hurt Sylvie more than it had hurt the Wexford corner forward.

"Was there a need for that?" Farrell asked.

There was a decent trickle of blood down the left-hand side of Sylvie's head, as Farrell probed, further, about what Sylvie was thinking.

Sylvie was silent.

"Are you alright, there?" Farrell added.

"I'm alright," Sylvie responded, finally. "He'll think about that," added

Sylvie. "He'll remember that the next time."

A few weeks further down the road, the Galway squad was getting it hard from Farrell on the training field. He was unrelenting, physically and mentally, reminding his players that they had lost four finals in 1986. Four finals. And what's more, Galway had lost them against four different teams.

Farrell wanted his players to know that four of their biggest opponents all believed that they had the upper hand on Galway.

The lads were hurting on the field. But, try as he might, Farrell could not bring Sylvie to a standstill. Sylvie Linnane was in a mood that Cyril Farrell had never seen before. In training, in the early summer, he started playing seventy minutes' work with the ball. Every minute was used. The field, as usual, was dotted with balls. And Farrell kept it going, harder and harder, as the final ten minutes arrived, at last, and then as the final five minutes counted down on his stopwatch.

In those final two or three minutes, Farrell was more demanding than he had been in the opening minute or two. On different evenings, he got different players in his sights, and pressured them, and doubled that pressure on them. Sylvie refused to give in. He refused to back down. Farrell's words and Farrell's whistle would not get the better of him.

In April, Sylvie had been in London, helping out with some association or other the night before a big night's training. It was intense that night back in Athenry. The pitch was cold. He picked on Sylvie from the very beginning.

Sylvie had extra runs.

There were laps that Sylvie, and his fellow tourists from London, had to finish off on their own. And Farrell goaded them.

"Welcome home to Athenry, boys," shouted Farrell.

Sylvie knew Farrell as well as Farrell knew him. He was looking at his manager, hard. And he was keeping that long look on him after runs.

He was staring hard as Farrell walked by.

"It's not going to happen, Farrell," Sylvie muttered, his hands on his hips, his head down.

"What?" replied Farrell.

"You know," said Sylvie.

• • •

In June, it was time for Galway to build.

They had a League title in the bag, but there was a better team to get on the field. Galway were playing the Munster champions on August 9.

Gerry McInerney and Pete Finnerty were in New York. McInerney had been there since the week after the 1986 All-Ireland final. Finnerty had gone out and joined up with him in April, before the League final. The Galway management team had given both players a deadline. It was July 1. If they wanted to be part of the county's Championship plans, then they had to be home a full month before the All-Ireland semi-final.

The clock was on the two young boys.

For one of the elders on the team, Farrell also knew that it might be a hit or miss end to the season. Noel Lane had played well below his own high standards in two successive All-Ireland finals. Farrell decided that building a team was not all about getting the right fifteen players out on the field for the start of the game. Galway needed something more.

He needed to talk to Lane. And he needed to convince one of the county's greatest forwards that his future as a Galway hurler might be confined to a shorter role, and a late role at that.

Farrell wanted to introduce Lane late in the second half of every game in the 1987 Championship. He wanted to have Lane as a card to play. He wanted him as a 'springer' or call it a 'super-sub'. And Cyril Farrell knew that Noel Lane was not going to be a very happy man once that conversation started.

He was going to look Lane in the eye, a man who had won an All-Ireland medal and a League medal, lots of Railway Cups, and two All Star awards, and he was going to try to convince him that it was best for Galway, and best for Noel Lane, if he accepted a jersey with a big number on it – one of those numbers that a man as proud as Noel Lane had looked down his nose at through his outstanding career.

• • •

In July, it was time for Galway to watch.

All-Ireland champions, Cork, had only managed to draw with Tipperary in the Munster final, in Thurles, on July 12. It was 1-18 each at the end. Everyone who watched the game marvelled and gasped for breath, at times.

It was brilliant, and nerve-racking, for the 60,000 supporters who packed into the stands and stood on the terracing surrounding Tom Semple's old field in the middle of the town.

Tipp felt that they had been robbed. Cork felt that they had never really played, but, in the sixty-seventh minute, they took the lead for the first time all afternoon when Kieran Kingston grabbed a goal. They had him, and John Fenton, who struck ten points from frees in a personal twelve-point haul, to thank for staying alive in the Championship.

Tipperary had been seven points in front after Nicky English scored a goal in the 15th minute of the second half, losing his stick, and kicking the ball into the net, to leave it 1-14 to 0-10. Cork scored six points to Tipperary's single reply in the next ten minutes. After Kingston's goal, Fenton pointed, to make it a two-point game with two minutes left. Two points from frees from Pat Fox had forced the replay.

Galway were still watching.

If the first game was a thriller, seven days later the second game was a true epic. In the strange surroundings of Fitzgerald Stadium in Killarney, Tipperary ended a sixteen-year wait for a Munster title by defeating the reigning All-Ireland champions by 4-22 to 1-22, after extra time.

The teams were deadlocked, 1-17 apiece, at full time. Then Tipperary, younger and hungry as hell, surged for the finish line. But 89 minutes of play had to pass before Babs Keating could enjoy watching his team take the lead for the first time. It was Donie O'Connell who put them in front, 1-22 to 1-21. It was the fourth minute of the second half of extra time.

An avalanche followed. There were three Tipperary goals in the last nine minutes. Michael Doyle, who had come on as a substitute, the son of the legendary John Doyle, scored two of them. O'Connell struck the third. Tears flowed. Richard Stakelum spoke of a great famine having ended. For hours, they danced and sang outside the ground, and the party jubilantly snaked its way from the stadium on high overlooking the town, right down the long straight hill into the heart of the lovely town.

• • •

Two years earlier, 8,200 people had turned up in Croke Park to see Galway meet Cork in the All-Ireland semi-final. In August of 1987, over 50,000 made their way to the ground. The whole of Tipperary seemed to be on the move.

Farrell was in no mood to allow Tipp to join the small, but still significant number, of 'old hurling counties' who felt that they had some God-given right to beat Galway whenever the notion took them. Cork, Kilkenny and Tipperary had a rich history, handed down from generation to generation.

It told the story of the county's successes, and part of that story included Galway as a team that was usually there to make up the numbers on the field, and take their beating like inferior hurling men should.

Farrell, pretty much, told his players that they were capable of eating the Tipperary team alive. He wasn't interested in a cautious note.

That sort of note hadn't done much for Galway.

• • •

It was bright and sunny as Miko Donoghue slowly crept the team coach closer and closer to Croke Park. It was like All-Ireland final day on the streets surrounding the old ground. And it was Tipperary's day out, more than anything else. Everyone in the Galway squad could see that, as soon as they made it safely to their dressingroom, and took up one of the match programmes, which were sitting in two large bundles on the table in the middle of the room.

The programme for the day was coloured blue and gold, and the front cover also had a dramatic photograph of Bobby Ryan. There was no Galway man beside him, surprisingly. Inside, there was a long article on Babs Keating, the new Tipperry manager, who had just led his county out of Munster and who, the same article stated in a very prominent manner, had personally scored 2-12 for Tipperary when they had defeated Galway the last time the two teams had met in an All-Ireland semi-final, back in 1971, in Birr.

It was a quieter Galway dressing room than usual. Before they got to their feet, and circled Farrell for his last few words, news reached inside that things had not gone too well for the Galway minors. Tipperary had beaten them by twelve points.

That was a pity for the young lads, but it also meant that, outside, the Tipperary supporters were already in noisy, jubilant mood.

Nicky English was named at left full-forward. The programme had Bobby Ryan at full-forward, but Farrell had told his players that there was no way Tipp were going to go through with that. Sylvie and Hayes expected English to position himself on the edge of the square. From there, it would be his job to use his speed and amazing powers on the turn, to make life ugly for Hayes.

Ryan, one of the toughest, and manliest of defenders, started up front alright, but was back in the last line of the Tipperary defence by the finish. Having his weight and strength amongst his own forwards did not offer any great help for Tipp, and Babs would discontinue that experiment in 1988.

English led the attack, as Galway knew he would, and, after fifteen seconds, he opened the day's scoring with a typically stylish point.

• • •

Galway needed to lay down the law immediately.

They could not afford to allow Tipp to grow in confidence. Babs already had his team in confident mood to begin with. If Tipp relaxed and really brought the game to their opponents, there was a chance that they could start the semi-final just like they had finished the Munster final replay.

The game had already got off to a blistering pace. And every ball was being fiercely contested in those opening few minutes, as though the next ball was the last ball a man might get the chance to take into his hand. But, after English's goal, John Commins struck a puck-out that sailed the whole way to 30 yards from the Tipp goal. Brendan Lynskey got on the end of it, and he found Martin Naughton, who, quick as a flash, whacked the ball past a hapless Ken Hogan. Galway might have had another goal in the fifth minute, but Eanna Ryan, not trusting his left hand side, switched to his right and took his point instead.

Naughton was on fire. Cooney and Ryan were already flying, but slowly, surely, John Kennedy settled down at centre-back for Tipp. Galway were lying deep in their own half for long spells. At times, they only had three men up front. A pattern finally developed in the game, and Galway looked to have their noses in front in most aspects of the game. They had been five points in front after eight minutes.

The lead was increased to seven, 1-10 to 0-6, after twenty-six minutes. But a penalty in the thirty-third minute brought Tipp closer. English had possession of the ball and the flurry of activity around him bordered on panic. He was taken down, and although Commins got his stick to Pat Fox's penalty, the ball sizzled into the roof of the net. It was 1-13 to 1-9 at half time, and a game to contend with either of Tipp's two Munster final outings against Cork, was clearly in the making.

Tipp started the second half even faster than they had the first. After fourteen seconds, Donie O'Connell pointed. Aidan Ryan added another. Next, Paul Delaney landed a '65' to leave it 1-13 to 1-12.

Tipp might have led a little later, but after Sylvie had uncharacteristically failed to clear at the first attempt, Martin McGrath was on hand and he saw his shot rebound off the post. Babs brought on Michael Doyle, the man who had dealt Cork two deadly blows in the final minutes of the Munster final replay. But it was not the forceful Doyle who plundered the goal that gave Tipp the lead, it was the wily, speedy Fox.

Sylvie saw Fox coming.

He was in two minds. He had set out to rattle Fox with a shoulder charge as the ball descended in his direction, but, at the last minute, Sylvie went to win the ball instead.

It would have been some collision.

Sylvie regretted not getting in his tackle, even though he knew that one of them, Fox or himself, might have ended up on their way to a hospital if they had met? Each man was flying at full speed, on a direct course for one another. Maybe the two men would have been carted off the field, if they had indeed collided.

Sylvie had missed man and ball.

It broke between Ollie Kilkenny and Fox, and the Tipp corner forward came away with it. He roofed the ball into the net. Sylvie kicked himself for not stopping Fox in his tracks.

It was the fastest game Sylvie, or any of the Galway defenders, had ever played in, in their lives. There was not a second to think twice.

Sylvie resolved not to do so again.

Tipp led 2-14 to 1-16. English was now drifting, as he did so effortlessly, on the right wing. He got the ball and swung over a brilliant point. Galway got back with one from Cooney, from a free, and another from Steve Mahon. Cooney was now at full forward. Lynskey was on the '40'. The game was there to be won or lost by either team, but the man who had the biggest say, all of a sudden, was Offaly referee Gerry Kirwan.

As English knocked over a point, to send Tipp back into the lead, Kirwan had noticed a late tackle on Commins. Hayes, from the resultant free, thundered the ball downfield. Lynskey grabbed it and expertly set up Ryan, who was on his way to a sensational Championship debut. Ryan raced down the throat of the Tipp defence, and hand-passed the ball by Ken Hogan. Instead of being a point down, Galway were three up.

Anthony Cunningham made it a four-point lead. Noel Lane had been sprung midway through the second half. PJ Molloy had also come on for Naughton, and it was Molloy who combined with Cunningham and Ryan to offer Lane the chance to send Tipp reeling. He cut the ball into the net from close range. Cooney tapped over the final point of the game. Galway were there, 3-20 to 2-17, a six-point advantage that did not reveal the full character of the game that had just ended.

Tears were flowing in the Tipp dressing room once more. Men, unashamedly, placed their heads in their hands. Captain, Richard Stakelum admitted that nobody around him, not for half a minute, had thought that they were going to lose. Babs, indeed, had informed his players that it was their duty, if not their birthright, to defeat Galway in an All-Ireland semi-final. Keating told the newspapermen tightly gathered around him that the referee's decision had decided the game, and that denying English his point, and awarding a free out instead, had turned Tipp upside down.

• • •

Seven days later, in Dundalk, the greatest upset in the history of the game, since Antrim had beaten Kilkenny 3-3 to 1-6 in the 1943 All-Ireland semi-final in Corrigan Park in Belfast, after earlier besting Galway 7-0 to 6-2 in their quarter-final in the same field, appeared quite possible. Antrim were at it again.

Antrim and Kilkenny were level in the 1987 All-Ireland semi-final, with ten minutes remaining. And Antrim had the greater momentum.

They had been in front 1-5 to 0-0, after 14 minutes, when Kilkenny got their first score of the day. It was 1-7 to 0-5 at half time. Kilkenny were being beaten in every part and parcel of the amazing game. The Kilkenny attack was non-existent, and only Christy Heffernan and Kieran Brennan were still in the same positions in which they had started.

Nothing was getting past Terence Donnelly, James MacNaughton, Dominic McKinley and Leonard McKeegan in the Antrim defence. The crowd only mustered 4,926 but they were watching something that had seemed wholly impossible. Danny McNaughton had scored Antrim's second goal. They had already shot twelve wides in the first half, and any sort of calmness on the ball, and Antrim would have been out of sight before the last ten minutes of the game ever arrived.

That ten minutes held only heartbreak for Antrim. For Kilkenny it was ten minutes of some form of redemption as they rifled off points in quick succession from everybody, and from all angles, to win 2-18 to 2-11.

Kilkenny had work to do, to get their heads back in perfect working order, for the All-Ireland final. But there was also an upside for their manager, Pat Henderson.

Kilkenny were absolute underdogs.

• • •

The thought of losing could not be suppressed within the Galway hurling squad. It had to be confronted.

If not, the thought of not just losing to Kilkenny, but the colossal fear of being known for evermore as a team that had lost three All-Ireland finals in succession, to Offaly, Cork and Kilkenny, and being classified as some form of freak by the game's future historians, might secretly overpower too many in the dressing room.

In 1985, and again in '86, speaker after speaker on the giant platform in the centre of Eyre Square, had promised the huge gathering in front of them that they would be back the following year.

"We'll be back ... NEXT YEAR ... WITH LIAM!"

How many Galway lads, at the top of their lungs, in desperation more than hope, had hollered those exact words?

Man after man, after man. Sylvie Linnane, too.

He knew that Kilkenny would be fiercely motivated. They were being told they had no chance, and they had the memory of losing to Galway in the semi-final the previous year. All the pressure was zooming Galway's way. Each day of the final week of the All-Ireland final was the longest day Sylvie Linnane had ever encountered as a Galway hurler.

Farrell had told them that Galway's will to win should be a hundred times larger than Kilkenny's. He kept reminding his players how often Kilkenny had beaten Galway in previous years, and how savage some of those defeats had been.

"We'd have to beat them ten times on the trot lads," Farrell had stated, "just to get the balance right."

Farrell was nothing less than masterful that week. There were the All-Ireland final defeats of 1975 and 1979 to be remembered. And the teams had met twenty times in All-Ireland semi-finals, and, before 1986, Galway had only managed to get by Kilkenny in 1953, and before that, they had to go back to the 1920s to see that Galway had defeated Kilkenny three times.

Galway owed Kilkenny.

Farrell made sure his players felt that in every single bone. Meanwhile, in Nowlan Park, Pat Henderson had words with newspapermen, which might have been aimed at both the Kilkenny, and Galway, teams.

"Desire for revenge is a bad thing," mused Henderson, five days before the All-Ireland final, "when you direct it at another team."

• • •

It was the longest wait Sylvie had ever experienced. But, once it began, the game demanded total concentration.

At one point Sylvie got the hardest punch he had ever received in his life, square on his jaw.

At the time, Sylvie was looking down the other end of the field, his hands by his sides, when the upper cut landed.

It was the full packet.

For ten, twenty seconds Sylvie's senses were rocketed somewhere far away. But he had not collapsed on the ground. In fact, instinctively, as soon as the punch had landed, Sylvie had swung with his stick in the direction of the shadowy figure in front of him. He pulled across the shadow. He gave it as hard as he could give it.

He knew he had connected with the other player across his chest, but Sylvie, still, was trying to clear his head. His teeth were sore, and they'd remain sore for the rest of the week.

He struggled to clear his head. He knew he had to concentrate on staying between his man and the goal.

He knew it had been a near one. An ounce more strength in the punch, and Sylvie knew he'd have been down. A second punch, of any kind, and he knew full well he would have been down, and would not be getting back up onto his feet.

He'd have been gone.

Game over.

• • •

Tony Keady had opened the scoring in the 100th All-Ireland final by sending a '65' soaring over the bar. The game was on, alright, but there were battles, of all sizes and shapes, being waged all over the field nearly all of the time.

It was torrid, and tougher and more blatantly physical, than any All-Ireland final that decade, or perhaps any decade before that. There were also precious few scores. Galway had hoped for a good, dry day, and did not want a repeat of the soaking the ground had received all through the 1986 All-Ireland semi-final with Kilkenny. But, the first Sunday in September, 1987, was another complete wash-out.

Kilkenny failed to score from play in the opening thirty-five minutes. Their four points from frees were all converted by Ger Fennelly. At the other end, Galway had fared only a little better in taking the few chances that came their way. There was Keady's '65', and two frees from Joe Cooney, in their five scores, as they led 0-5 to 0-4 at half time.

By the end of that first half, Kilkenny had nine wides totted up, while Galway, over the entire seventy minutes, would only fire the ball wide six times.

It was a numbers game, in so many ways, and that included the men who were entering the little black book of Limerick's Terence Murray. By the finish, Kilkenny's Ger Henderson, Richie Power, Ger Fennelly and Liam Walsh would be booked, while Brendan Lynskey, Martin Naughton and Conor Hayes would also have to formally give their names to the referee.

A tidy total of seven men, though Murray, by the very end, would also have harsh words to say, at some time or other, to practically every other player on the field.

By the end of that first half, Ger Henderson's hand would be a bloodied mess.

• • •

Twenty-two-year-old Joe Cooney was marking thirty-three-year-old Ger Henderson. The Kilkenny centre-back had been his boyhood hero.

The Kilkenny No.6 was an old-style defender, and he had the great old game's finest character traits imbued in everything he did on the field. Henderson was a rock. Cooney had played against him a handful of times, but, in an All-Ireland final, when two men went toe-to-toe, their meeting in the last game of the year was usually recorded as the defining and ultimate judgment of all.

On the Cooney farm, in Bullaun, one of the two townlands that formed the Sarsfields' GAA club, little Joe always told anyone who was prepared to listen to him that he was 'Ger Henderson'. Every time he played in an imaginary All-Ireland final, in the backyard, or out in one of the field, he was 'Ger Henderson'.

Nobody else got to be 'Ger Henderson', not unless they wished to tease Joe, and have some fun at his expense.

Joe was fifteen years old when he was brought to Croke Park to watch Galway win the 1980 All-Ireland final. It was a proud, memorable day, and even mightier for the Cooney's since Joe's older brother, Jimmy, was in at left corner-back that afternoon. Five years later, Joe would be on the team. And, in the two years that preceded the 1987 All-Ireland final, Joe Cooney had played in every forward position on the team, as well as the centre of the field.

Centre-forward was always his favourite position, however. To play centre-forward on a huge field was best of all. Joe had all the skills and tricks that any man could wish for in his hurling game, but he also had a rare speed. To play centre-forward, on a big field, and a field as big as Croke Park, was where Joe Cooney looked like he had been born to play.

His greatest display at centre-forward for Galway, in his own head, was the 1985 All-Ireland semi-final when Galway had beaten Cork, and he loved every minute he spent in the company of Tom Cashman. His worst display, he reconciled, was twelve months later, also against Cork in the All-Ireland final, when Richard Browne seemed to know everything Cooney was about to do.

There was a long career, and dozens of big games, still lying in wait for Joe Cooney, but when he walked out the dressing room door and trotted onto the field for the 1987 All-Ireland final, he felt, same as the oldest men in maroon shirts around him, that he was about to play in a game that would be talked about forever.

One way or the other!

And, after Farrell's final few words, he had walked in the direction of Ger Henderson. The Kilkenny centre-back was waiting for him. There was a big, clumsy, firm handshake.

There were no words.

• • •

From the earliest minutes, blood had been flowing from Henderson's hand, and no matter what the Kilkenny medical team did to stop the bleeding, and cover up the wound, their good work came to naught.

In those tense opening minutes, Joe Cooney had pulled on the ball, without hesitation. He had the right to go for the ball. Henderson had the right to try to catch the ball. It was that sort of game.

A hurler did what a hurler had to do.

Looking down the length of the field, Sylvie reckoned Kilkenny had come out to shake up Galway. He had personal knowledge of that already. But he could see that every single Kilkenny player was laying into his opponent at every opportunity. Galway had to stand up to it.

Sylvie's head, and his whole body, was filled with a complete belief that if Galway stood up to Kilkenny physically, and refused to be pushed around, anywhere, then they would win.

Fennelly was having an off-day, it looked, with his frees. That made Sylvie even more bullish. Nothing warmed any defender's belly as much as watching a free-taker drive the ball wide.

Fail to stand up or, worse still, stand back?

It spelled disaster.

• • •

It was a day in which a goal, surely, would be the killer punch.

Kilkenny were finding it hard enough to score points, never mind goals. They would finish the game with nine points. No goals. Only three of those Kilkenny points would come from play, and only one of Kilkenny's starting forwards would manage to score. That was Harry Ryan, Sylvie's man, and it came early in the second half, a superb effort from the right at the Canal End. There was nothing Sylvie could do about that one. But, other than that, Harry Ryan was getting no more than a sniff at it, same as all Kilkenny's forwards. Ger Fennelly, who finished with seven points in total, grabbed the first Kilkenny score from play thirty seconds after the restart. A substitute, Tommy Lennon scored their third from play, three minutes from the end.

It was an All-Ireland final in which backs were powerful, and punishing, at both ends of the field. The scoreboard was level once in the first half. It would be back level four times in the second half.

Joe Connolly lifts the Liam MacCarthy Cup after Galway's glorious breakthrough victory over Limerick, in 1980.

The Galway team which defeated Limerick in the 1980 All-Ireland final; and (above left) Sylvie Linnane takes up his position on the goal-line, and (above right) John Connolly fought harder than any Galway man to win his first All-Ireland medal.

Sean Silke (above) was a master craftsman in the Galway defence, but he also played an instrumental role in bringing Sylvie back onto the Galway squad after he had quit the team in the early '80s; Sylvie in action in the National League, in 1984.

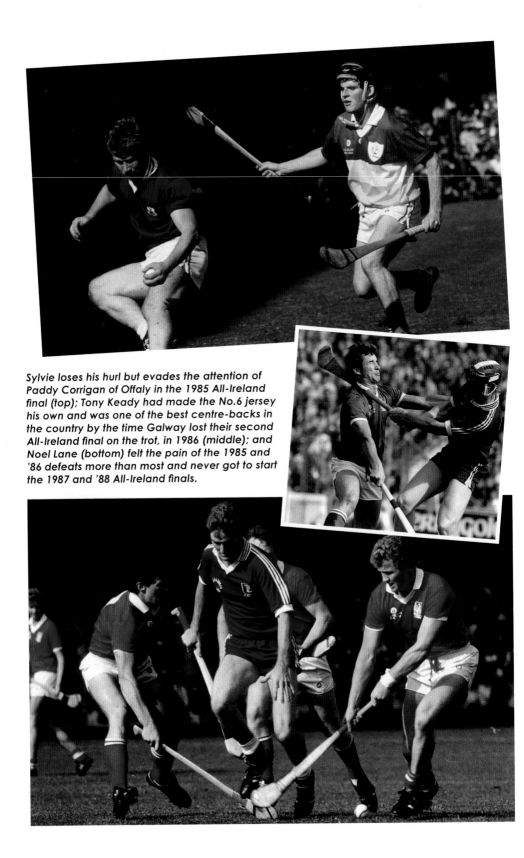

Sylvie loses his hurl but evades the attention of Paddy Corrigan of Offaly in the 1985 All-Ireland final (top); Tony Keady had made the No.6 jersey his own and was one of the best centre-backs in the country by the time Galway lost their second All-Ireland final on the trot, in 1986 (middle); and Noel Lane (bottom) felt the pain of the 1985 and '86 defeats more than most and never got to start the 1987 and '88 All-Ireland finals.

Galway's Anthony Cunningham gets clear of Clare's Ger Loughnane in the victorious 1987 National Hurling League final (top); Michael McGrath tortured defences with his running style and is photographed (middle) in the 1987 All-Ireland semi-final win over Tipperary; and (bottom) the inimitable Joe Cooney was the classiest finishing touch to Cyril Farrell's double winning All-Ireland team.

Conor Hayes proudly lifts the Liam MacCarthy Cup after Galway's hard-fought victory over Kilkenny, in 1987.

Sylvie Linnane was dispatched to look after some of the greatest forwards in the game, as Galway marched to their double All-Ireland wins in 1987 and '88. Here he gets to grips with Liam Fennelly of Kilkenny (top), with Cork's legendary Jimmy Barry Murphy (middle) and the magnificent Nicky English of Tipperary.

With the All-Ireland final victories, the good times also rolled off the field for the Galway squad. Sylvie and Noel Lane (top) entertain the huge crowds in Galway's Eyre Square; Sylvie and colleagues are as relaxed as can be outside the Ashling Hotel in Dublin before heading to Croke Park; with John Connolly, Tom Hynes and Brendan Lynskey in New York; celebrating with the team boss, Cyril Farrell; and (bottom) a group of players relax for the camera in Los Angeles.

Margaret and Sylvie take the old train in style, with Gerry Curtin, in Disneyland; Sylvie makes a quick visit behind bars in Alcatraz during the team's stop-over in San Francisco; and Sylvie says hello to Frankenstein.

The Galway team which retained the Liam MacCarthy Cup by defeating Babs Keating's Tipperary in the 1988 All-Ireland final.

Tipperary's famous full-forward line needed plenty of minding, and Sylvie had the best of company in the Galway full-back line playing alongside Tony Kilkenny (top) and Conor Hayes.

Brendan Lynskey never backed down from the challenges which stood in his or Galway's way, and celebrates with a bloody hand and stick after the 1988 All-Ireland final.

Joe Cooney in action in the 1989 NHL (top) and Conor Hayes has double trouble on his hands with Nicky English and Pat Fox in the 1989 All-Ireland semi-final.

Sylvie suffers the roughest of justice of being sent to the line, after a collision with Nicky English, in the 1989 All-Ireland semi-final defeat, and Tipp's big-hearted Bobby Ryan stops Michael McGrath and Galway from their dream three-in-a-row of All-Ireland titles.

Cyril Farrell gave 10 years of his life to guiding Galway to three All-Ireland titles but was back for more hard work in the late '90s (right).

Galway were honoured as the 'Jubilee Team' on the day of the 2012 All-Ireland final, as Anthony Cunningham's young squad came so close to dethroning Brian Cody's Kilkenny. On the field (inset), before the game, Sylvie waves to the packed stadium in Croke Park.

Though, Kilkenny had three slim opportunities of goals. Harry Ryan had struck the crossbar in the eleventh minute of the opening half. And Liam Fennelly had two chances of getting that goal in the second half, but, on each occasion, he was expertly foiled by John Commins in the Galway goal. The first time was in the fifty-fifth minute as he stopped the ball with his body as Fennelly tried to palm it home to the net, and, one minute later, the full-forward shot hard from the right but Commins managed to get his stick to it.

Noel Lane had been introduced early. He came bounding onto the field in the 40th minute, with the energy of three or four men. He didn't get too many chances coming his way, however.

Not until the sixty-third minute.

Galway led 0-11 to 0-9. It was a line ball to Kilkenny, under the Cusack Stand and close to the Canal End. Ger Fennelly struck it. Steve Mahon got his stick to the ball, batting it down, and then doubling on it. The ball zipped straight to Eanna Ryan. He slipped by Sean Fennelly, and took off.

Eanna Ryan had the ball on the end of his stick. And he was making ground. He carried the ball all of forty yards from deep in the middle of the field, before passing it off to Cooney.

Cooney wove his way through two, three, four defenders, and just managed to lay the ball off to Lane. His shot was simple, his touch light enough, and the ball was deflected into the net from Kevin Fennelly's hurley, squirming its way over the goal line.

Keady belted over the last point of the game. 1-12 to 0-9.

• • •

Gerry McInerney was voted the Man of the Match. Every Galway defender was in the running for the award, and one or two Kilkenny defenders, if the result had bounced the other way, would have been in with a shout.

But McInerney was imperious.

He was swashbuckling, and heroic, and Farrell took special delight in watching McInerney every single minute of the match.

Farrell never felt happier in those closing minutes. He had announced the previous Sunday, that he would be stepping down as Galway manager. Win or lose in the All-Ireland final, he stated it was time for him to go.

He felt emotionally drained as he watched the scoreboard declare that there were five points between the teams, and then six points. He was happy and satisfied and relieved, more than anything else, but, for his players, he was absolutely thrilled. Gerry McInerney was close to the top of that list.

One of the Sunday morning newspapers had him classified as the weak link in the Galway defence. The Cork coach, Johnny Clifford, had rated all of the players from both teams, and he had singled out McInerney for special mention, for all the wrong reasons.

When Farrell had spotted it, over the breakfast table, he quickly made for McInerney who was on the far side of the room.

"See that?" said Farrell.

The Galway manager did not need to say anything else, as he left the newspaper next to his wing back, and walked back to his own table.

"Had a poor semi-final and will need to show a huge improvement," wrote Clifford. "… if Galway are not to find themselves in trouble in this area. Kilkenny may well choose to pressurise him because he is vulnerable."

McInerney also read Clifford's comments on his opponent, Kieran Brennan. "If he hits form, he could go to town on McInerney," stated Clifford. "Wouldn't surprise me if he ended up Man of the Match."

The pair had clashed early in the game.

Every pair had clashed very early. McInerney and Brennan were no different, but they had fairly bashed into one another, and both needed the attention of the Galway and Kilkenny medical teams.

McInerney was shook up. Brennan was in bits, it seemed, and got back onto his feet, but never settled into the game, and never hinted at doing any great damage.

• • •

Back at the Ashling Hotel, Miko Donoghue could barely find room to park the Galway team coach. The place was alive and hopping. There were thousands of people out on the street.

That morning, Miko had carried the team from their hotel the mile or two up the road and into the Phoenix Park. It was wet and far too miserable for anyone to be walking in the park, or even looking out the window of a passing car. As usual, Farrell requested a little puck around in the park after breakfast, to allow the players to unwind that little bit more, and relax ever so slightly.

There was nobody about.

Farrell got the players out of the bus, against their will, but a few minutes later the Galway team manager was standing under a big tree with a bunch of his players, seeking some form of shelter from the sheeting rain.

Other players had taken a small walk.

Miko saw them all come running back to his bus, twice as fast as they had left it. There were only three hours to go before the All-Ireland final.

Farrell had a little chat with them on the bus, on the way back to the hotel. He told them to eat what they could, from their light lunch.

"Tuck in!" Pete Finnerty had advised, as they arrived back to a quiet hotel. "It'll be a long time before we eat again and the MacCarthy Cup is heavy," he joked, though not too many lads managed a laugh.

Everybody, Farrell could see, was wound up so tightly. They were holding themselves in, physically and emotionally. And when the bunches of supporters, who were found inside the hotel lobby, and huddled against the building back out on the street, shouted encouragement in the direction of any player, all they received back in reply, if they got a reply at all, which was seldom enough, was a nod of the head.

By early Sunday evening, the place was a riot of noise and celebration. Everybody looked soaked to the skin, but nobody seemed to care. And Farrell's players were making more noise than any large group of delirious supporters.

• • •

Farrell's speech in Kilkenny's dressing room had been short. The 1987 All-Ireland final had been shockingly tough, and brutal at times, but once it was over, neither team had an ounce of regret. And their respect for one another, immediately, was equally intense.

After his words, Farrell made his way over to Ger Henderson, who was still receiving attention as he sat on one of the wooden benches at the far end of the room. He saw Farrell coming. The Galway manager gave the towering Kilkenny centre back a hug. Henderson wrapped one arm around Farrell.

Back in his own dressing room, his players were either laughing or fighting back the tears, some of them having already lost that fight, and not giving a damn. PJ Molloy, who had come into the game shortly after Lane, had a carton of milk that he could not get into himself quickly enough.

"The best of all!" Molloy said to Farrell.

Farrell's loyal friend and ally, Bernie O'Connor – who, on Farrell's orders, had stated boldly to everyone he had met all week long, that Galway were sure to win – was waiting for him.

"We now have the Railway Cup, the National League Cup, whatever it's called, and the Liam MacCarthy Cup!" shouted O'Connor. "And anyone who likes can come looking for them!"

When asked, and he was being asked repeatedly, every time he looked to his left or to his right, was he still retiring, Farrell said he was, for sure. His three-year term as manager was over. The 44 Galway hurling clubs had already been asked by the Hurling Board to nominate a manager for a new three-year term.

The board chairman, Tom Callinan, and everybody around him – now that Galway had won, now that Galway had avoided three losing finals in a row – knew that there would only be one name on the lips of all of those clubs. Farrell left nobody in any doubt.

"I'm gone," he laughed, heartily. "I'm out of here!"

• • •

In the Burlington Hotel the next day, both teams sat down to lunch. Sylvie ate quickly. He was hungry. Winning All-Ireland teams, and losing All-Ireland teams, forget to eat for twenty-four hours after the game.

Both teams were famished. Kilkenny were quiet, and they looked a sorry lot. Galway were even quieter, conscious of how Offaly and Cork had behaved in their company, on the Mondays after the 1985 and '86 All-Ireland finals. Offaly had been extra respectful. Cork had done their best to keep it all in for the couple of hours they had to spend in Galway's company.

Farrell didn't need to tell his players what was expected of them. They'd been there. They knew the ground, the unwritten rules. But, rules or no rules, there were two Kilkenny boys whom Sylvie Linnane needed to find.

And he had no intention of sparing them.

He would not need to say very much when he did find them, just a couple of words. A few words and a great big smile. As a matter of fact, he had decided that when he found them, he would let them do most of the talking.

He could not see Paddy Prendergast at any table.

No sign of Ger Henderson either!

The whores, thought Sylvie.

After eating, he walked through the two bars in the hotel. Both were full and doing the soundest of business in the middle of the day. But Sylvie did not want to give up, and when Margaret asked him where he was going he said he had to see a couple of lads.

"To see two men about a dog." he told his wife.

He stood in the foyer, talking to people, always keeping on the lookout, trying not to miss the large main doorway as groups of people barrelled in and out of it. There was no sign of Prendergast, no sign of Ger.

• • •

Miko Donoghue was ready to head for home.

Everybody was aboard his bus. All the women, wives and girlfriends were in the bus behind him. The Liam MacCarthy Cup was sitting on the giant dashboard to Miko's left. Sitting directly behind him was Cyril Farrell.

"Will we go, boss?" asked Miko.

Farrell could hardly remember one single hour of the long, cruel, brilliant journey home seven years earlier.

"Let's do it, Miko!" replied Farrell.

CHAPTER
17

Tipperary were back home.

When the team raced out onto the field on September 4, 1988, in front of their awe-inspiring and often flamboyant manager Babs Keating and his backroom team, the whole stadium received them as though every last soul in Croke Park had been in their seats, waiting seventeen years to greet them.

Blue and gold appeared to spread across the entire stadium. The people wearing those colours, and waving them, had energy to burn, whereas anyone in the ground parading the colour maroon were awaiting their fourth All-Ireland final on the trot. Farrell had warned his players it might look like that, and sound like that, like some giant homecoming for Tipp.

The night before, he moved through the foyer of The Ashling Hotel, and sat in a quieter corner of the bar for some time, talking to Bernie and Phelim, and different lads. Some of the team, he knew full well, would be going out to find some quiet place for a calming pint.

And Farrell had no problem with that. By now, after perhaps the hardest year's training of their lives, nobody was going to be foolish. They were a serious bunch. And experienced too.

If one or two of them wished to have a pint or two, no harm would be done. He doubted that the Tipperary players were relaxed. He knew what a first All-Ireland final was like, and he saw how his players had reacted in so many different ways to the sneakiest of pressures on their first big day, and the night before that day.

Babs wouldn't be letting anyone take a drink.

He'd have his whole team bottled up in their team hotel, and every last man in the place would be watching every single hour, casually, pass by. It would be excruciating for some. Distracting for others. Everyone in the Tipperary squad would fear a fitful sleep.

The following week, he'd heard that, on the Saturday evening before the game, Conor Hayes had only cared to walk the one hundred yards down the road to Ryan's public house. He'd heard that Hayes had a couple of pints, as usual. On one of the television sets behind the bar, RTE's Up For The Match was halfway through, with supporters and officials from both counties already starting their weekend's celebrations a little bit early.

Farrell had heard that, as Hayes was sipping his second pint, the television show was dramatically eulogising the man he was due to mark the next day, Nicky English. On the screen, English was moving in slow motion. There was some fancy music keeping pace with his movements.

But, when Hayes' attention was drawn to the television screen by his friends, he took one quick look, shrugged his shoulders, and took another sip of his pint, seemingly without a care in the world.

Farrell knew that Hayes was one hundred per cent ready.

• • •

The rival captains, and direct opponents, Hayes and English, were due to meet in the centre of the field for the coin toss.

Farrell had told Hayes to be in no hurry.

English was brand new to the business of captaining a county team. He'd been given the job, when Babs and his selectors took the tough decision to drop their 1988 captain, Pat O'Neill, for the last game of the season. When the officials in the green coats started prowling the Galway end during the pre-game warm-up looking for Hayes, he ignored them. When they called him to come to the middle of the field, he told them he'd be with them in a minute.

Hayes went over to talk to Sylvie, about nothing in particular. Farrell had told him to keep English waiting. Let him stand in the middle of the field all on his own for a few minutes, and see how he likes it.

That was Farrell's message.

Eventually, Hayes walked in the direction of English and the referee, Gerry Kirwan from Offaly. He did so in his own time.

English won the toss. And he chose to play against the wind in the first half, which surprised Hayes, and surprised Farrell even more when his captain informed him of Tipperary's decision. Farrell had told Hayes to play with the wind, if they had won the toss. He wanted to take every single advantage over Tipperary from the very start, and anything that helped to ensure that they were chasing the game, and chasing Galway, was a good thing.

The room for self-doubt, and little errors, were far greater for a team chasing down an All-Ireland final, in Farrell's experience.

• • •

The year had not been without its own distractions for Galway. Some troubles as well, and, close to the end of it all, as the weeks and, finally, the days counted down to the All-Ireland final, Farrell and his players appeared to be at a more peaceful place than they had been in almost twelve months.

By the close of 1987, Galway had played thirteen competitive games, winning ten of them, and drawing three times. They had never been beaten.

No manager in the game, in such a long time, ever had the opportunity to walk away with such a record nailed to the wall behind him. Phelim Murphy was telling Cyril Farrell that all of the hard work with the team was done. Bernie O'Connor was agreeing, and neither man was prepared to let Farrell say his goodbye to the players.

Farrell never called that meeting.

Galway had won the Railway Cup, in October, beating Leinster 2-14 to 1-4. In the National League they had beaten Kilkenny by two points in Nowlan Park, when Sylvie Linnane appeared to keep control of most of the home team's forwards all on his own. They drew with Tipp, beat Limerick by three points, tore Clare apart, and drew with Cork.

In five of their six games, they had won by three points or less.

Clearly, Galway felt that they had the edge on every other team. And, just as naturally, every team they played felt that it was unlikely they were actually due a victory over Galway.

That double-edged sword was in Cyril Farrell's hands, for the first time.

• • •

The honeymoon period for the All-Ireland champions came to a halt when, in Fraher Field in Dungarvan, for the first time in fifteen months and since losing to Westmeath in the League in the autumn of 1986, Galway were beaten. A three-point result went the other way. Waterford won 4-10 to 3-10.

That was February. In March, a Seamus Fitzhenry point thirty seconds into injury time, grabbed a late draw at Wexford Park. At the end of the same month, Galway played Offaly, who had taken all of their points from their seven games in Division Two, in the League quarter-final.

It was a scrap right to the end. By then, Joe Cooney had one of the nastiest head injuries Sylvie had ever seen, and Offaly had somehow won the game by one point. Losing in Croke Park hurt, as did surrendering the National League title in front of Offaly, of all teams.

• • •

Farrell felt he needed more.

On the day that Gerry McInerney was married, he had instructed his players to leave the reception in Hayden's Hotel, Ballinasloe, just after the meal. He wanted them on the training field.

By the start of June, Sylvie and the lads were training with their clubs on Tuesdays and Thursdays. They were with Farrell on Mondays and Wednesdays. If there was a club game on a Sunday afternoon, Farrell would try to squeeze in a challenge game the same weekend.

By the end of June, Farrell had them four nights every week, and Saturdays were also his. The team had a head of steam up. All everyone in the dressing room really wanted was to get to the All-Ireland final, and the faster the better.

• • •

The 1988 All-Ireland final was less than two minutes old when Farrell noticed that Colm Bonnar and Joe Hayes, in the Tipperary midfield, were lying deep for Galway's puck-outs. With the wind at his back, they expected John Commins to be sending the ball long.

Word was quickly dispatched from the sideline to Pat Malone and Michael Coleman to come short for Commins' deliveries. Coleman was playing in only his second Championship match for his county, having been picked to play against London in the quarter-final. Brendan Lynskey and Malone were given the two jobs in the centre of the field for the semi-final. But, in the final, Coleman was into that long stride of his straight from the off.

Farrell knew that if anyone could find a man with a ball, even on the most crowded street in Galway city centre, it was his goalkeeper. Galway started winning easy ball in the middle, and Coleman and Malone had more room than they had found all year.

Farrell looked in Babs' direction.

The Tipp manager didn't seem to be taking any notice. Farrell reminded himself that All-Ireland finals were, indeed, strange animals, and even someone like Babs Keating would not necessarily be able to put two and two together – not all that quickly in the pressured, noisy, always confusing atmosphere of All-Ireland final day.

The first ten minutes were ruled by Galway, by the slimmest of margins throughout the field, but the next ten minutes were even more important. Galway had settled. Every man looked to have his head on his shoulders. In contrast, Tipperary were simply trying too hard.

Galway had a six-point lead. It was 0-9 to 0-3, and the most satisfying of those points was scored by Hayes. It was a long-range free, which should have been Tony Keady's to take, but the Galway captain told his centre-back in no uncertain terms that he'd look after it. Keady looked over to the Galway sideline, at Farrell, wondering what was happening.

Hayes, meanwhile, stood over the ball, raised it high, and struck a mighty point, before running back in the direction of Nicky English.

Farrell knew what Hayes was at, alright.

A couple of minutes later, Galway were awarded another free, in roughly the same place. Keady looked at Hayes, and looked at the Galway sideline again. Hayes stayed in his goalmouth.

He signalled to Keady to go ahead.

Keady whacked the ball over the bar. Only then did it dawn on him what Hayes had been doing. His captain wanted to show Nicky English that he was going to score some points too. And after sending over an inspiring score, Hayes did not wish to take the chance of trying it a second time.

He didn't need to.

Babs had Aidan Ryan vacating his left corner-forward position, and roving deep down the field. But Farrell instructed Sylvie to ignore him. He knew Tipperary wanted to take Sylvie out of his corner, and then use that extra space for English to run onto long passes delivered inside. As Ryan raced all over the field, and even appeared once or twice in his own full-back line, Sylvie stayed put.

He cleared anything that came near him, but spent most of the half sweeping in front of Hayes and English. Sylvie started winning more possession than he had ever imagined. In front of English and Hayes, and behind them, he was picking up lots of loose ball.

English was growing frustrated. But Babs left Aidan Ryan wandering for the rest of the half.

• • •

The drama of mid-summer, typically, had Galway at the centre of the action. Once more, for a team that did not have a provincial championship on which to concentrate its thoughts, Galway surprisingly dominated the sports pages.

The half-back line, as usual, was in the thick of it.

Finnerty had taken a twelve-month career break from the Garda Siochana in April of 1987, and, when he played against the All Stars on their spring tour in 1988, he decided to stay put in New York once again. The team came home without him.

Farrell had to hope that Finnerty would be home, in time, and fit and well. Steve Mahon was also off the team by the end of the spring, recovering from a cartilage operation. Then, in July, with the All-Ireland quarter-final against London coming down the tracks, Brendan Lynskey looked to be in some trouble. He'd been sent off in a seven-a-side tournament in Dublin, playing for the Galway Association against a Tipperary selection in a competition organised by the Offaly Association.

It was all very complicated.

Worse still, word then emerged that the competition was unauthorised, and all of the players competing were liable for heavy suspensions. The sending off even had its own name for several weeks, becoming known as 'The Lynskey Affair'.

It could only happen to Lynskey, thought Farrell. By the end of July, however, Farrell was not seeing the funny side of it. His sergeant-at-arms in his forward division was handed down a three-month suspension. Two weeks later, however, his suspension was lifted with immediate effect by a meeting of the GAA's Central Council.

A flurry of phone calls every single night, and a couple of trips in the direction of Croke Park each week, had Farrell on his toes, and more than he needed to be. There were also trips south to see, first-hand, how the Munster championship was going, and the usual visits to Croke Park to keep an eye on what was happening in Leinster.

• • •

After beating Kilkenny, Wexford had been favourites for the Leinster title. But, Offaly, loving the shadows, got themselves together and had a hold on their ninth successive Leinster final that Wexford could do nothing about. It was 3-12 to 1-14 at the final whistle.

Wexford were over-anxious. And they knew no luck on the day. Just as they had settled into the first half, George O'Connor cleared the ball hastily from his own square, but only found Michael Duignan on the 50-yard line. Duignan centred. Wexford goalkeeper Paul Nolan had time to come and grab the ball. He hesitated, and fell to his knees to smother the dropping shot.

Joe Dooley was in like a light, punishing the Wexford defence with a goal that could not be properly explained.

In Munster, Tipperary held onto their provincial crown, and quite majestically at that, beating Cork 2-19 to 1-13 in the final. They got a right fright, however, against Antrim in the All-Ireland semi-final, when they never raised the tempo of their game. Olcan McFettridge scored 1-5 for the Ulster side and could have doubled that tally with a little slice of luck, and it was not until the twentieth minute of the second half, when Pat Fox scored Tipp's third goal, that Babs or anybody around him could breathe more easily. A final scoreline of 3-15 to 2-10 did not tell anything like the full story of the afternoon.

• • •

Galway had secured their first meeting with Tipperary in an All-Ireland final since way back in 1958, when they also made hard enough work of it against Offaly in their semi-final. Farrell's forwards found it hard to gain their rhythm and, while it ended with big numbers on the scoreboard with Galway winning by 3-18 to 3-11, it was classified as a bad day out for everyone concerned.

Galway were defending an All-Ireland title, and that semi-final was not entirely about beating Offaly, and seeking to redress the 3-1 advantage that Offaly held over them in semi-finals and finals over the previous eight seasons.

The teams had been level four times in the first half and, yet, at the end of that 35 minutes, Galway had their three goals, leading 3-8 to 1-7. Noel Lane, who was one of the few men who could have been highly delighted with his performance, made a triumphant return to the starting fifteen at full-forward, and scored one of those goals, and four points as well. Martin Naughton and Eanna Ryan scored the other goals.

Lane had done everything that was asked of him, but he had more than an inkling what was in Farrell's mind for the All-Ireland final. And he was quite correct.

Farrell held him in reserve again.

• • •

In the 1988, All-Ireland final, there were four points in it at half time.

Galway looked good enough, but only just, to hold onto their All-Ireland title. It was 0-10 to 0-6. Galway had seven wides. Tipperary had six. Both half-back lines looked in formidable shape.

McInerney, always a man for the biggest of occasions, had latched onto the ball in the twenty-third minute and scored one of his trademark points, which didn't make all that much difference to his own game, but sent a surge of electricity through every other maroon shirt on the field. In the twenty-seventh minute of the second half, 'Mac' would do the same again, after clutching a high catch and driving up the field.

Malone and Coleman were still dominating in the middle of the field. Malone also took three telling points over the seventy minutes. Joe Cooney had lined out at full-forward, with Lynskey on the '40, and the two swapped positions for periods of the first half, but, most worryingly of all for Farrell, and for every Galway defender watching from the far end of the field, Cooney had not quite settled. He'd been far too quiet through the first half, and remained so for the first fifteen minutes of the second half.

Martin Naughton was finding it hard to break free from Bobby Ryan, and, on the right wing, Anthony Cunningham was not making much of an impression on either John Kennedy or John Heffernan.

Galway's natural speed game was not making itself felt.

Lynskey was getting through a ton of work.

And just as well.

At the other end, the Galway full-back line had refused to let go of the firm handle they had on their opposite numbers. By the end of the game, Conor Hayes had held English scoreless from play. The Tipp captain would score from five frees, and a penalty. Aidan Ryan would score one point. Pat Fox, in the other corner, was held scoreless by Ollie Kilkenny.

• • •

Margaret Linnane could not watch it any longer.

Tipperary were too close, and were staying in touch. She feared a Tipp goal. Quickly, the fear became quite suffocating.

Sylvie, it appeared to her, was now taking up English.

Margaret's heart was in her mouth. She was terrified that Sylvie would let him slip, just once. That's all that might be needed. She had to leave. She had to get out of her seat in the Hogan Stand, and try to get away from the game.

She told her family she had to go.

But people were climbing out of their seats all around her. There was a wall of people to her left, and to her right. Margaret could not move. The wall of people was descending down the steps, towards the fencing, and the field beyond.

Margaret was being swept downwards.

She reached the old wired fence. She could not fight to get back up the steps, and the pressure at her back was now growing heavier and heavier.

She was on the sideline. Before she knew it, she found herself there, amongst a horde of spectators watching the final minutes of the match.

• • •

Sylvie never looked sharper.

Ollie Kilkenny was as steady as a rock in the other corner. Keady had been growing stronger, and more unbelievably forceful, with every passing minute of the second half.

Farrell had his worries.

But his team were on top where it mattered on the field. And he still had Lane, whom he had put into the game for Cunningham after forty-three minutes, to make his dramatic mark on another All-Ireland final, perhaps?

Galway also had that little bit of luck. Paul Delaney was off target with a couple of long-range frees. Commins made a fantastic save from Fox. John Leahy had the ball in the net, but the referee pulled play back, judging that he had been fouled before he shot, and awarded a free in instead.

Tipp could not get their noses in front. With two points still between the teams, Commins made another breathtaking save, parrying a Cormac Bonnar shot from close range, and then, with lightning reflexes, clearing the bouncing ball out for a '70', which Delaney shot wide.

It was still too dangerous for Galway. However, the mortal blow for Tipperary was just around the corner. Substitute Tony Kilkenny sent a long ground shot through to Lane.

Lane had moved into the centre from the left corner. Tipp full-back, Conor O'Donovan turned, but the ball spurted away from him. O'Donovan was in no man's land. Lane moved by him, and with a crisp ground stroke he buried the ball by Ken Hogan.

English's penalty, which was a fortunate award in the first place, was slewed over the bar. Time was up. Galway were leading 1-15 to 0-14. Penalty or no penalty, they could not be caught.

• • •

Farrell was ready to retire, again.

And he promised that nobody would talk him out of it this time. Conor Hayes assured anyone who asked him, that it would be time enough to knock on Farrell's door a few weeks down the road.

A three-in-a-row was a tempting quest.

But, after losing two All-Irelands, and winning two All-Irelands, the Galway manager also knew full well that surprising his players, pushing them that extra inch or two in 1989, or getting them to work out in their own heads why exactly they needed to win a third All-Ireland title, was not going to be any less arduous than any season that lay at his back.

A third All-Ireland?

Farrell knew it was easy to talk about 'three-in-a-rows', but the winning of the last one was usually twice as hard as the winning of the first.

He'd tried out new things all through the summer of 1988, like training sessions at 9am on a Saturday morning. They had gone well enough. There was lots of grumbling, which he was prepared for, but the early starts had been a novelty. The training was done, and everyone had a late breakfast together, and the rest of the day was theirs to do with as they saw fit.

Farrell was, naturally, an early riser. As a non-drinker, it was never a problem jumping out of bed, any morning of the week, any time of the year. All the same, those early morning starts had added to his busy diary.

It was as hard for him to retain a bounce in his stride as the next man. But it was his job to be out in front, all the time. The year had been as enjoyable and successful as he could ever have hoped, through there were weeks when he felt the going particularly wearisome. And times when he was not in the best of form. One weekend, in June, particularly stood out for him.

They had trained on the Friday evening, in Athenry, and it was a dull, uninspiring session. The lads were dragging themselves. Farrell struggled to get a pep into his own stride.

"Right!" he blasted from the hip, as soon as he had them all back in the dressing room. "That was awful lads. It's not good enough and I want you all here at 10 to 9 in the morning. And I want everyone, EVERYONE, YOU HEAR ME? on time! Have you got that?"

The following morning, Farrell slept in. The road from Woodford to Kenny Park in Athenry was only touched on the occasional spot as he drove like a mad man. It was 9.15am when he got there.

The car park was full. Hardly one car missing as far as he could tell and then, suddenly, it dawned on Farrell that all of the sliotars were in the boot of his car. He'd taken them all with him the previous night.

They'd be waiting for him. Standing with their hands on their hips, or sitting in groups on the ground. When he reached the top of the small hill looking down upon the field he could see them, some of them were stretched out, getting a little bit of the early morning sun, but, as soon as they spotted his head, a slow handclap began.

It grew louder and louder.

There were days with the team that he'd miss and there were days he would not. That Friday night and Saturday morning in the middle of June fitted into both categories.

• • •

Sylvie Linnane was tired, and sore.

For the third time, he was making the long, slow, altogether mesmerising journey home from Dublin with the Liam MacCarthy Cup. By Ballinasloe, they still had much less than half of the journey over. Ballinasloe to Eyre

Square could take another five or six hours, he knew full well, perhaps longer.

At Willie Connaughton's public house, in Cornafulla, there was great difficulty in any member of the All-Ireland winning party getting within two or three yards of the bar. Half of the lads stayed outside.

From Ballinasloe, the team would be getting off Miko Donoghue's bus, and climbing up onto open trucks. Their arrival into their own towns and villages would not be in the height of style, but it would be dramatic. Sylvie thought to himself that he must, indeed, be getting old.

The third journey had him whacked. He could not remember being as tired a year earlier, but in 1987, he also remembered, he had not been awoken in the dead of the night before the All-Ireland final by a wicked screeching, and shouting. God knows, it was always hard enough to get to sleep the night before the big game. He was never tired. And then there was a strange mattress to contend with.

He'd been sharing a room with Steve Mahon the night before. They had their little chat, and both had agreed it was time to try to sleep at least. Sylvie had just gone off. Suddenly, there was a right row going on, on the street, beneath his window. Sylvie and Mahon were on the third floor of The Ashling Hotel.

Sylvie made his way over to the window, thinking that the row might be the work of some Galway people, or even a few supporters from Tipp deciding to wake up the entire Galway team.

But, on the street below him, he could see only a young woman, and a man, who was way out of line. He was hitting the woman.

Sylvie shouted to Mahon.

"Where's the basket, the waste paper basket?" he asked.

Mahon helped him find it, quickly, and Sylvie dashed into the bathroom. He filled the basket with water. Mahon had the window opened.

Sylvie took careful aim.

And, then, he tipped the basket upside down and, quick as a flash, ducked back inside the window.

He heard the splash, just before he also heard another mighty roar. Mahon told him that the man had been drenched. But the job was a success. The same man had forgotten about his wife, or girlfriend or whoever the poor woman was, and he was now intent on climbing the drainpipe.

He was shouting all sorts of threats, and the most vicious of promises. Sylvie turned the light off in their room. Mahon had already closed the window. Sylvie pulled the curtains together, tightly.

The two of them lay on their beds laughing.

The drainpipe climber had stopped at the window below them. He was hammering away at the same window. The man inside the window was, at the same time, telling his visitor what he would be happy to do with him, if he didn't slide back down the bloody pipe.

Sylvie and Mahon chuckled their hearts out. And they chuckled, repeatedly, though it only made sleep all the harder to come by.

CHAPTER
18

It might have been someone else's worry.

But when Cyril Farrell picked up his newspaper on a Tuesday morning, early in January 1989, and read that Galway's 26-year-old centre-back Tony Keady was emigrating to the United States, he knew that everyone would immediately turn to him for a solution.

Farrell had known about Keady's intentions. He told his manager that he was heading off, the morning after the All Stars' banquet. He'd be gone on February 4, and Galway would be all a fuss.

Cyril Farrell was back for more.

He was still Galway hurling manager for another year.

• • •

There was no good reason why the year should become a ball of trouble, for Farrell more than anyone. But, it did.

And it was a ball nobody could quite control.

The season had started off so well. Galway had remained unbeaten in the 1988-89 National League, twice getting the better of Tipperary. Though, on each occasion, Babs Keating did not have anything like his full side on the field. Babs picked a skeleton team when the sides met in March in Ballinasloe,

and, by the time they were back in each other's company for the L
Tipperary showed up without Pat Fox and Nicky English, who w
injured.

Galway officials were not pleased that Babs decided to play wit
English or Fox, nor Ken Hogan, Bobby Ryan, Declan Ryan, John Kenenc
and John Leahy, in their first meeting. An attendance of close to 20,000 was
expected in Ballinasloe. There might have been a good few bob in it for the
Hurling Board, if Tipp had decided to take the game seriously.

In the end, 8,000 people turned up in Duggan Park to see Tipp put up a
real fight, and go down by only 0-12 to 1-7. Joe Cooney had steered Galway
to victory with seven points.

"We put it up to them!" Babs, heartily, informed reporters after the game.

And Tipp did so, a second time without their deadly inside duo, in the
League final on the last Sunday in April when they were defeated, for the
second time, by only two points. Galway won 2-16 to 4-8.

Tony Keady played in both games.

He never did head off to New York as planned. Sylvie Linnane was also
on the field for the League final, though he was fortunate. Various newspaper
reports stated that he had received either fourteen stitches, or sixteen stitches
or seventeeen stitches, to close up a gash on the inside of his mouth after a
clash in training, which was completely accidental, with Brendan Uniake.

Sylvie was in no position to clarify the number of stitches. And when the
less sympathetic members of the Galway squad added up all the different
number of stitches, and asked Sylvie had it taken forty-seven stitches to keep
his mouth closed, for once there was not much he could say in reply to that
question either.

The League final was indeed a thriller.

It was also tough as nails. Three times, Brendan Lynskey was floored, but
it was only after the third time that he had to leave the field, to have a one-
and-a-half-inch gash across his lip dealt with, with some stitches of his own.

"Who measured that gash then, Lynskey?" Sylvie asked him, afterwards,
when hearing that the cut was said to be exactly one-and-a-half inches.

Silence suited Lynskey on this occasion.

When Lynskey went off, Farrell brought Cooney to the '40' and brought

'd. Galway were dominant, but Tipp were in a
title with some vengeance; however, Joe Hayes
the first half, and team captain Pat McGrath
ond half.

..e goaled for Galway. John Leahy, Michael
...ar, and McGrath goaled for Tipperary. The game had
...d whetted everyone's appetite for more of the same from the
..ounties.

When Tipperary chairman, Noel Morris was leaving the victors' dressing room, after thanking them and congratulating them once more, he was met by Phelim Murphy at the doorway.

"Good luck, now," said Murphy. "… I'll see you back here in August!"

• • •

Sylvie was well used to not having Pete Finnerty and Gerry McInerney around the place at the start of the summer. Losing Keady, however, might complicate matters. There was also talk of Brendan Lynskey taking off.

Newspaper reports had him going to London or New York, but they did announce that he, too, was definitely thinking of emigrating.

Sylvie was in the dark.

Most of the squad were slightly confused about what was going on. Farrell could not help them as much as he would like. By the middle of the summer, he was looking to get Steve Mahon back into full action, after the midfielder had been out all winter long with a cruel knee injury, and then, one Sunday evening Martin Naughton went high to pull the ball out of the air, but fell to the ground awkwardly, and was left there writhing in pain. His knee was a mess.

The summer had promised so much.

• • •

Galway were reigning All-Ireland champions, and new League titleholders, and they'd been out to New York to play the All Stars on successive Sundays in Gaelic Park. Everyone had a good time. And that's all Farrell had wished for. He didn't go on the trip, deciding to catch up on things in his own life while the lads were away. The team was left in the safe hands of Bernie O'Connor.

Farrell waited for their return.

He had gone very light on them for the first few months of the year, and they had sailed through the League campaign despite being slightly out of condition. Farrell had planned to do something about that in the months of June and early July, and have everything running smoothly in his camp for the second half of the season.

Galway lost both games to the All Stars, on May 7 and 14.

Sylvie had been on the trip with Margaret, but he knew that some of the lads were thinking of staying behind for a few weeks. He did not know, exactly, what their intentions were, as he flew home.

On May 21, Tony Keady, Aidan Staunton and Michael Helebert, lent a hand as Laois defeated the Tipperary club, 4-14 to 3-6, in a New York senior championship game. It was a game Sylvie, and everyone else on the Galway squad, knew nothing about until they read about it a week later in the newspapers.

By the end of the month, all hell was about to break loose.

The three players were standing accused of playing in the game without the official sanction of their club secretaries, the Galway County board secretary, or the Director General of the GAA. The trio were threatened with twelve-month suspensions. By the middle of June, the executive committee of the New York GAA Board sat and decided that all three should be suspended for two games only. Keady, in particular, seemed safe.

And lucky.

But, then, the Games Administration Committee, sitting in Croke Park, decided to get their teeth into the untidy business, and, by the end of the first week of July, it was announced that Keady, and the other pair, were receiving the full twelve months!

Galway kicked up. An appeal had to be made. Also, there was talk of the defending All-Ireland champions withdrawing from the 1989 Championship in protest. Though, Sylvie didn't have any time for that kind of talk.

• • •

Sylvie was never one to believe in threats.

And he also believed that if a man said he was going to do something, then he damn well better be prepared to do it.

Simple.

Galway had no intention whatsoever of withdrawing from the All-Ireland Championship, and hearing that sort of stuff, and reading about it in the newspapers, simply annoyed him.

All the players were sitting in the mart canteen, in Athenry, after training on the last Tuesday before the All-Ireland semi-final against Tipperary, when a phone call came through, informing everyone that a special meeting of the Central Council had turned down Keady's appeal. The appeal was defeated, 20-18.

Sylvie felt sorry for Keady. At the same time he realised that their centre-back had made his own bed by accepting the word of local officials in New York, in the first instance, that he was allowed to play in the foolish game the previous May. Keady should have known better than that.

And Galway should have handled the whole business, in a smarter, more determined way. They should have withdrawn from the Championship, and informed the GAA of their decision. Or else, they should have accepted the bad news, and got on with the defence of their All-Ireland title, without thinking twice about the injustice of it all, and with one hundred per cent faith in Keady's replacement, Sean Treacy.

Sylvie hated seeing the team left in a ridiculous state of limbo. He also disliked the fact that Treacy also had his future thrown up into the air. Treacy had served his time. Sylvie had absolute belief in him, and his ability to get the job seen to in the centre of the Galway defence. Treacy had played left half back in the League final against Tipperary, in Gerry McInerney's absence. He liked his style as a hurler, and he especially like the bullish strength of the man.

• • •

Martin Naughton was out, and Noel Lane was in the throes of rehabilitation after an unfortunate knee injury.

Galway had their backs to the wall, before the 1989 All-Ireland semi-final even began, and with Croke Park packed to the rafters there was a mood in the Galway dressing room that bred utter defiance. If some people thought that the champions were being led to their slaughter, then they'd soon find out how wrong they were in their presumptuous thinking.

The first of the day's semi-finals had Antrim and Offaly, and Farrell and his selectors didn't need their men to know that the Ulster champions had finally, for the first time since 1943, worked their way into an All-Ireland final.

Antrim had rocked Offaly in the final handful of minutes, winning 4-15 to 1-15, but Farrell didn't want to hear very much about it at all.

Hearing that might just, dangerously, and mischieviously, leave a man thinking for half a second that Galway were even closer to the coveted three in-a-row. It might appear at the team's fingertips.

Seventy minutes away.

Sylvie Linnane never had his head so full of what had to be done. He heard something or other about Antrim, but loudly shooed that conversation well away from his corner in the dressing room. Tipperary had stopped trying out different things with English in the full-forward line. They now had Cormac Bonnar starting at No.14. English was in one corner, Pat Fox in the other.

Sylvie knew that he, Ollie and Hayes had their hands full. People had been saying they might be over-run. People had been saying they didn't have the pace any more. He knew what people were saying.

They'll soon see! he thought.

• • •

After five minutes, Galway were 1-1 to 0-1 in front.

Eanna Ryan grabbed the early goal, taking a pass from Pat Malone and tapping it past Ken Hogan. And, just before half time, Ryan was again on hand, always the opportunist, and deadly with half a chance, to score his second. Gerry Burke and Lynskey set up the attack, and when Ray Duane's shot came back off the post, Ryan met it first time in the air and gave Hogan no chance whatsoever. In between the two goals, however, Tipperary had definitely ruled the proceedings and Galway had failed to get a score for seventeen minutes.

Farrell felt that the referee, John Denton from Wexford, was helping them rule with some of his split-second decisions falling in Tipp's favour.

But, Tipp were only two points in front at half time. It could have been far greater. Cormac Bonnar had rounded Hayes and, with a goal seeming quite certain, Commins somehow stopped the full forward's blazing shot.

It was, amazingly, 0-11 to 2-3.

It was helter-skelter in the Galway full-back line, and the pressure was continuous. With not enough possession being won in the middle-third of the field, and with too many Tipperary men enjoying breathing space, the line was in danger of being torn apart. By the end of the day, the Tipperary full-forward line would take enormous pride in having plundered 1-12 of their team's total of 1-17.

• • •

English would score eight of those points. Three of the eight came from frees, and one from a penalty, but the moment in the afternoon that brought most attention upon English, came in the eleventh minute of the second half.

The ball was dropping down between himself and Sylvie.

Sylvie raised his stick to bat it down but he had no idea what happened next. English was on the ground. Sylvie didn't believe he had touched him at all, not unless, by complete accident, he had made contact with the handle of his hurl.

He looked down at English.

There was no trace of blood or any damage.

He then bent over him and told him to get up off the ground. Sylvie grabbed at his shirt and tried to pull English up off the ground, to prove there was life in him. He then went tumbling to the ground himself.

Cormac Bonnar had pushed him over.

Sylvie was confused. He could smell trouble, and he wanted to let everyone know, Galway defenders especially, but also Tipperary men, and the referee, especially the referee, that he had done nothing.

He turned to head back to English, but Bernie O'Connor was on the field. And he grabbed Sylvie, and began pushing him back.

"Get up out of that!" roared Sylvie.

The first sight Sylvie caught of the referee, he was sending him off the field. He felt disgusted. Anger was welling up inside him. The game was a blur in front of him. He felt completely disorientated, and still confused. There was nothing he could do.

He had done nothing wrong but there was nothing at all he could now do, sitting there, surrounded in the dug-out by other players and officials, with Tony Keady next to him, all of them already lost in the absolute fury of the game.

He looked up at the scoreboard.

Tipp were a good few points in front. It was 1-15 to 2-6. It was going to take a miracle, either that or something crazy from somebody up front for Galway.

Sylvie could not understand what he was doing there. The next thing that registered was the sight of Michael McGrath, coming walking in his direction. The 'Hopper' was also off.

Sylvie had no idea what was left in the game. 'Hopper' had been sent off for a frontal charge on Conor O'Donovan. Galway were down to thirteen men. It was over.

There was no hope. They were gone. Gone, surely? Sylvie was looking out at the field, but his brain was numbed. His body was full of energy, and intent, but he could not move. Everyone around him was roaring and shouting. Sylvie couldn't form any words. He felt locked away.

• • •

Pat Fox had broken through for a fine goal three minutes into the second half, finishing off a brilliant pass from English. That goal, and Sylvie's dismissal eight minutes later, had knocked Galway off their feet.

Tipp led by six points and, with fifteen minutes left, they looked strong all over the field. But Galway held on. Somehow, they had brought it back to a three-point game. Commins made another breathtaking save, this time denying English a certain goal.

With three minutes left on the clock, the champions were only two points behind. Eanna Ryan had a chance at one end, but the ball went wide. English pointed at the other end.

It was 1-17 to 2-11.

Slightly after the stroke of seventy minutes, the referee blew the full-time whistle.

• • •

The referee had sent off Sylvie and McGrath, and booked ten other men. He had also seen fit to take the name of Cyril Farrell when the Galway manager blew his top at the sight of Sylvie being sent off.

It was a battle and a half.

But it was also a game that Sylvie felt had been wrongly taken from Galway. The champions had not been allowed to defend their title.

From the middle of the summer, until the referee's final whistle, which was blown without any thought being given to the amount of injury time that might have been totted up, events had conspired to stop Galway.

Tipperary, at the same time, were a worthy team.

Sylvie couldn't deny them that, even though it was hard to stomach watching them carve up Antrim in the All-Ireland final, winning 4-24 to 3-9, and lifting the Liam MacCarthy Cup with greater ease than any team in living memory. They were a strong and manly bunch, and that included Nicky English. Though Sylvie could never forgive him for what had happened, not until some years later, when they met and shared a few words.

• • •

It was all too late then. Sylvie Linnane had played his last match in Croke Park on August 6, 1989, though he did not know it at the time.

It would also be the last occasion in which he would wear a Galway jersey. Years later, he would remain saddened, and a little angry, that it had all ended as it did, getting sent off in his very last game in an All-Ireland semi-final.

Almost ten years had passed since he had being sent off in the 1980 All-Ireland semi-final. The two events were the wrong sort of coincidence, and not something he ever would have wished to have ceremoniously book-end his long career.

But he would have to live with that ending. It didn't matter to a great many people that the sending off had been unjust.

The fury that had taken hold of Galway, on the field, and up and down the sideline, remained for days, and never quite went away as the weeks passed. Two weeks after the final, two carloads of Galway officials and players were summoned to Croke Park to answer questions from the Games Administration Committee.

Eventually, Farrell would be suspended for another two months, for speaking his mind once more. Phelim Murphy was warned about his future comments, but Bernie O'Connor was also suspended for two months. And, before the month was out, Galway had two officials, and six players, Tony Keady (twelve months), Michael Helebert (twelve months), Aidan Staunton (twelve months), Michael McGrath (two months), Brendan Lynskey (two months) and Sylvie Linnane (one month), under suspension from the GAA.

• • •

"OUT, OUT, OUT."

The headline in *The Connacht Tribune* surprised Sylvie Linnane. It also annoyed him. Nobody had told him he was 'out' of the Galway squad.

He had received no phone call. Nobody had called to his door. No letter, either.

He was never as mad with Cyril Farrell as he was that day when he picked up the local newspaper and saw his name, and his photograph, with two or three others, under the heading...

"OUT, OUT, OUT."

It had never dawned on him that the 1989 All-Ireland semi-final would be his last game for Galway. And that, as it turned out, he would not even get to finish that game, and walk off the field in his own time, in his own manner.

Nobody died that day. But the dressing room had been like a morgue, for the solid hour that it took everybody to let it all sink in. And shower. And sit there. And, finally, get dressed and get ready to meet their families waiting outside, just down the corridor, the other side of the two large steel doors that were made for players and officials only.

Sylvie had no idea that, for that hour, he should have been mourning the finish of his own hurling career.

He had a bit of a groin injury in the months that followed but he had been waiting to get the phone call, to tell him to get his backside back in gear and get back to training. It was well over ten years since he had waited for any sort of phone call from a Galway official, and he was not waiting in the first few months of 1990 for any call that might deliver some bad news.

He was thirty-two years old. There were miles on the clock, sure there were, and his body was banged up. It had been banged up for years. That was a price he had willingly paid to be part of the Galway defence for so long. He knew it would be time to go, to say his goodbyes in the dressing room soon enough.

Another year? Maybe two? Something like that.

When he picked up the *Tribune,* that evening, he felt shocked initially. There was also some disbelief. There was a good chunk of anger at work within him. And, mostly, he was mad as hell with Farrell for not telling him anything.

He felt the scapegoat.

He had started his career with Galway, by being handed an empty box, with no Oireachtas medal inside. And, after so many big wins, and so many agonising defeats, after making so many friends, and taking hold of the most unbelievable and brilliant of memories, he was back where he started.

Getting his backside kicked by his own people.

• • •

Sylvie had a front-row seat.

He watched as the Galway team broke up before his eyes and, everything, slowly but surely came to a shuddering halt. Conor Hayes would be on substitutes' bench for the 1990 All-Ireland final. He played against London in the quarter-final, but Farrell had to call it a day for Hayes. And Hayes agreed.

All of the older lads seemed to be landing back on the team for that

London game at the end of July. Hayes was back at full-back, after being dropped from the National League panel, and at full-forward Noel Lane started against London and grabbed himself three points. Martin Naughton was back in the squad after missing the guts of a year with his knee injury. Ollie Kilkenny was in contention for his place despite breaking a finger.

Tony Keady was also back. Keady was in the centre of the defence for his first big game since playing for the county against the All Stars in New York, back in May of 1989.

Sylvie went to Ballinasloe to see Galway struggle past London, winning 1-23 to 2-11 in the end, and he was in Croke Park for the semi-final, when Galway powered through his old enemies and old pals from Offaly, winning 1-16 to 2-7, and made it through to the county's fifth All-Ireland final in six years.

The full-back line in the 1990 All-Ireland final would be made up of Dermot Fahy in Sylvie's old corner, Sean Treacy at No.3 and, in the other corner, Ollie Kilkenny. They were all strong hurlers, and Sylvie wished them well.

That All-Ireland final was as hard on Sylvie as some he had played in and, by the end of the game, he knew it would be a long time before he could sit peacefully, or even close to it, in the Hogan Stand.

Sylvie had watched his old team-mates outscore Cork, and completely take command of them in the second quarter of the game, by 1-8 to 0-2. Galway had gone in at half time five points up. Nothing had prepared the lads out on the field, or Sylvie in his little seat, for what was to come.

Galway then conceded 4-3 in a nineteen-minute period when every part of the team's performance seemed to collapse. They finally lost to Cork by three points, in a whirlwind game that finished 5-15 to 2-21.

He felt so sorry for the lads, for all of his friends, and especially the team captain, Joe Cooney. To see Cooney lift the MacCarthy Cup over his head would have been the perfect ending to a year that had been all so disappointing for Sylvie.

He had watched Peter Finnerty and Dermot Fahy in his old No.2 shirt through the Championship. That was hard.

Harder to sit there, and accept, than Sylvie had ever expected.

He wanted Galway to win. But Sylvie still wanted his old jersey back, even though he now knew that it was hardly going to happen. He knew he had better get used to his seat in the stand. Worse than that, he had better get used to looking for tickets for himself and Margaret and his family for Championship games in the future.

He could see that things were not going well in 1990, from the very start. Like Cork in the All-Ireland final, Kilkenny had put five goals past Galway in a League game in Nowlan Park in February. Sylvie had gone down to that game as well. He went to all of the League games. All of the Championship games. It had been a long year.

• • •

Galway faced a campaign in Division Two of the National League in the winter and spring of the 1990-91 season. The team defeated Munster to win the Railway Cup, and made it to the League quarter-final, where they met Kilkenny in Thurles. Kilkenny scored 1-4 in a rapid-fire closing burst to win 2-11 to 2-9.

Galway never recovered from that Sunday.

The writing was on the wall for a large number of people in the Galway dressing room. And that included the Galway manager. Farrell had stayed on, for far longer than he had ever intended. He had been talked out of retiring so often. But, now, he was returning to a point in his life where he knew that some of the very same people were thinking it might be a good idea for him to go.

Cyril Farrell would not need to be pushed.

The team was wiped out in the 1991 All-Ireland semi-final by Tipperary. Only eight members of the 1987 and '88 All-Ireland winning teams took the field at the start of that game. Pete Finnerty was in at full-back. Tipp were 2-3 to 0-1 in front after fifteen minutes, with Cormac Bonnar and Michael Cleary cutting through the defence and scoring the goals.

Tipp beat Galway by 3-13 to 1-9.

Farrell was happy to say thank you and goodbye. And, with Galway winning the All-Ireland Under-21 title, with excellent performances against Cork and Offaly, it was quite obvious that it was the turn of Jarlath Cloonan, a successful businessman, and an exceptional coach and manager from Athenry, to try out life at senior inter-county level.

• • •

Cloonan's Galway would lose out to Kilkenny, by four points in the 1992 All-Ireland semi-final, and by five points in the 1993 All-Ireland final.

It was Cloonan who had to be clear-eyed, and perfectly unsentimental, in reaching judgment on some of the greatest hurlers Galway had ever known. Newspaper reporters were now calling them the 'old-timers'. Pete Finnerty was dropped to the substitutes bench for the 1993 All-Ireland final. Tony Keady was already sitting on that bench.

"Worse things have happened to better," were Finnerty's sober words, when asked to describe the feeling of being dropped.

Four of Farrell's lads started the 1993 semi-final. Six of them were named for the All-Ireland final. Treacy at full back, McInerney at centre back, Coleman and Malone in the centre of the field, Cooney at wing-forward, McGrath at corner-forward.

Cloonan had viewed the heavy All-Ireland semi-final defeat in 1991 as the game that formally brought the curtain down on Farrell's old team.

"That game was the end of a natural life cycle," he explained.

It was Cloonan who had to bring to a close the most intriguing and electrifying period in the history of Galway hurling. It had also been the most successful ten years the county had ever experienced.

• • •

Three All-Ireland titles!

Sylvie Linnane felt that it had not been enough, however.

For all of the hard work that was put in, and for the incredible depth and range of talent, it was not nearly enough. Sylvie believed that Galway should have won five All-Ireland titles. That would have been a fairer return. He understood that the team had met with bad luck in some of those years, in semi-finals and finals, but he also felt that Galway had under-performed on the field, and had been out-smarted on the sideline, on at least two big occasions.

Without Cyril Farrell, there might have been no All-Ireland titles.

But, equally, with Cyril Farrell being as brilliant and thorough as he was in every facet of the team's preparation, there also should have been more.

But Sylvie could live with three.

He got to play in seven All-Ireland finals. And he got to travel Ireland, and travel vast tracks of the planet, as one of the greatest hurlers the country had ever produced. He had so many people to thank for that.

Cyril Farrell would be close to the top of that list. The time would, indeed, come when Sylvie would have his say and let Farrell know directly, and honestly, how annoyed he had been at the manner in which his career was closed down.

He felt it had been terminated.

Farrell and himself would, a couple of years down the road, have that discussion, which would conclude as a warm chat between two men who always expected so much from one another.

For a few of those years, together, they had demanded perfection.

EPILOGUE

Sylvie and Margaret were heading off.

They were going back to the United States, to the west coast, to experience some of the amazing delights there.

They were going to hire a car and hit the highway. Las Vegas was one of their targets. Death Valley and Mount Rushmore were two more, as well as Yellowstone National Park and the Battle of The Little Bighorn. They were going to be staying for a while in San Francisco and Los Angeles.

It was the trip of their dreams, to mark their twenty-fifth wedding anniversary, though there were always surprises when Margaret Linnane travelled far afield with her husband.

• • •

Margaret and Sylvie were in their seats on the plane in Shannon, closer to the back than the front. They had five memorable weeks ahead of them.

One of the Aer Lingus stewardesses had spotted Sylvie on the quick flight from Shannon to Dublin, where they had to stop for an hour or so. She had been friendly and was keen to ask them some questions about where they were going.

As they arrived in Dublin, the stewardess came back down the aisle and, in a low voice, asked Sylvie and Margaret to get out of their seats.

"I've got a much nicer seat for you and your wife, Sylvie," she promised. Sylvie and Margaret were brought up to the front of the plane and invited to take up two seats in first class.

"Thank you very much," said Margaret, understanding that the stewardess had recognised Sylvie and wished to get their big anniversary celebration off to the best possible start.

"This is very kind of you."

"It's the least I can do," replied the stewardess. "When you won the All-Ireland you did something special for my father and my little brother. You don't remember, do you? Of course, how would you," continued the stewardess.

It was explained, hurriedly, to Sylvie and Margaret that the stewardess's father had asked Sylvie if he could get some of the players to sign the little boy's hurl. The little boy was clearly unwell.

Sylvie had taken the stick out of the father's hand and then taken the boy out of his father's arms. He carried the boy onto the team bus and told the father to follow. As they travelled on the team bus for the next mile as it, ever so slowly, made its way one hundred yards at a time, Sylvie insisted that every last man on the bus sign the hurl.

"You made every single player sign it," confirmed the stewardess. "My father never forgot you. You're a hero in our house!"

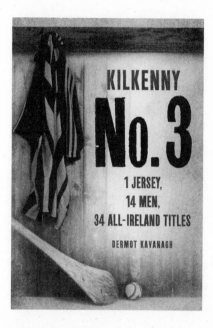

THE MOST precious territory in Kilkenny is the 75 square yards that front the county's goalposts. It is the heart of Kilkenny hurling and, down through time, it has always been the most safely guarded.

For more than a century of Kilkenny hurling, a princely total of 14 men have done everything asked of them – stretched every sinew, flexed every muscle, shed tears and often blood – to defend and protect that prized rectangular piece of ground.

In total, those 14 men have brought home to Kilkenny 34 All-Ireland senior titles. They are, indeed, men apart. From the light figure of Jack Rochford, the 5'7" Paddy Larkin, the 6'2" Pa Dillon, the burly Jim 'Link' Walsh, the tall and languid presence of Brian Cody, the granite-like 5'10" of Noel Hickey to the fleet-footed JJ Delaney, all of these men have handed the No.3 jersey down to one another with great pride and conviction.

This is the remarkable story of those 14 men and the story of how they safely brought home to Kilkenny an amazing 34 All-Ireland titles.

ISBN: 978-0-9573954-0-4
Price: €14.99

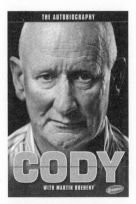

Cody: The Autobiography
Martin Breheny
ISBN 978-0-9563598-0-3

Doyle: The Greatest Hurling Story Ever Told
John Harrington
ISBN 978-0-9563598-5-8

Life Death and Hurling
Michael Duignan
ISBN 978-0-9563598-6-5

Cody is the remarkable story of the most successful GAA manager of all time. Cody has led Kilkenny hurlers to unprecedented success. Here he explains the philosophies and motivations underpinning his achievements and gives a unique insight into the life of a man whose name has become a symbol for all those who strive for success.

John Doyle hurled 19 Championship campaigns in the blue and gold of Tipperary. In that time he won eight All-Ireland senior titles and 10 Munster Senior Championships. His haul of 11 National League medals has never been equalled.
John Doyle was a one off – he was a hurling hero. This is his story.

In his autobiography, Michael Duignan lays bare the events, both personal and professional, which have gone into shaping him over the years.
A strong, true voice that speaks on sport, life and death with authority and compassion, *Life, Death & Hurling* is an exceptional work by any standards.